Mistaking Order for Anarchy

Mistaking Order for Anarchy

TERRITORY, MOBILITY, AND SECURITY IN THE SAHEL

Casey McNeill

STANFORD UNIVERSITY PRESS
Stanford, California

Stanford University Press
Stanford, California

Library of Congress Cataloging-in-Publication Data

Names: McNeill, Casey, author.

Title: Mistaking order for anarchy : territory, mobility, and security in the Sahel / Casey McNeill.

Other titles: Territory, mobility, and security in the Sahel

Description: Stanford, California : Stanford University Press, [2026] | Includes bibliographical references and index.

Identifiers: LCCN 2025023402 (print) | LCCN 2025023403 (ebook) | ISBN 9781503644977 (ebook) | ISBN 9781503644267 (cloth) | ISBN 9781503644960 (paperback)

Subjects: LCSH: National security—Mali. | Territory, National—Mali. | Security, International—Sahel. | Geopolitics—Sahel—History. | Mali—Politics and government. | Sahel—Politics and government.

Classification: LCC UA869.M42 (ebook) | LCC UA869.M42 M364 2026 (print) | DDC 355/.03306623 23/eng/20250—dc14

LC record available at https://lccn.loc.gov/2025023402

Cover design: Susan Zucker

Cover art: Body wrap, Zarma, Minneapolis Institute of Art. Gift of Richard L. Simmons in honor of Lotus Stack, Accession Number: 2011.90.27

The authorized representative in the EU for product safety and compliance is: Mare Nostrum Group B.V. | Mauritskade 21D | 1091 GC Amsterdam | The Netherlands | Email address: gpsr@mare-nostrum.co.uk | KVK chamber of commerce number: 96249943

For West

Contents

Acknowledgments

I have benefitted from the generosity and wisdom of many people over the course of this project, without whom this book would not exist. I am grateful to my professors at American University, especially Randolph Persaud, Patrick Thaddeus Jackson, Christine Chin, Amy Oliver, and the late Andrea Tschemplik, for their generous engagements with my undergraduate work, their encouragement to pursue graduate school, and their modeling of a scholar-teacher vocation.

The Johns Hopkins Political Science Department provided a collegial and stimulating environment for this project to take seed. Early versions of ideas in this book developed in conversation with my colleagues, especially Hitomi Koyama, Tim Vasko, Nate Gies, Derek Denman, Chad Shomura, Anatoli Ignatov, Jacqui Ignatova, and Ben Meiches. Michael Hanchard, Naeem Inayatullah, Isaac Kamola, Sara Berry, and Jennifer Culbert were close readers of my work and pushed my thinking. Siba N. Grovogui has influenced this book immeasurably, especially through his guidance and feedback in its conception but also through my continuous return to his work in the years since. At Hopkins, Siba also introduced me to Amy Niang, whose groundbreaking work on questions of order, space, justice, and security in the Sahel has been a major influence on this book. I am grateful to Amy for her feedback on early versions of ideas in this book and for introducing me to key interlocuters in Bamako.

This book draws on interview research that I conducted in Germany, Mali, and Niger. This research was funded by the Baden-Württemburg Stipendium, the Smith Richardson Foundation's World Politics and Statecraft Fellowship, and the Nicole Suveges Fellowship. While based at the University of Mannheim, I benefitted from the camaraderie and hospitality of Adam Scharpf, Benjamin Engst, Caroline Wittig, Moritz Heß, and Katrin Paula. Many people in Bamako and Mopti, Mali, and Niamey, Niger, were generous with their time, experience, and insights. Special thanks are due to Nana Touré, Dr. Hamidou Magassa, the late Dr. Naffet Keïta, and Dr. Aghali Abdelkader. Hamidou Guindo, Ibrahim Laouali, and Agalher Alhassane provided research assistance. I am grateful to Point Sud in Bamako and Laboratoire d'études et de recherche sur le dyanmiques social et le developpement local in Niamey for providing institutional affiliations for my research stays. In Bamako, Lamine and Diaffe Bagayoko provided valuable logistical and research assistance, not least connecting me with my home away from home. Korotoumou Diawara and family welcomed me with open arms and kept me comfortable, safe, and healthy. *Aw ni ce.* I am especially thankful for my host brother and friend, Siriman Troaré, who helped me in countless ways to navigate life and work in the city.

The ideas in this book have been presented in various stages and forms at different conferences, workshops, and seminars, and I am grateful to the organizers and participants, who are too numerous to name here. I have especially benefitted from workshops focused on the contemporary Sahel, where I have had the privilege to meet and learn from many brilliant scholars across disciplines and specializations. In particular, I thank the organizers, Amy Niang, Baz Lecocq, and Isaie Dougnon (now also my colleague at Fordham), and participants of the 2016 workshop "Sahelian Identities in Times of Crisis," held at Point Sud in Bamako. Since moving to New York City, I have been fortunate to participate in and learn from workshops organized by Gregory Mann at Columbia. I also thank Patrick Jackson and the Department of Global Inquiry at American University, who provided a forum to present parts of this manuscript in its later stages, where I benefitted from excellent comments and questions.

I would not have been able to complete this book without the support of a Fordham Faculty Fellowship. Fordham's Department of Political Science also provided funds for a manuscript workshop, which was invaluable. I thank the participants, Isaac Kamola, Kevin Dunn, Sam Opondo, and Cecilia Lynch, for their generous and close readings, critical feedback, and generative conversation, which guided my revision process. Special thanks are due to Isaac, whose enthusiastic support for this project goes back to its very beginnings and who has provided feedback on more versions of it than anyone else. I am grateful to my colleagues in the Political Science Department, who have provided a supportive environment to present work in progress. Robert Vitalis generously served as an external discussant in that context and provided valuable comments on a chapter. Comments from two anonymous reviewers also improved the manuscript. It has been a pleasure to work with Stanford University Press, and I thank the editorial and production team members, especially Dan LoPreto, for their support and guidance.

I am indebted to my friends and writing group comrades, Tim Vasko and J. Mohorcich, who kept my spirits up as we weathered the pandemic and its wakes in New York City and who helped me to reimagine this project in light of canceled fieldwork plans. Their feedback on multiple book-proposal and chapter drafts was critical in moving the project forward. I am also grateful for the ongoing support of my National Center for Faculty Development and Diversity Faculty Success Program small group, which has continued to meet since the summer of 2020. Megan Ennes, Hannah Krimm, and Kameron Moding have offered advice and commiseration as we have all navigated the tenure track.

Finally, I thank my family for their love and support, which saw me through challenges at all stages of this project. I am grateful to my parents, Martha and John, who have always encouraged my curiosity and my academic pursuits no matter where they took me, and to my brother, Michael, who is a model of creative perseverance and integrity. My partner, Patrick Austin, supported me throughout the writing and revision of this book, and its completion is thanks in no small part to his loving encouragement and good humor. My twin, West, inspires me always, and I dedicate this book to them.

Map of Mali

Source: United Nations, "Mali," Geospatial Network, February 1, 2020, https://www.un.org/geospatial/content/mali.

Mistaking Order for Anarchy

Introduction

In December 2023, the United Nations' decade-long Multidimensional Integrated Stabilization Mission in Mali (MINUSMA) withdrew at the request of Mali's military government. On many fronts, it left conditions of even greater instability than when the mission was deployed in 2013 in the wake of armed groups' occupation of northern Mali and the fall of the civilian government to a coup d'état. After a period of decline during internationally mediated peace negotiations, violence increased sharply beginning in 2017. New armed groups claimed to defend populations who were excluded from the peace process, victimized by the state, and neglected by MINUSMA and its international partners. Government corruption—notably, interference in legislative elections—amidst declining security conditions led to mass protests in Bamako in the summer of 2020, which culminated in a widely celebrated coup d'état in August. A planned transition to civilian rule was foiled by another coup nine months later. Even amidst escalating violence, the military government's vocal opposition to Western-led political and military intervention in Mali and in the region has been a source of popular support.

The failure of the United Nations (UN) stabilization mission in Mali is not an outlier. International stabilization interventions in so-called fragile states have failed everywhere they have been tried. This book aims to shed light on these failures by examining relationships among space, political order, and collective security in Mali from the nineteenth century to the beginning of the current crisis in 2012. I approach this case as a vantage point from which to rethink the spatial logics and imaginaries that ground diagnoses of fragile states and interventions to stabilize them. These have been premised on the assumption that international security is an effect of territorial governance: security at the international scale is produced and maintained through states' capacities to secure territory at the national scale. Fragile states are thus a problem for global security to the degree that the absence of state territorial control creates spaces where threats can incubate and circulate. From this perspective, Mali and the Sahel region of which it is a part represent a particularly stubborn challenge for international security. Here, arid ecologies, low population densities, and limited infrastructure make the consolidation of state control over territory difficult and expensive.

The latter characteristics of the Sahel have shaped popular imaginaries of the region as a space of endemic crisis and insecurity. The Sahel came to international attention as a distinct—and troubled—geographical and political space in the 1970s and 1980s when severe droughts, famine, and displacement prompted an international humanitarian response. It was in this context that the Sahel "became part of the lexicon of governments and international NGOs" as a symbol that "would evoke poverty for the world at large."[1] In the early 2000s, when counterterrorism strategies sought to identify "ungoverned" spaces that could become the "next Afghanistan," the region again became an international signifier of poverty and weak states— this time, as a source not just of humanitarian concerns but also of global threats.[2] Sahel strategies proliferated across governmental, intergovernmental, and nongovernmental organizations. These strategies have warned that the region's geographic, demographic, and institutional contexts may pose persistent threats to international order. Unless and until states are able to foster economic development, provide infrastructure and public services, and control movements within and across their borders, the Sahel will remain a "weak link" in the international state system and a perennial source of crisis.

In relation to contemporary international order and security, then, the Sahel has often been identified with conditions of lack and deficiency: geographical remoteness, economic deprivation, and institutional weakness. Accordingly, the region, its populations, and its histories have rarely been recognized as sources of relevant knowledge and experience about international order and security. In short, the Sahel is a space of "security consumers," not "security producers." But such discourses of lack are themselves brightly flashing signals pointing to productive avenues for critical inquiry. This book takes them as such. It starts from the premise that investigating conditions that have come to signify international *dis*order is a means of interrogating the theories and practices that define and defend international order.

In this sense, the book follows postcolonial approaches that theorize international order from the perspective of its "constitutive outside."[3] The constitutive outside refers to relational processes of identity formation through which "Self" is recognizable in its difference from "Other." The processes of colonialism and imperialism that shaped the modern international order were also processes of identity formation, through which Europe and then the West constituted itself as the global subject and agent of world history through its differentiation from other, purportedly less agential, regions and peoples. As "Other" to the world-historical West, non-Western spaces, peoples, and perspectives have been situated as constitutive outsides vis-à-vis the material relations of a hierarchical world order *and* the ways in which the history and development of this order are narrated and theorized. To the extent that theories and histories of international order adopt the perspective of the imagined world-historical "Self" apart from the relational and hierarchical dynamics that constituted it (in other words, treating the "outside" as actually external and *not* constitutive), they are necessarily partial and distorted ones. Theorizing from the constitutive outside is thus a heuristic that responds to the ways in which power relations distort perceptions of relationality and obscure processes of mutual constitution.

As a constitutive outside, the Sahel's identity of lack and deficiency in relation to international order can be a jumping-off point to investigate the relational processes through which that order is (re)produced in particular ways and not others. More specifically, this book examines the Sahel as a context in which the spatial imaginaries and practices shaping international order can be put into relief. Like other arid zones, order and security in the Sahel have depended more on the preservation of mobility through space than control over space. This has generated distinctive ways of organizing authority, populations, and resources, characterized by flexible and overlapping sociopolitical and economic geographies. This orientation toward space contrasts with territorial modes of order, in which political identity, belonging, and authority are mediated by a sovereign's capacities to control bounded, contiguous space. In the context of European imperial expansion in Africa in the late nineteenth century, this difference was defined by colonial discourses that ultimately equated the absence of territorial order with anarchy and the project of international ordering with territorial development (chapter 2).

The book traces how nonterritorial modes of order were thus produced as a constitutive outside, in relation to which territorial administration has been recognized as a precondition for security in "underdeveloped" parts of the globe and thus for the security of international order in general.

By examining relationships among political order, security, and the production of space in the Sahel, this book problematizes the modern equation of international order and security with capacities for territorial control and containment. As we will see, this case illustrates not only that stable forms of social and political order do not necessarily require territorial control or definition but also that the territorialization of order is itself a disruptive political process, whose relationship to security is variable and contingent. Evidence from the Sahel suggests that the relationship between the territorial state and conditions of (in)security depend not on the strength or even legitimacy of the state but instead on how it affects populations' capacities to respond to conditions of interdependence, uncertainty, and contingency. Multiple ways of organizing political community can be compatible with the latter capacities, and in some contexts, the territorial state impedes rather than enables them. In a world of intensifying climate crises and associated population movements, it is increasingly important to recognize conditions where the political arrangements of the territorial state are especially maladapted and/or harmful to these capacities. This book contends that understanding and responding to global security conditions thus requires delinking security, conceptually and practically, from the project of territorial control and containment.

Territorialization and Modern International Order

It is increasingly acknowledged that political science and international relations (IR) research is often caught in what John Agnew first called the "territorial trap": assuming that the state is a spatial container for society, that sovereignty is inherently a power over territory, and that the territorial boundaries of sovereignty divide the "domestic" and "international" as two distinct political spheres with different ethical possibilities.[4] On the one hand, the territorial trap describes a scalar problem: "space is viewed as a series of blocks defined by territorial boundaries," and "other geographical scales (local, global, etc.) are disregarded."[5] On the other hand, the territorial trap points to a more fundamental problem of conceptualizing and historicizing space itself. The conflation of space with territory has figured space as a naturally occurring object, as "brute, physical terrain."[6]

The perception of space as ahistorical and apolitical terrain is itself a product of political and historical practice. As Henri Lefebvre writes, "If space has an air of neutrality and indifference . . . it is precisely because this space has already been occupied and planned."[7] Lefebvre understood territorialization—the production of space as territory—to be a state strategy. In his account, the basis of this strategy is the abstraction of space from its lived social and ecological diversity into an homogenous and calculable grid. State territorialization produces and represents space as naturally divisible into jurisdictional and logistical containers. This facilitates and legitimates the expansionary and homogenizing forces both of the state and of capital. The projection of space as territory figures land, resources, humans, and their activities and relations as calculable according to economic, bureaucratic, and/or military logics.[8] In Lefebvre's words, this "serves those forces which make a *tabula rasa* of whatever stands in their way, of whatever threatens them—in short, of differences."[9] Projecting space as a geometrical plane becomes a basis for comparative calculation, and difference can be refigured as deviation—for example, as inefficiency, danger, or disorder. The state's territorialization of space also works to "naturalize its own transformative effects on socio-spatial relations":[10] it creates landscapes, infrastructures, and routinized practices through which space is experienced as always already territorial.

Lefebvre's focus on the state's and capital's production of abstract space theorizes territorialization as a technology of European state building and capitalist industrialization. More recent research situates the development of the territorial state in its global context of colonialism and imperialism. This connects the development of the "territorial trap" and its associated logics of security to Eurocentric ontologies of time, space, and political subjectivity, which sheds light on the origins and durability of theories of fragile states and ungoverned spaces and their relationship to international order.

Imperial and colonial conquest shaped—and was shaped by—novel ontologies of space and time. Replacing earlier notions of cyclical time, Enlightenment thought conceptualized time as universal, progressive, and linear, which was influenced by interpretations of societies in the "New World" as signifying Europe's long-ago past.[11] Related theories of history depicted time as civilizational and evolutionary and imagined Europe further along an evolutionary trajectory than less civilized non-European societies. As Naeem Inayatullah and David L. Blaney write, this philosophy of history was also a novel interpretation of geography that legitimated colonial conquest: it functioned as "a conversion of space into time" in which "the spatially distinct other is converted into a temporally prior self."[12] Difference as it materializes in space could thus be read not as evidence of geographical and human diversity but as historical backwardness. This was premised on conceptualizing space itself (nature) as ahistorical and apolitical raw material.[13]

For example, recent research has shown how colonization of the Americas produced new techniques for defining political claims in relation to geography based on colonizers' construction of indigenous lands as vast empty spaces. This facilitated the innovation of new mapping and surveying techniques as a basis to claim jurisdiction and property.[14] Jordan Branch identifies the papal bulls of 1493 and the 1494 Treaty of Tordesilla—which introduced a linear division through the Atlantic Ocean and granted Spain and Portugal rights of "discovery" on either side—as the first examples of "global linear thinking." As colonization in the Americas expanded, claims to political authority were negotiated and adjudicated according to novel "'legal cartographies' of charters and grants" that mapped colonial dominion onto abstract lines of latitude and longitude. These techniques were developed in response to Europeans' nonrecognition of indigenous claims to land. "In the Old World . . . an invader would conquer a people and claim the same authority that the previous ruler had held. In the New World, the absence of recognized authorities demanded a new means of claiming authority vis-a-vis other European powers: linearly defined territoriality, expressed abstractly in maps or cartographic language."[15] As Karem Nisancioglu emphasizes, the territorialization of colonial sovereignty materialized not just in relation to abstract geometric reasoning but in the violent "colonial crisis" that this reasoning produced. Colonizers' appropriation of land and assertion of political control utilized techniques of spatial segregation through which white settlers would be secured by preventing or controlling the movement of indigenous people past circumscribed borders.[16] While the imagined emptiness of the Americas was a condition of possibility for "global linear thinking," violent attempts to actually empty those lands entangled the production of territoriality with that of racialized boundaries between "civilization" and its outsides.[17]

The homogenization of space as territory circulated from the colonial world to Europe. According to Branch, the emergence of modern territoriality in Europe, which was consolidating in the late eighteenth and early nine-teenth centuries, should be understood as a process of "colonial reflection."[18] Spatial strategies for sublimating and securitizing difference that were first developed in the colonial context were deployed in Europe in the context of sovereign-legitimation crises. The territorialization of sovereignty contrib-uted to resolving these crises by abstracting sovereignty from the person of the ruler to the state itself.[19] This abstraction could be materialized through the territorial performances of the state, for example, in surveying and taxing land and defining and defending territorial borders, which were depicted in increasingly familiar cartographic representations of political authority and identity. The location of sovereignty in the territorial state facilitated a strengthening norm of equality and mutual recognition among western Eu-ropean sovereigns and produced the first concepts of modern international order as a European "society of states."

First understood as a continental society, the international was reimagined to describe the space of the planet as industrial globalization advanced in the late nineteenth and early twentieth centuries. In a context of globalization, many internationalists anticipated that the primacy of territorial jurisdiction and associated national political identities would become obsolete.[20] But, as I elaborate in chapter 2, resurgent imperial interests shaped political and legal theories of modern international order that reinforced territorial sovereignty as its foundation. Arguments about the absence of territorial sovereignty in Africa and Asia justified incorporating these spaces into the international order as objects, not subjects, through colonial rule and international trust-eeship. In this context, territorial administration and its absence became the key signifiers of order and its absence—anarchy.

In postwar IR theory, this history of territorialization was narrated as one of technical adaptations to objective material conditions, which deter-mined what political communities would survive and thrive. For example, the territoriality of states in the Concert of Europe has been taken as evi-dence of the capacity of those states to secure themselves individually and collectively, which enabled the reproduction of a stable "balance of power" and of Europe's global dominance. John H. Herz writes that nineteenth- and early twentieth-century depictions of non-European spaces as an anarchical frontier zone, where the laws of war and peace did not apply, "had its *non-ideological* foundation in the actual difference between European and non-European politics so far as territoriality was concerned. European states were impermeable[,] . . . while most of those overseas were easily permeable by Europeans."[21] The "nonideological" basis of European supremacy in this context can seem self-evident based on the material presence in European states of a physical infrastructure, including standing militaries, urban industrial hubs, state bureaucracy, etc., which signifies state strength and which can, in fact, be leveraged to assert coercive control over distant spaces.

However, as Herz himself also recognizes, the conditions under which this territorial infrastructure was, for a time, a source of stability rather than instability in Europe was based not on states' territorial capacities themselves but on the consensus among European sovereigns to recognize and protect each other's authority *as* territorial—that is, to treat each other's territorial borders as impermeable despite their actual permeability by growing military capacities. European sovereigns' mutual recognition of their own spaces as territorial and civilized and non-European spaces as nonterritorial and thus anarchical was a mechanism through which "it was relatively easy to divert European conflicts into overseas directions."[22] The balance of power, then, was reproduced not by territorial impermeability—the militarization that signified territorial impermeability also made European states, and much of the planet, highly vulnerable to increasingly extreme forms of violence—but by a framework of international subjectivity and morality that justified "diverting" violent conflict to other geographies.[23]

This account of the development of modern territoriality connects its spatial imaginaries and practices to colonial relations of hierarchy and inequality *and* to an ontology of international order according to which that hierarchy signifies objective differences in communities' capacities to secure themselves. The project of ordering the space of the international is equated with the project of territorialization, and territorial capacities are read as proxies for state "strength." This fills out a geographical imaginary of the international as made up of zones of order and zones of disorder, while obscuring the ways in which these zones have been mutually constituted.

Accordingly, research on international security has commonly treated the relationship between territorialization and national and international security conditions as a theoretical given rather than an empirical question. But the latter empirical question is a crucial and urgent one, as the failures of successive international state-building and stabilization missions make clear. As this book will show, rethinking the relationship among security, space, and political order requires greater attention to the diversity of ways in which humans interact with, experience, and produce their material and ecological surroundings. The next section introduces the space of the Sahel as a context that is particularly generative for this inquiry.

Mobility, Order, and Security in the Sahel

The Sahel is known as such—as a shore—because of its position and function as a border between the vast Sahara Desert, where conditions become dramatically harsher for humans, and the more populated savanna to its south. Situated in a "transitional zone" between arid and humid climates, its ecology is shaped by high variability and uncertainty in terms of rainfall volume, timing, and location. As the desert shares characteristics with the sea (in terms of the challenges it poses to human life), the Sahel shares characteristics with other shores and port economies, including abundant commercial activity, high degrees of intercultural interaction and mixing, concentrations of wealth and capital, and a dependence on inter- and intraregional trade and mobility. The Sahel's cosmopolitanism reflects the interdependence of communities located across different rainfall zones and ecological niches and the historical development of social, political, and economic ties among them.

The paradigmatic example of this interdependence is relationships between nomadic pastoralists and less mobile cultivators, with pastoralists connecting savanna-side populations to salt, animal products, and desert-side trade and cultivators providing grain and access to water and pasture during the dry season and in periods of drought. These relationships help mitigate particular risks and uncertainties associated with production in an arid ecology, like the Sahel. Sahelian ecology can be understood as a nonequilibrium system, meaning "populations [and] other components are not in a long term balance with other elements of the system."[24] In equilibrium systems, human production can be calibrated to predictable variations in the resource base, and sustainable production systems are sensitive to the "carrying capacity" of the land to avoid resource degradation.[25] In a nonequilibrium system, resilient production systems are instead flexible and opportunistic, taking advantage of favorable conditions where and when they materialize.[26]

Opportunistic production relies on both spatial mobility and diversity in production goals and economic activities across a socioeconomic network or system.[27] For example, for pastoral production, diversity in herd composition and size means that the breadth of forage available can be converted by different animals into human food as milk or meat, and herds can be split up to redistribute surplus wealth or respond to lower levels of pasture or water resources. Diversity of economic activities means that when herd sizes must be reduced in response to climatic variability, labor can be redirected toward agriculture, trade, transport, and other wage labor and commercial activities. When larger herds can be sustained, labor can again readjust to support this activity. These diversification strategies rely on animals' and people's ability to move.

The mobility and diversity that characterize Sahelian livelihood strategies have been conducive to the growth of prosperous trading networks and to states and empires that were able to control part of this trade and gain the allegiance of the populations that sustained it. Sahelian commercial networks and market towns became nodal points within the trans-Saharan caravan trade. High volumes of trade, especially in salt and gold, fueled the rise of three successive empires in the western Sahel from around the seventh through the sixteenth centuries: Ghana, Mali, and Songhai. The Middle Niger region, most of which is in present-day Mali, has been a particularly important zone of contact linking long-distance and regional desert-side trade with populations and economies of the savanna and forest. This stretch of the Niger River, beginning around Ségou (figure 1), runs northeast toward the desert, bending along the southern edge of the Sahara before crossing through present-day Niger on its southward trajectory toward the Atlantic. It is navigable most of the year and thus serves as a commercial thoroughfare connecting populations across tropical and arid climates. Towns and cities along this part of the river, including Jenne (Djenné), Timbuktu (Tombouctou), and Gao, grew as commercial hubs and as centers of political, cultural, and intellectual influence. The Middle Niger was at the eastern edge of the Ghana Empire and at the heart of both the Mali and Songhai Empires. As I discuss in chapter 1, after a period of climatic shifts and political instability in the seventeenth and eighteenth centuries, the region was again home to multiple projects of political centralization, state building, and empire in the nineteenth century.

States and empires in the Sahel have been characterized by high degrees of diversity, decentralization, and subsidiarity. Power and wealth depend on regional and long-distance circulations of people, animals, and goods. The routes and networks enabling this circulation have been maintained by groups with specialized skills in mobility and with extended social ties, including pastoralist elites, merchants, and Islamic scholars. Expertise in mobility as well as its political and economic value have protected varying degrees of autonomy for these groups from the centers of political power.

Pastoralists' mobility and the networks that make it possible have been foundational to economic life across much of North and West Africa. Animal products from transhumant and nomadic herding remain a significant source of protein for the region's populations, and pastoralists have played a pivotal role in commerce. Historically, the mobility of pastoral elites depended on relationships of protection and dependence between more and less mobile groups, where hierarchies of prestige and freedom were tied to relative mobility. At the top, noble families and lineage groups traditionally owned the largest herds and moved freely across the broadest spaces, while nonnoble groups managed smaller herds and supplemented pastoral production with other activities. Relatively settled agricultural producers sat at the bottom of this sociopolitical hierarchy. Elites secured their wealth and freedom of movement by maintaining formalized relationships with dependents, both slave and free, which allowed herders to adjust to climate, ecological, and political conditions by accessing labor and resources maintained by geographically dispersed dependents.

Sahelian states and empires have relied on alliances with pastoral elites, and these alliances have typically entailed recognition of nomads' authority over their "vital space"[28]—that is, the places and itineraries that sustain pastoral production and its associated social, political, and economic ties of protection and dependence. One of the ways in which nomadic elites' autonomy was reproduced and regulated was through raiding, or *razzia*, in which a raiding party seizes goods, animals, and/or people from camps, villages, or caravans. The institution of *razzia* is guided by shared understandings of legitimate and illegitimate uses of violence and is a means through which relationships of authority and hierarchy are contested and/or normalized and wealth and resources are redistributed.[29] *Razzia* developed among desert societies as a way of regulating the use of raids according to an ethic of reciprocity. To carry out a raid was to invite a counterattack, and raiding a target that lacked the capacity to retaliate (whether themselves or through a protector) was dishonorable. As Amy Niang explains, the institution of *razzia* helped prevent the centralization of control over resources and circulation in an ecological context where such control would impede populations' capacities to adjust to dynamic conditions. Raiding "served to maintain political stability in a context of economic precariousness and political competition, but also to stem attempts at direct governance, ordering, control, and exclusion from zones of commerce, exchange, and interactions."[30] Reciprocal raiding was a means through which nomadic elites and state rulers both recognized and constrained each other's spheres of authority. For example, the capacity of Tuareg confederations in the southern Sahara to raid Timbuktu or to protect it from raids was a point of leverage in their political relationships with the states and empires that claimed authority over that city, including the Malian and Songhai Empires and the Islamic states of the nineteenth century. In general, states' and empires' access to trade through Timbuktu depended on their recognition of relative autonomy for these confederations and for the city itself. Where this autonomy was challenged, the economy of the region suffered.[31]

The example of Timbuktu also highlights the role that Islamic scholars and merchants have played in reproducing capacities for mobility across North and West Africa, facilitated by a tradition of relative autonomy from political rule.[32] From at least the tenth century, trade in the Sahel was shaped by merchants' adoption of Islam, which facilitated access to commercial networks based in North Africa and the Mediterranean. Islam spread further over the eleventh and twelfth centuries with the influence of missionaries from the Almoravid movement, which promoted adherence to the Maliki school of Islam and resulted in the widespread adoption of Maliki jurisprudence. This provided shared standards that furthered the expansion of regional and long-distance trade. Due to this influence, West African rulers increasingly came to rely on Islamic scholars and clerics as advisers and mediators.[33]

Based on its wealth from the salt trade, Timbuktu had become a renowned center of Islamic learning by the fourteenth century, and it drew Islamic scholars and Maliki experts from other commercial towns along the Niger. Though Timbuktu formally recognized Malian sovereignty from the early to mid-fourteenth century, this period saw the emergence of "patrician" families, who were the effective authorities of the city through their appointments of scholar-judges, or *qadis*. This autonomy was challenged but ultimately reinforced under the Songhai Empire in the fifteenth and sixteenth centuries. Its first ruler, Sunni Ali, perceived Timbuktu's elites as rivals and targeted key figures with imprisonment and execution. This led to a mass exodus of Timbuktu's merchants and scholars—at great cost to regional trade and thus to imperial coffers.[34] Sunni Ali's successor, Askia Muhammad, reversed course, attracting Timbuktu's elite back to the city by recognizing the city's relative autonomy over its internal affairs under its local *qadis*.[35] In addition to a recovery in trade, repaired relations with the scholars of Timbuktu would have given broader legitimacy to Askia Muhammad's claims to authority as a Muslim ruler.

The mobility of Timbuktu's elite—which could be a tool of political opposition and a means of asserting independence—reflected merchants' and intellectuals' embeddedness within extended networks. Islamic training and long-distance trade connected individuals to commercial and scholarly diasporas across the Sahel and into North Africa. Students of Islam traveled to study with esteemed scholars and, once educated, used those scholars' connections and the wide-reaching demand for their skills to find work across the region in Koranic education, negotiating and interpreting contracts, mediation, and political and legal consultation.[36] These services were valuable to trade, and merchants and scholars often came from the same families and lineage groups and thus maintained overlapping networks. Merchants and scholars typically claimed political neutrality, which was reinforced by differentiating lineage groups associated with political rule from those associated with scholarly and religious expertise. This delineation between the spheres of scholarly and religious expertise and political rule situated the former in an important role as trusted mediators, consultants, and power brokers. It also facilitated their mobility even during periods of conflict as traders and scholars were often given free passage because of their recognized neutrality.

Overall, mobility is a signifier of prestige in the Sahel. Accounts of lineage and ethnic identities commonly center stories of migration, celebrating ancestors who were once outsiders and recounting "records of trajectories and long lists of way stations" that marked the ancestors' journeys.[37] Capacities for hospitality, too, are important to social standing and identity. Hospitality is itself an investment in mobility as guests (or their associates) serve as hosts in the future. Hospitality can also, like raiding, function as a countervailing force against the centralization of power and as an assertion of autonomy. For example, the tribute, or tax, owed in the context of a hierarchical relationship could at times take the form of hospitality and gift giving, with the weaker party playing the role of extravagant host and the stronger party, the role of dependent guest. As Judith Scheele writes, hospitality in this context reflects a broader "political vision . . . not of centralized, homogenized sovereignty but of a multitude of smaller protected spaces where guests can be accommodated, with the assumption that the roles of guest and host are determined and hierarchical for the moment but reversible and reciprocal over time."[38] Norms of hospitality and reciprocity mediate relationships among identity, authority, and space in ways that privilege powers of inclusion over powers of exclusion. This facilitates outsiders' access to space, recognizing that everyone becomes an outsider vis-à-vis essential resources at some point.

Capacities for mobility in the Sahel were compromised by European imperial expansion and by colonial and postcolonial states. This was also the case, to varying degrees, under prior imperial and state-building projects in North and West Africa, as I discuss further in chapter 1. But European conquest in the Sahel, undertaken by French and British forces at the end of the nineteenth century and beginning of the twentieth, was especially disruptive in that it aimed to reorient the region's political economy away from desert-side connections and toward the coasts. Economic-development policies, under colonial regimes as well as postcolonial states, were focused on the production of cash crops for export to Europe, trade networks were disrupted by colonial and then postcolonial borders, and colonial and postcolonial administrators sought to sedentarize nomads and expand agricultural production into historic rangelands. Nevertheless, mobility remains vital to Sahelian livelihoods and identities, and networks associated with pastoralism, desert-side trade, and Islamic affiliations have persisted, in changing forms, across colonial and postcolonial states.

Despite being frequently neglected by state and donor development policies, pastoralism remains the foundation of rural livelihoods in arid zones, with approximately 60 percent of Sahelians dependent on livestock production.[39] Relationships between pastoralists and agricultural producers have become strained over the last fifty years in the wake of major droughts, as agricultural production has expanded into rangelands, and as wealthier agricultural producers have invested in their own herds. The last decade of conflict in the Sahel has exacerbated existing tensions, and some localized conflicts between pastoralists and agriculturalists have been absorbed into broader armed struggles. At the same time, intercommunal ties rooted in complementary production strategies have also proved to be as much a resource for resolving social and political conflicts as they are a driver of conflict. As I discuss in chapter 3, such ties were the basis for the peace-building process that prevented a rebellion in Mali from escalating into a broader civil war in the mid 1990s. Rebuilding these intercommunal ties will almost certainly be a requisite foundation for peace building in the contemporary context, though this faces barriers that were not present in the 1990s, including an increasing stigmatization of pastoralists as terrorists or terrorist sympathizers.

Desert-side trade, too, remains a source of wealth, prestige, and social and political influence in the Sahel. Much of this trade is illegal in that it avoids official border restrictions and customs duties. In northern Mali, for example, people rely on foodstuffs and fuel from Algeria that cross the border in violation of legal limits on the types of goods that can be traded over land. Many traders have multigenerational familial ties to trans-Saharan commerce and to markets in North Africa, the Mediterranean, and the Middle East.[40] Since the 1990s, when refugees from political repression and drought returned to northern Mali and Niger, relative newcomers have also entered the business. Many pastoralist families lost their herds in the 1970s and 1980s, and returnees, particularly young men, turned to smuggling as an alternative livelihood, which was potentially very lucrative while also socially and culturally connected to a nomadic way of life. In the 2000s, volumes of trans-Saharan trade increased, attracting a new generation to desert trade, due to several factors: technologies that made desert crossing somewhat safer, including 4x4 vehicles, GPS and satellite phones, improved security with the end of rebellions in Mali and Niger and the civil war in Algeria, and shifts in supply routes for illicit goods due to increased security measures at European ports of entry. The latter development in particular led to the Sahara becoming an important transport route for cocaine.

The growth in Saharan trade has, on the one hand, contributed to a revitalization and enrichment of the social networks and logistical infrastructures that enable mobility. On the other hand, relatively rapid shifts in the types of products crossing the Sahara, especially the growth of the narcotics trade, and in the demographics of traders have strained and circumvented these networks. Desert crossings no longer require as extensive a social network or as much experience with navigation as they have in the past thanks to access to GPS and 4x4 vehicles. Lower costs to entry mean that elite families that have historically dominated long-distance trade face competition, including from groups that they have traditionally seen as subordinates.[41] The narcotics trade in particular has infused huge amounts of capital through new channels. In Mali, competition over trafficking routes and their increasing militarization since the mid-2000s were major factors in the outbreak of armed conflict in 2012 and continue to shape the organization and objectives of armed groups, as I discuss further in chapter 4.

In sum, security for both livelihoods and social and cultural identities in the Sahel is deeply entangled with capacities for mobility and with the reproduction of economic and social ties across diverse groups. As it has in the past, in the contemporary context, requirements for mobility have put Sahelians' security interests in conflict with states' efforts to control circulations both within and across their borders and to reorient productive activities and social, cultural, and political identities toward identification with the nation-state. This conflict has only become more acute in the context of international security interventions aimed at counterterrorism and migration and border control.

Recognizing the Sahel as a cosmopolitan and productive space—not in spite of but in relation to its geographical, historical, and ecological context—reframes its relationship to international order and security. This relationship is not defined by lack or deficiency but by collisions and contestations between different visions and practices of political order.[42] The project of the sovereign, territorial nation-state has variously competed with, accommodated, displaced, or destroyed other political formations that have different legitimating structures and rationalities, different relationships to political and social identities, and different relationships to space. This goes unrecognized within frames of political recognition that conflate political order with territorial state sovereignty.

As Niang and Scheele highlight in studies of order in the Sahel and Sahara, the exclusion of nonstate institutions and practices from understandings of political order has made histories of state building in North and West Africa largely illegible. For example, Niang analyzes the relationship between state and nonstate authority in the case of Mossi state building in what is now Burkina Faso. Governing institutions reflected the reconciliation of two distinct realms of authority: *naam*, the realm of political authority, and *tenga*, the realm of social and moral authority. The negotiation and performance of the relational extent and limits of these realms—for example, through ritual practice—produced political formations with varying degrees of centralization and decentralization.[43] These constitutive limits to the state reflect different understandings of what political order is for. Scheele, for example, contrasts justifications for state apparatuses in Morocco and Algeria with rationalities of sovereignty. The former system "was more concerned with the circulation of wealth than with the direct governance or administration of people," and its authorities were oriented toward "protection and arbitration as much as . . . command." In the latter contexts, state formation has been grounded in relations of allegiance vis-à-vis other identities and subjectivities that preexist and outlast the state, in contrast to relations of sovereignty, where political subjectivity is contingent on recognition by the state.[44] These limits on the centralization of political power have been important to populations' strategies for relating to an environment characterized by high uncertainty and diversity.

Attention to relationships and traditions of recognition between state and nonstate forms of order and authority sheds light on contemporary political conflicts in the Sahel and on the failures of national and international attempts to control them. The contours of these conflicts are not simply defined by support for or opposition to the state but reflect different visions of the objectives and justifications for political order. The territorial nation-state has never fully encompassed or subordinated nonstate institutions and practices in the Sahel, which have been important for the reproduction of forms of circulation that do not adhere to the political and legal regimes of the nation-state and the state-based international system. As I examine further in chapters 3 and 4, order has been reproduced through accommodations between states and elites, who are sometimes aligned with the state and sometimes in opposition to it.

Georg Klute and others analyze these relationships in northern Mali using the concept of heterarchy (and similar concepts, such as hybrid order).[45] The concept of heterarchy was first used to describe the nonhierarchical ordering of neural pathways in the human brain and was subsequently adopted by archaeologists and anthropologists to describe nonhierarchical structures of social and political order in complex stateless societies.[46] Applied to analyses of political order, it describes "fluid and changing relations within a political organizational form whose components may divide and again unite in new constellations."[47] Contrary to its characterization as an "ungoverned space," analyses of heterarchy in northern Mali show it as a site of proliferating and overlapping ordering projects, including by national and international military interventions, by trading and trafficking networks, by tribal authorities, by armed groups, and by humanitarian and nongovernmental organizations.

In relation to international counterterrorism and countermigration security interventions, the political space for accommodation between state and nonstate ordering practices has narrowed. Rather than consolidating political order under the authority of the territorial state, as envisioned by international security interventions, this narrowing has produced more acute political crises for Sahelian states, not least the growth of armed groups, who, in contrast to past rebellions, are not demanding recognition from the international state system but rather freedom from this system altogether. Significantly, armed groups active in Mali have explicitly challenged the legitimacy of the nation-state and the international state system with reference to precolonial models of political order. In central Mali, for example, the jihadist leader Hamadou Koufa invokes the history of the Diina, which I discuss in chapter 1, to legitimate his struggle against the state.[48] In Kidal, jihadist groups have instituted an administrative structure called the *husba* in rural areas, which is organized in accordance with pastoral geographies and under the authority of *qadis*.[49] The jihadi organization al-Mourabitoune, based in Gao in northern Mali, named itself with reference to the Almoravids, who ruled the western Sahara in the tenth and eleventh centuries.[50]

All these groups have articulated critiques of the state that emphasize the illegitimacy of its constraints on free circulation and trade. Koufa has especially targeted the Malian forest service, which is infamous for restricting pastoralists' land use and imposing predatory fines.[51] In Gao and Kidal, jihadist groups declared state border controls and customs duties to be a violation of Islam and outlined a vision of political authority that is "restricted to justice and security" and otherwise does not interfere with trade and circulation.[52] These practices of and justifications for political rule indicate that conflicts in Mali and in the Sahel more broadly concern not just who controls and is represented by the state but what the state is (and is not) for. More fundamentally, they represent challenges to "the legitimacy of the linkage between territoriality and political rule."[53]

For Niang, the failure of international security interventions, most recently in the Sahel and in Afghanistan, indicate that dominant frameworks for conceptualizing international order and security have been inadequate to the task. In both contexts, these frameworks have, at best, discounted and, at worst, pathologized "existing modes of life, relationality, governance, and cultural forms that resist statist designs and external modes of ordering." Addressing these inadequacies requires more empirically grounded accounts of the diversity of ways in which people secure their livelihoods and identities in relation to their social and material environments. Beyond deconstructing the "territorial trap" and its effects, Niang calls for reconstructing a different notion of geopolitics that "functions as a template for thinking interconnectedness and interdependence" in relation to physical space, ecology, and the "subjective experiences and life-worlds" they produce.[54]

In line with the latter research agendas, this book situates contemporary dynamics in the Sahel not as disruptions on the margins of international order but as indicators of core problematics shaping international security, especially concerning the (re)production of space and its relationship to territorialization. *Mistaking Order for Anarchy* examines how nineteenth-century political communities in the Sahel engaged with problems of (in)security, how these practices related to those of colonial and postcolonial state building in the twentieth century, and how the contemporary production of the Sahel as a threatening "ungoverned space" has materialized in this context. The study relies on evidence from existing historical, anthropological, and economic research into the western Sahel, data from over one hundred interviews I conducted in Germany (at the headquarters of the US Africa Command), Mali, and Niger, and scholarly, governmental, and nongovernmental analyses of contemporary conflict in the Sahel.

The following chapter explores relationships between collective security and political order in the Middle Niger in the nineteenth century. Focusing on the Diina system in the inland Niger delta and the Iwellemedan confederation in the Niger bend, I show how security production required the maintenance of high degrees of both diversity and interdependence. Navigating conditions of diversity and interdependence relied in turn on populations' capacities and strategies for mobility, which shaped the ways in which political authority was understood and legitimated. Authority and prestige correlated with higher capacities for mobility, and this mobility depended on maintaining relationships of protection and dependency with less mobile populations. The chapter examines how state-building projects associated with the Diina and Iwellemedan confederation encountered these features of security, focusing on how initiatives to centralize political authority engaged with the decentralizing effects of security strategies and practices linked to mobility. These cases illustrate how flexibility in the boundaries of political spaces and identities was central to security, while attempts to fix these boundaries corresponded with crises in security and prosperity.

ONE

Ordering Interdependence in the Middle Niger

Life in the Sahel has been shaped by climatic variability and uncertainty. In addition to short-term rainfall variability, the Sahel has also seen long-term shifts in climatic conditions, with cycles of relative humidity and aridity. Variability in climate, ecology, and conditions of production have influenced distinct ways of living on the "desert frontier," which closely link desert-side communities with producers on the less arid savanna.[1] Social, economic, and political institutions have ordered the relations among and between these groups in more and less conflictual ways but overall facilitated their close interdependence. This chapter examines how these institutions developed and were contested in relation to nineteenth-century projects of political centralization in the Middle Niger. This period saw attempts to consolidate political order following a period of relative political instability after the fall of the Songhai Empire and increased aridity. In the Niger bend, a Tuareg political confederation, the Iwellemedan, established wide-reaching political authority by maintaining relations of protection and dependence across an expansive multiethnic network. In the inland Niger delta, successive jihadist movements sought to establish Islamic states that could encompass the region under a universalizing vision of Islamic law. These political projects defined and engaged with conditions of interdependence in different ways, which shaped the characteristics, reach, and durability of their political authority and its effects on the collective security of populations in the Middle Niger.

Ecology and Interdependence in the Middle Niger

Pastoral production is central to livelihoods in the Sahel because it makes arid environments habitable as animals convert water and fodder otherwise unsuitable for human consumption into nutrient-rich milk. Because of high variability in the availability and value of land and water, pastoralism requires capacities for mobility. Adaptability to arid ecologies and expertise in mobility situate pastoralists as important links between communities in the desert and savanna. In addition to specialized skills in interpreting and tracking changing environmental conditions, mobility requires the maintenance of social and economic relationships both with other pastoralists and with less mobile cultivators. As I elaborate further below, relations between desert-side and savanna-side populations have been characterized by different forms of hierarchy, protection, dependence, and reciprocity that contribute to ordering mobility.

Pastoralism in arid contexts depends on rules and norms of communal-resource use and management, which enable the flexible and opportunistic use of resources in response to environmental changes.[2] For example, access to resource patches is commonly mediated through tiers of priority users who are responsible for the maintenance of the resource—for instance, the regulation of grazing access or the upkeep of hand-dug wells. Priority users grant other users access to land and resources based on rules and norms of reciprocity. Lower priority users might pay a fee or, more commonly, provide reciprocal agreements assuring access to lands or resources in the future. These systems rely on the recognition of flexible and overlapping geographical boundaries, which are subject to regular negotiation. Boundaries are typically oriented around points, such as a water source, with increasing flexibility and overlap of access and ownership at greater distances from those points. Authority over different scales of land and resources have historically corresponded with different social and political institutions from the household to larger kinship structures and political groupings. General agreements over reciprocal movement and resource access are often long-term and sustained over generations, with details renegotiated in relation to ecological, social, and political conditions.[3] Pastoralists' collective dependence on these regimes creates tangible costs to violating them—namely, being excluded from or bearing higher costs for accessing crucial resources and information.

Pastoralists' mobility also depends on relationships with less mobile pro-

ducers, including cultivators, fishers, craftspeople, and merchants. During
the dry season and in periods of drought, herds need access to water and
pasture in areas with higher rainfall, which brings them into regular contact
with areas of long-term settlement. In addition to accessing water and pasture, pastoralists have historically relied on less mobile populations for grain
to supplement their milk-based diets, textiles, metal and leather products,
and labor and storage. Pastoralists, in turn, provide animal products and
fertilizer and connect savanna populations with desert-side trade. Overall,
the complementarity of desert-side and savanna production can provide in-
surance against the effects of drought, disease, and overall climatic volatility.[4]
For example, relationships between more and less mobile populations facilitate herd splitting—a strategy of distributing the animals of one's herd across
as wide an area as possible to manage risk.[5] While mitigating pastoralists'
losses from drought or disease, herd splitting can also serve as a form of investment in agricultural villages, which reinforces ties of mutual obligation.

Complementarity across ecological niches and climatic zones situates the
Sahel as a vital commercial crossroads. The Middle Niger region in particular has long been the site of prosperous and politically influential market
towns and cities. Here, the course of the Niger River facilitates both trade
and settlement. In the present-day city of Mopti (figure 1), the Niger inter-
sects the Bani River, forming a broad inland delta with wetlands, lakes, and
floodplains. Since at least 250 BCE, the delta region has been home to prosperous population centers, notably Jenne-Jeno (Djenné-Djenno), thanks to
its fertility and biodiversity as well as its proximity to both the desert and
the savanna.[6] North of the delta, the river turns east, carving a fertile valley
through the southern Sahara Desert. Southern Saharan cities with proximity
to the Niger, like Timbuktu and Gao, developed as nodal points in the long-
distance trade between savanna gold producers and desert salt producers.[7]

Beginning in the seventh century, growth in the gold and salt trade fueled
the expansion of three successive empires with influence over the Sahel:
Ghana, Mali, and Songhai. These empires had decentralized structures with
"social and economic [heartlands]" and "tributary [zones] with fluctuating
boundaries."[8] Taxation on trade and food production across these spaces
funded the administration of the heartland, the maintenance of fighting
forces to secure trade routes and collect tribute, and the provision of gifts to
maintain rulers' legitimacy. While the Middle Niger was at the far eastern
edge of the Ghana Empire, it was central to the Malian Empire for much of

its tenure—from the early fourteenth to early fifteenth centuries—and was at the heart of the Songhai Empire, whose main capital was at Gao, from the mid-fifteenth century to the end of the sixteenth century. The geographies of these empires reflected their interests in the commercial centers of the gold and salt trades. Their eastward shift from the twelfth to fifteenth centuries correlated with the movement of the desert frontier as the Sahel's climate dried. As this frontier—where desert-side and savanna-side production are in closest proximity—shifted, centers of commercial activity and the networks that sustained them shifted as well.

Long-distance trade in salt and gold depended on the maintenance of regional trading networks between the desert and savanna that ensured populations' basic needs and enabled adaptation to climatic volatility. While imperial rule depended on the profit margins and access to luxury goods made possible by long-distance trade, most people's livelihoods hinged on the higher volume trade in foodstuffs, and the infrastructure of this shorter-distance trade provided the foundation for the trans-Saharan trade.[9] This encouraged subsidiarity in relationships of social, economic, and political authority. In particular, political rulers recognized varying degrees of autonomy for groups with specialized capacities for mobility, including Islamic scholars and clerics, merchant communities, and nomadic pastoralists. Centers of commerce and of Islamic study asserted varying degrees of independence. For example, later histories report that Malian kings would not enter the scholarly town of Diakhaba without invitation even though it was located within their imperial realm, making it a place of asylum from political oppression.[10] When the first ruler of the Songhai Empire, Sunni Ali, threatened the autonomy of Timbuktu's elite, they left the city, returning when Ali's successor, Askia Muhammad, affirmed the authority of the city's own scholar-jurists.[11]

Relative autonomy for merchant elites overlapped with strong norms of independence between political and religious/moral authorities.[12] Differentiation between political rulers and religious authorities was shaped by broader norms in West Africa defining relationships among ethnocultural identities, lineage groups, and occupational specializations. Diversification of production techniques (which, as discussed above, secures livelihoods in conditions of ecological uncertainty) corresponded with diversity in ethnic identities, which served to regulate access to protected resources. As Richard L. Roberts summarizes, "[Ethnic] boundaries were not rigid, but in order to

acquire the protected resources on a regular basis, producers needed to con-
form to the dominant social characteristics associated with the ethnic group
that controlled those resources."[13] Within common ethnocultural identities,
relationships to lineage also differentiated specialized occupational roles,
particularly for elites. Political rulers typically claimed ties to lineage groups
with recognized warrior traditions, and religious authorities, to groups with
scholarly traditions.

Norms of religious and scholarly autonomy played an important role
in facilitating mobility and exchange across the Sahel. Islamic clerics were
among the most mobile people. Training typically required relocation to the
home of a teacher, and teacher-student relationships often translated into durable familial ties, with teachers arranging marriages for successful students
from within their communities or even their own families.[14] After completing
training, young clerics would often relocate again to open their own schools
and provide other religious services. Islamic education thus produced durable "webs of affection, kinship, and scholarship" across the Sahel.[15] Scholars'
neutrality protected their freedom of movement even during periods of conflict, and this neutrality protected trade as well given the close ties between
merchants and scholars, with many coming from the same families. In addition to protecting mobility, neutrality positioned Islamic experts as trusted
mediators, negotiators, and advisers.[16]

In sum, related to ecological and geographical conditions in the Middle
Niger region, prosperity and security have long depended on reproducing relationships of interdependence among diverse population groups and across
complementary ecological zones. In this context, securing the material and
social conditions for mobility was vital. This shaped geographies of identity,
belonging, and authority characterized by flexible and overlapping boundaries and different forms of hierarchy, dependency, and subsidiarity.

Political and Ecological Change in the Seventeenth
and Eighteenth Centuries

In 1591, Timbuktu was conquered by forces of the Saadi dynasty of Morocco, and the Songhai Empire collapsed. This inaugurated a period of significant political and ecological change in the western Sahel, characterized
by political fragmentation, ecological crises, and widespread vulnerability to
violence. After its successful displacement of the Songhai Empire's rule, the

Saadi dynasty was unable to consolidate its authority over the Niger bend (which it had hoped would enable Moroccan control over the salt trade). Subsequent political fragmentations and transformations were also shaped by climatic shifts. After a period of increased rainfall in the sixteenth century, the climate became significantly drier from about 1630 until the mid-nineteenth century, with several major droughts affecting the entire Sahel.[17] These changes drove populations toward higher-rainfall zones to the south and east and shifted the geographies of encounter and exchange among pastoralists and cultivators. Political fragmentation and social and economic uncertainty in the drying Sahel often favored the former over the latter.[18] In a context of decentralized violence, mobile groups typically had an advantage over more sedentary cultivators with the capacity to strike on camel or horseback, expropriate animals, grains, or slaves, and flee into the desert. These political and climatic shifts also coincided with the growth of the Atlantic slave trade as well as an increased demand for slaves in the Maghreb.[19] Successive droughts and famine over the eighteenth century increased the slave population by making sedentary cultivators more vulnerable to predatory raids as well as incentivizing people to sell themselves or their children into slavery to avoid starvation. Slaves could be exchanged for arms and horses, which further bolstered the capacities of slave raiders.[20]

Even at the height of the Atlantic slave trade, most people who were enslaved in the western Sahel remained in North and West Africa.[21] Islamic scholars and jurists largely agreed that the sale of Muslims to Christians should be prohibited, and efforts to exclude Muslim populations from the Atlantic slave trade protected the political and economic power of Sahelian elites, who relied on the labor of enslaved persons.[22] In contrast to the chattel slavery of the Atlantic trade, Islamic law recognized enslaved persons as human beings entitled to moral and legal protections and characterized most conditions of enslavement as temporary.[23] Nevertheless, the racialized exploitation that was foundational to chattel slavery marks slavery and its legacies in the Sahel as well. As I discuss further in chapter 3, hierarchies distinguishing noble, free, and slave status in the Sahel and Sahara were racialized according to understandings of genealogy as a marker of connection to Islam. With French colonial rule, existing understandings of race were influenced by European regimes of white supremacy.[24] Moreover, representations of African slavery as benign were themselves shaped by colonial rule. Even as they justified colonization as an effort to abolish so-called Arab and

indigenous slavery in Africa, colonial administrators relied on the cooperation of slave-owning elites and the continuation and even expansion of slavery to maintain social control. In this context, administrators were interested
in defining different indigenous categories of dependency as distinct from
slavery.[25] In sum, while conditions of slavery and dependency in the Sahel
were very different from those of racialized chattel slavery, the former also
depended on violence, exploitation, and hierarchical constructions of ethnic
and racial difference, which have ongoing effects.[26]

Indeed, fear of enslavement and demands for protection shaped reconfigu-
rations of power and authority in the inland delta and along the Niger bend as
they developed over the eighteenth and nineteenth centuries.[27] Warrior groups
offered protection from raids in exchange for tribute. As warrior groups expanded their networks of protection and dependency, their access to resources,
labor, and fighting forces expanded, which further increased their capacities
and the credibility of their protection. Networks of protection overlapped with
networks of exchange across different rainfall zones and productive activities.
In the upper Niger bend, between Timbuktu and Gao, a new ethnic-political
grouping, the Arma, resulted from intermarriage between Moroccan occupi-
ers and the Songhai. The Arma increasingly asserted their independence from
Morocco by developing relations of protection and dependency with populations along the Niger River.[28] For most of the seventeenth century and into the
eighteenth, the Niger bend was nominally under the authority of the Arma
Pashalik of Timbuktu, which maintained a network of garrisons in otherwise
mostly autonomous towns, like Jenne, Bamba, and Gao.[29] In Timbuktu, the
Arma found (as had the Malian and Songhai Empires before them) that their
authority was contingent on accommodating the city's scholars, who approved
the pasha and appointed the *qadis*, who actually administered the city.[30]

Beginning in the seventeenth century, influenced by the drying climate,
Tuareg populations who had been based to the north in the drier Adagh
and Tilemsi Valley regions moved south. Like the Arma, Tuareg groups also
sought to establish themselves closer to the Niger River valley through raiding and offering protection from raiding. Conditions of generalized insecurity
and mutual raiding in the early eighteenth century gave way to increasing
political centralization in the latter part of the century as demand for protection strengthened political coalitions.[31] As I elaborate below, a Tuareg confederation, the Kel Ekummed, emerged out of this period as a hegemonic
force across much of the Niger bend.

South of the Niger bend, the insecurity and famine of the eighteenth century also empowered warrior elites. In the inland delta, Fulani warriors' historic dominance of the area was challenged by the growth of the Segu state to the southwest, led by young Bamana warriors, who overthrew the traditional leadership structure around 1712.[32] The state's productive base was built on slave raiding. Captured populations sustained the state by providing agricultural and domestic labor, joining slave raids themselves, or being traded for arms, horses, and luxury goods from Europe or North Africa, which could be distributed as patronage to sustain political support.[33] The Fulani elites, the *ardobé*, ultimately maintained relative autonomy by paying tribute to Segu while reciprocal raiding between Segu and the delta continued.

This context of increased insecurity also altered the terrain of Islamic authority and its relationship to political authority. To the east and west of the Middle Niger, in the Senegambia and Hausaland, Islamic clerics attracted diverse followings with critiques of exploitation by and collusion among political rulers, merchant groups, and religious leaders.[34] Revolutionary clerics challenged longstanding norms of independence between religious and political authority and established states led by Islamic scholars. In the Senegambia, Islamic states were established in Futa Jallon in the 1720s and in Futa Toro in the 1770s. In Hausaland to the east, Usman dan Fodio founded the Sokoto Caliphate in 1804.[35]

By the turn of the nineteenth century, life in the Middle Niger had been transformed by a long period of insecurity and vulnerability to drought and to violence. Across the Sahel and West Africa there were movements toward forms of political centralization. To the west and east, jihadist states had successfully overthrown the status quo of accommodation among commercial, political, and religious elites. The next sections examine forms of political centralization and their relationship to security conditions in the Niger bend and the inland Niger delta.

The Iwellemedan in the Niger Bend

At the turn of the nineteenth century, political authority north of the Niger bend was consolidating under the leadership of a Tuareg political grouping, the Iwellemedan. The authority of the Iwellemedan (and more specifically the Kel Ekummed confederation) came from a diverse network of relations of protection and dependence, and these relationships enabled their freedom of movement across a vast area. This freedom of movement served in turn to reproduce reciprocal ties of protection and dependence. This section examines how the mobility of Iwellemedan elites related to collective security in the Niger bend.

Before discussing the role of the Iwellemedan in the Niger bend, it is useful to summarize features of identity, belonging, and authority that were common across Tuareg society in the Sahara and Sahel. As predominantly nomadic pastoralists, Tuareg communities oriented their social relations toward facilitating mobility. Elites who owned the largest herds and could move relatively freely across the broadest spaces maintained that wealth and mobility through their relationships with groups lower down on the social hierarchy who were less mobile. These relationships facilitated an opportunistic model of pastoralism, where herders had maximum flexibility to adjust to climate and ecological conditions. Less mobile groups managed parts of the herd and worked in villages and oases, providing agriculture and commerce-related labor, which could buffer the effects of ecological and climatic variability. Investing in and maintaining distant villages and oases maintained nomads' freedom of movement, ensuring access to water and pasture along nomadic itineraries, providing reliable storage facilities and connection points where information could be shared and transactions negotiated, and offering alternative sources of income when conditions for herding were unfavorable.

Social hierarchies were reproduced via lineage and kin-based identities, which signified distinct social and productive roles (e.g., warriors, herders, or religious experts) and the relative prestige of a group's origins (noble, free, or slave). The primary sociopolitical grouping was the *tewsit* (pl. *tewsiten*), which can be defined as a clan or lineage group. *Tewsiten* signified relatively stable collective identities, but they also facilitated social and political flexibility and reconfiguration; they were amenable to being "both split and bundled." Membership in a *tewsit* was not exclusive: individuals could be encompassed within multiple *tewsiten* through different individuals in their lineage or through different familial or labor arrangements. Alliances among *tewsiten* constituted larger political groupings, including military confederations, or drum groups (*ettebel*), under the authority of a chief. Familiarity with *tewsiten* identities and relationships helped situate individuals and groups in relation to broader social, political, and ethical frameworks. This knowledge was a tool for navigating encounters with neighbors and strangers and reproducing broader social cohesion across long distances. As Baz Lecocq explains, "In times of scarcity it is vital to be able to leave one's territory and dwell on that of neighbors. In this particular environment, knowing people, and the relation to them over space as well as time, is essential to survival."[36] Connections to *tewsiten* provided a script for how strangers related to one another and an accountability mechanism for individuals' behavior. The interdependence of social groups created tangible costs to violating norms and expectations.

These sociopolitical groupings facilitated flexible relationships to space and to resources. *Tewsiten* and confederations thereof negotiated and claimed spatial rights and responsibilities in relation to both residency and the requirements of pastoral production. In Tamashek, these conceptions of space are distinct: *akal* refers to a space of belonging or zone of security, and *ihenzuzagh* refers to the geographies in which nomadic livelihoods are sustained.[37] The latter "indicates a bundle of rights held by a particular family, clan or federation of clans to exploit the natural resources in certain places at certain periods."[38] These routes were formally negotiated among *tewsiten* leaders. *Akal* refers to a space in which one can reside without special permission. The borders of these spaces were flexible and overlapping, their geographies extending out from key points or nodes at their center rather than being contained within fixed boundaries. Lecocq summarizes, "They can best be seen as a maze of frontiers, tied up in residential nodes of individual clans or federation members, overlapping and interspersed with similar mazes of other clans or federations. . . . The more power and status a clan had, the larger the space they could move in at ease."[39] *Tewsit* identity, status, and membership in broader alliances or confederations granted varying degrees of mobility tied to a group's ability to claim dependents or dependency. This provided a logic for adjusting who had access to and authority over what in a context where climatic variability meant that any given space could accommodate varying numbers of people from season to season and year to year.

The Iwellemedan emerged as a distinct sociopolitical identity in the late eighteenth century among *tewsiten* who claimed the seventeenth-century leader Karidenna as an ancestor. Karidenna is remembered as a great political leader and alliance builder during a period of social and political upheaval as Tuareg communities migrated south from the mountainous Adagh toward the Niger River. Under his leadership, the nascent Iwellemedan established themselves in the Niger River valley by forming alliances with warrior and clerical elites, both Tuareg and non-Tuareg. After his death at the turn of the eighteenth century, each of Karidenna's three sons became a leader of their own *tewsit*, which together formed an alliance known as the Kel Ekummed. Each expanded their political influence through intermarriage with the families of warrior elites. In the late eighteenth and early nineteenth centuries the Kel Ekummed translated their expanding network of alliances into military capacity under the leadership of Kawa, the fifth chief since Karidenna. Kawa's ability to mobilize fighting forces from among the Iwellemedan's allies enabled the Kel Ekummed to expand a network of dependent villages and populations. Over the rest of the nineteenth century, the Iwellemedan were known as *"les maîtres du pays"* across a vast area stretching along the river from Bamba (east of Timbuktu) to Ayoru in present-day Niger and north of the river between the Tilemsi Valley, Adagh Mountains, and Azawagh Valley. At its most expansive, the Iwellemedan's network of dependents stretched between four and five hundred kilometers east to west and north to south (at least eight days of travel by camel along both axes).[40]

Iwellemedan power was tied to their freedom of movement over a large space, which facilitated their accumulation of capital and their access to fighting forces. This was enabled by alliances and relationships of protection and dependency across a multiethnic network of populations and villages. The greater the number of dependent groups with which the Iwellemedan could establish reciprocal ties, the larger was the geographical scope of their movement. Charles Grémont has produced an extensive analysis of the Iwellemedan's political network in the nineteenth century using available written sources as well as interviews conducted in the region of Gao in the 1990s and early 2000s. His account highlights the diversity of relationships that constituted the Iwellemedan's authority. The Iwellemedan and the politically and militarily dominant Kel Ekummed did not have the numbers or capacity to directly assert their authority across the areas and populations they claimed. Instead, they exerted influence through a range of intermediaries who had their own claims to authority vis-à-vis diverse communities and interests at different geographic scales. These intermediaries typically had their own fighting capacity or religious and juridical expertise through which they offered protection and services to dependent groups. As the regional influence and military capabilities of the Iwellemedan grew, aligning with them could reinforce existing authorities' credibility and legitimacy in relation to their own dependent populations.[41]

Through intermediaries, the Iwellemedan's power was intertwined with overlapping relationships of protection, dependency, and socioeconomic complementarity. For example, the Shiyukhan were an intermediary of the Iwellemedan at the western edge of their network in the area of Bamba. Their history recounts their ancestor Shekh Almoner forming an alliance with Karidenna based on the former's Islamic training and expertise. In exchange for religious counsel and services, Karidenna and the Iwellemedan provided security for their camp. This security enabled their small camp to grow into a village that attracted other groups, including Songhai and Tuareg families seeking protection from raids. This positioned the Shiyukhan themselves in a role of protector because they could intercede with Karidenna and the Iwellemedan on behalf of new dependents. Other intermediaries were connected to the Iwellemedan through marriage ties. For example, east of Bamba in the region of Zomgoy was the Kel Tabankort, a warrior lineage group, who intermarried with the Kel Ekummed and functioned as their principle intermediary. The Kel Tabankort maintained tributary relationships with the villages in the area, all headed by Songhai chiefs. The Iwellemedan then received part of this tribute. Grémont's interviews with the Sheriffen, a Tuareg group whose presence in the area around Gao predated the Iwellemedan's arrival, describe a different model of relationship with an intermediary. The chief of the Sheriffen could be counted on to provide for the Iwellemedan's needs in the area, while the Iwellemedan would not demand their own tribute from the villages already under Sheriffen protection.[42]

Vulnerability to violence was the foundation of many of the relationships of protection and dependency that constituted the Iwellemedan's authority. Under Kawa, the Iwellemedan established their authority over an expanding area because of the credibility of both their threats of violence and their guarantees of protection from violence. In Grémont's research, many groups described their relationship to the Iwellemedan and their intermediaries as that of providing tribute, typically a portion of the annual harvest, in exchange for protection from raiding.[43] However, relationships of protection and dependency were also shaped by other dimensions of socioeconomic complementarity, shared vulnerability, and interdependence. Routine interactions between protector and dependent groups were oriented around exchange between specialized production activities, with more mobile and militarily capable groups typically connected to the desert-side production of animal products and the salt trade and less mobile and militarily capable groups connected to river and agricultural production. The exchange of desert-side and river- or savanna-side products formed a foundation for other sociopolitical and economic ties, such as religious training and services, social and political mediation, and longer-term capital investment—for example, in storage facilities, manufacturing, or herd splitting.

The term *arkawal*, in both the Songhai and Tamashek languages, characterizes this interdependence within a relationship that is also unequal. *Arkawal* is defined by one of Grémont's interlocutors as "fidelity to an oath, to something woven together, whose transgression would bring misfortune."[44] *Arkawal* describes a relationship of mutual obligation whose maintenance is not reducible to its material instrumentalities. For example, in one description of *arkawal*, a respondent explains that it entitled each party to the goods of the other according to need. But even when there was no economic benefit, superficial exchange would take place simply for the purpose of maintaining interaction and reproducing mutual trust. "Ils avaient un intérêt économique bien sûr, mais pas seulement. Des familles qui possédaient les mêmes biens faisaient aussi des échanges. Cela permettait d'entretenir les relations, de consolider la confiance." Grémont notes that in his research, *arkawal* was most likely to be used when describing relations among groups with an inequality in status.[45] This speaks to its role in protecting subordinate groups from the risks of abuse. The relationship between protector and dependent was not just defined materially but also socially and politically in terms of the relational identities through which groups' material rights and obligations were recognized. Protector groups' prestige as protectors required them to adhere to social and moral criteria of *arkawal*.

Given their reliance on intermediaries, the Iwellemedan's authority as *les maîtres du pays* was not based on their own control over the means of violence. Quite the opposite: the Iwellemedan's political legitimacy relied on their recognition of others' rights to use violence. Among groups recognizing the Iwellemedan's authority, mutual raiding remained a social, economic, and political tool to reinforce or reshape relationships of power.[46] Raiding was an important source of sociopolitical prestige for warrior *tewsiten*, and this was associated with ethical and cultural constraints on its use. Raiding was shaped by practices of *razzia*, which originated in Bedouin societies. *Razzia* structured the legitimacy and illegitimacy of the use of violence in the desert and reflected an overall context of relative scarcity and uncertainty: the *razzia* was a quick, typically nonlethal, incursion into a settlement or a camp to seize livestock, goods, and/or people, and then the raiders would flee back into the desert.[47] Raiding was "framed by two requirements: it was to be *normal and necessary,*" meaning that it adhered to mutually understood rules about the appropriate targets of raiding and the degrees of violence that could be used, and it was to be "equitable where provision is made for 'retaliation' and reciprocation," meaning that counterraiding was legitimate and expected. Rather than a source of conflict, raiding can be understood as a "regulatory mechanism" for mitigating the risks associated with the centralization of political and economic power in an arid environment.[48]

Within the Iwellemedan's confederation, raiding was used as a redistributive mechanism, as recourse against a group that was not fulfilling its obligations to dependents, and as a way for groups to increase their relative political influence or challenge that of a rival.[49] For example, less powerful warrior *tewsiten* commonly used raiding and counterraiding to reproduce their relative autonomy vis-à-vis the Iwellemedan while also recognizing the Iwellemedan's dominance. In this context, raiding and counterraiding was an accepted alternative to tribute: on balance, the weaker group was at a net loss from this raiding relationship, but they maintained a sociopolitical identity distinct from that of formally dependent groups.[50] Dependent groups were vulnerable to raiding as proxies for conflict between protector groups. In these raids, which targeted goods, animals, and sometimes slaves, dependent groups typically received compensation via their protectors through counterraiding.[51] Religious *tewsiten*, who were external to the dynamics of raiding and counterraiding, also played a central role in the regulation of violence as mediators and negotiators in the event that raiding threatened to escalate or exceeded accepted constraints.[52] Overall, the security benefit associated with wide recognition for a common authority, like the Iwellemedan, was not based on the monopolization over the means of violence but rather the legitimation of shared rules and norms around its use.

Raiding and counterraiding were also conducted at the edges of the Iwellemedan's geographical reach—between groups within the Iwellemedan's confederation and those outside it. These raids were more extensive in terms of the number of fighters used and the amount of booty seized. Exposure to violence from outsiders reinforced a collective sense of belonging within the Iwellemedan's confederation. In Grémont's interviews, many groups recount participating in fighting to defend villages from incursions by outsiders. The willingness to join these campaigns increased a group's prestige, which could translate into a less hierarchical relationship with the Iwellemedan— for example, no longer requiring the payment of tribute.[53] In general over the

nineteenth century, raiding and counterraiding with groups outside of the
confederation was less of a threat to the Iwellemedan's authority (though it
threatened lives and livelihoods in dependent villages on the margins) than a
means through which this authority was defined.

Prior to the French conquest, the greatest external threats to the Iwellemedan's power came from Fulani-led jihadist movements. The first con-
frontation, which was with an offshoot of the Sokoto Caliphate in 1816, was
significant in reinforcing the role of the Iwellemedan as the predominant
protection force in the Niger bend, capable of protecting existing elites from
Islamic revolution. This movement emerged in the years following the founding of the Sokoto Caliphate and was led by Muhammad Eljilani ag Ibrahim. Eljilani became an influential religious figure within the Kel Denneg,
a Tuareg confederation centered north of Sokoto. Inspired by Usman dan
Fodio's success, Eljilani had political ambitions of establishing an Islamic
state that would unite the Tuareg of the central and western Sudan. After
securing the support of Sokoto, he began a series of military campaigns
against Tuareg and Hausa populations north of the caliphate, gaining key
allies based on his claims to religious authority. For other religious and military elites, including within the Kel Denneg, Eljilani's revolutionary project was seen as a grave threat, especially in light of the Sokoto Caliphate's
success in transforming the sociopolitical order across much of Hausaland.
Key allies of the Iwellemedan—notably, those among the religious Kel Es-
Suq and the Kunta of Timbuktu—appealed to Kawa to mobilize his *ettebel*
against Eljilani's continued expansion. Kawa assembled a significant fighting
force and led an expedition east to the region of Aïr, where they defeated Eljilani's troops, inaugurating his rapid decline. Kawa was killed in the battle.
In Grémont's account, the defeat of Eljilani's forces and Kawa's battle death
were likely significant events in the growing recognition of the Iwellemedan's
authority in the Niger bend.[54] The Iwellemedan subsequently were a check
on the expansionary aspirations of jihadist states based in the inland Niger
delta, which I discuss below.

The Iwellemedan's military capacities also enabled them to influence
events beyond the western edge of their network based on their relationship
with elites in Timbuktu, specifically members of the powerful Kunta clan.
The Kunta, an Arab-Imazighen clan with significant interests in the salt
trade, came to prominence in Timbuktu in the early eighteenth century as
the Arma Pashalik was in decline. In 1737, Arma forces were defeated by the

Tuareg Kel Tadamakkat federation, which brought an end to the Pashalik, and the Kunta negotiated their surrender. In addition to their wealth and trading connections, the Kunta were known for cultivating broad scholarly and juridical expertise, and they were sought-after mediators.[55] This situated them as an important resource for multiple constituencies in Timbuktu and throughout the Niger bend.[56]

The Kunta relied on the military capacity of the Iwellemedan to support their interests—for example, when they called for a military response to El-jilani's political ambitions. For the Iwellemedan, their alliance with the Kunta gave access to commercial opportunities in the salt and tobacco trades. It also gave legitimacy based on the Kunta's religious authority and position as trusted mediators and advisers. With the rise of Ahmad Lobbo's (also known as Seku Amadou) caliphate in the inland Niger delta and his expansionary campaigns north, the Kunta relied on its relationships with the Iwellemedan and the dominant confederation to its west, the Kel Tadamakkat, to protect Timbuktu's autonomy. More broadly, these relationships constituted a barrier between the revolutionary forces of the jihadist movements and the Niger bend. As I discuss below, these movements aspired to bring the entire region under the authority of a single state and interpretation of Islamic law. This challenged existing social and material infrastructures connecting the delta and arid environments to its north.

Islamic States in the Inland Niger Delta

Upstream from the Niger bend, the river expands into a wide delta and floodplain with a uniquely diverse and productive ecosystem. The delta sees annual flooding and connects an arid zone to the north and a semiarid zone to the south. Since the fifteenth century, Fulani pastoralists had been the dominant political influence in the delta, intermarrying and establishing relations of protection and dependence with agricultural producers and fishing communities. The dominance of a warrior class, the *ardobé*, became increasingly formalized over time around the authority of clan leaders, or *ardo'en*, and their influence over the production activities of subordinate groups.[57] The *ardobé* regulated shared access to delta resources among fishing communities, cultivators, and pastoralists and invested in artisan production. During the flood season, fishing and agricultural groups had priority rights to land and water in the delta. After the waters retreated, entrance to, use of, and exit from exposed pasture was regulated by the *ardo'en* of four main clans, each of whom exercised authority over separate pasturing zones. Access to these zones was based on kinship and political relationships or on the payment of a fee. The system became more complex as the population in the region increased. From the fifteenth to seventeenth centuries, the *ardobé* established subordinate settlements of agricultural producers, or *rimaibé*, whose use of the land was tied to their provision of cereals and dry-season pasture to meet the needs of the pastoralists and nomadic elites.[58] Chiefs of allied Fulani clans were incorporated into this system as subordinates, or *jowro'en* (sg. *jowro*), who managed herds on behalf of the *ardobé* and had authority over pasture use in the villages where *rimaibé* lived and worked.[59]

When the founder of the Diina, Ahmad Lobbo, was born in the early 1770s, the *ardo'en* maintained their power by paying tribute to the militarily dominant Segu state, which provided imperfect protection against raids. The authority of Segu's kings and the delta's *ardo'en* was also supported by Islamic authorities in the wealthy commercial towns of Sinsani and Jenne, which connected the Middle Niger to the desert-side economy.[60] Discontent with this status quo was increasing at the turn of the nineteenth century, likely affected by drought and famine in the 1790s as well as continued vulnerabilities to raiding.[61] By the 1810s, as a marabout in Jenne, Ahmad Lobbo began to build a following based on his critiques of the religious authorities in Jenne and, by extension, the broader order of the Middle Niger. Like the other West African jihads, Lobbo's movement challenged longstanding norms distinguishing the political roles of warrior and clerical elites.[62] The jihadists instead envisioned a polity whose legitimacy was based on rulers' own spiritual authority and expertise in Islamic theology and jurisprudence.

Tensions between Lobbo and his followers and the existing religious authorities grew over the 1810s, coming to a head around 1817 when a dispute between one of Lobbo's disciples and a member of the *ardobé* escalated to violence. Lobbo's supporters were confronted by Segu's military, which had mobilized in defense of the *ardo'en*, and won an improbable victory in 1818. The victory inspired new recruits to Lobbo's cause, and in the following months, the *ardo'en* capitulated, and Lobbo asserted himself as the new leader of an Islamic state—the Diina.[63] In 1821, he established Hamdallahi as the administrative capital, from which he raised revenues to fund expansionary efforts in all directions.

The Diina institutionalized many of the existing practices of the *ardobé* but replaced the *ardo'en* and non-Islamic or otherwise resistant *jowro'en* with loyal clerics and scholars. It established thirty-seven distinct pasturing zones, managed by a *jowro*, and mandated that access to and use of resources be regulated based on users' established residence in one zone.[64] This included requiring nomadic Fulani herders to establish residence in existing or new villages, partially sedentarizing them. Rules concerning dependency were centralized and fixed—for example, the tribute owed by *rimaibé* and independent fishing and agricultural villages.[65] Herding practices, including access dates to pasture and herding routes and entry points, were codified. However, the day-to-day management of common resources in the delta saw minimal transformation with the creation of the Diina except where existing *jowro'en* challenged its authority and were replaced.[66] Each *jowro* remained accountable, as they had under the *ardobé*, to herders residing within their pasturing zone through a group called the *suudu baaba*. These groups continued to have decision-making power—as long as they did not challenge the ultimate authority of the Diina to raise revenues for the state.[67] This was the responsibility of new administrative authorities assigned to each pasturing zone, who were clerics and scholars loyal to Lobbo. Overall, the codification of property and resource management increased the relative power of what was previously a lower class of Fulani herders and rural clerics over warrior elites and their religious and commercial allies in Jenne.

The Diina is often described as a system that sedentarized formerly mobile pastoralists in fixed territories. Indeed, materials from the time report frustration from pastoralists about increased constraints on their movements. However, Pascal Legrosse and Matthew D. Turner emphasize that this often exaggerates the degree of sedentarization, wrongly associating the pastoral-management strategies of the Diina with Western range-management strategies oriented toward the carrying capacity of a particular range territory.[68] In fact, the Diina's system of differentiating pasturing zones embraced existing spatial regimes, which organized a nested framework of communal property and access rights with "a fluid geographical definition of the territory's boundary related both to ecological exigencies and political power plays" that could enable the "opportunistic use of boundary resources within certain agreed socio-cultural bounds"—in this case, mediated through the roles of the *jowro'en*.[69]

While the management of productive activities showed continuity with the *ardobé* system, Lobbo's creation of a centralized and expansionary state was novel to the inland delta. The delimitation of pasturing zones facilitated the collection of state revenues, which funded courts, mosques, and madrassas that aimed to promote populations' support for the state's interpretation of Islamic law and thus reproduce its legitimacy. These revenues also funded a standing military, most importantly cavalry forces.[70] With these forces, Lobbo sought to expand south and west into the Bambara states of Segu and Kaarta and north and east into Timbuktu and the Tuareg-dominated Niger bend. Ultimately, these campaigns were never fully successful. Segu and Kaarta maintained their autonomy. While Timbuktu fell to the Diina's forces several times, the latter's authority in the city and across the Niger bend was always tenuous.

The Diina's relationship with the southern Sahara was shaped by the interdependence of livelihoods in the delta and the desert. Lobbo and his successors consistently sought expansion to the north because of its importance to pastoral production (herders needed access to drier pasture when the delta flooded) and the state's dependence on access to desert-side trade.[71] The health of the latter trade depended in turn on desert-side populations accessing food produced in and transported through the delta. Connections between the delta and the desert were facilitated by the mobility of pastoral, scholarly, and commercial elites, who expected recognition of their distinct spheres of authority. Lobbo's aspirations for the Diina, however, sought to transform the status quo of mutual accommodation, situating himself as final arbiter of the law. This proved to be a costly project and one that never fully succeeded. While the Diina had the military capacity to subdue resistant populations and authorities in the Niger bend, these campaigns were unsustainable because they disrupted production and trade on which the Diina's wealth ultimately depended.

Islamic scholars repeatedly appealed to Lobbo to adapt his vision of jihad to the material conditions of diversity and interdependence in the Middle Niger. They argued that security and prosperity for the region's Muslims could not be achieved through the armed imposition of an Islamic orthodoxy but rather depended on protecting the region's traditions of religious pluralism. For example, a leading scholar, Ahmad al-Saghir, of the Saharan oasis town of Tishit protested disruptions to trade caused by the Diina's war on Kaarta in the 1820s. The Diina's forces had halted a caravan from

Tishit when it sought to enter Kaarta. In a letter, al-Saghir praised the Diina's broader cause of jihad but argued that long-distance trade must be protected for the well-being of Muslims and of Islam. He wrote, "[Tishit] is the center of gravity of this land, all the people come to Tishit to seek [Islamic] knowledge but it has no markets to obtain supplies. And the region of Kaarta is the granary of the people of Tishit."[72] Because of Tishit's dependence on trade with nonbelievers, al-Saghir argued that it was not consistent with Islamic law for this trade to be forbidden. Lobbo rejected this reasoning, arguing that trade with nonbelievers made the traders themselves legitimate targets of jihad.

From the 1820s through the 1840s, the relationship between the Diina and its northern neighbors was marked by cycles of conflict and accommodation. Initially, the Diina found support among the religious and scholarly elite in Timbuktu and the Niger bend. Lobbo's success in consolidating his authority across much of the delta and the Middle Niger brought stability, and his enforcement of Islamic law was attractive to merchants because of its clarity and consistency in tax policies.[73] Letters between Lobbo and the Kunta Shaykh Muhammad al-Kunti, for example, show willingness to support each other's interests. Lobbo mediated on behalf of al-Kunti with merchants in Jenne, and al-Kunti, in response to appeals from defeated Fulani elites to aid a revolt against Lobbo, affirmed the legitimacy of the Diina.[74]

But this relationship became fraught with disputes over the nature and extent of the Diina's authority over Timbuktu and the Niger bend. The Iwellemedan and the Kel Tadamakkat confederations consistently resisted attempts by the Diina's forces to claim villages in the vicinity of Timbuktu and further east along the river. The Kunta were sometimes in the position of mediating between these groups, especially as conflict disrupted trade. But at other times, the Kunta were in more direct conflict with the Diina, specifically over Lobbo's insistence on banning the sale and consumption of tobacco—a key commercial interest. At several points during his rule, Lobbo's forces had military successes in the Niger bend that led to nominal recognition of the Diina's authority only to then face resistance against taxation and the tobacco ban, which would prompt subsequent military expeditions.[75] This caused more general disruptions to trade and movement.

Lobbo's relationship with al-Kunti broke down in 1826 after the Diina's forces successfully claimed control of Timbuktu. After this success, Lobbo attempted to position the Kunta shaykh as a direct client to solidify the Diina's rule over the city. Al-Kunti refused, invoking his autonomy as a religious authority with a specific political role, writing in a letter, "I already have another legacy that is not compatible with politics. . . . We are obliged to collaborate but everyone in his domain for the smooth running of Shari'a. . . . I have always assisted you with useful advice and I will continue it; but to govern the city, this I cannot." Emphasizing the independence of political and religious roles, the shaykh reiterated the illegitimacy of the ban on tobacco, arguing that Lobbo's interpretation of Islamic law did not take precedence over the consensus of other scholars and jurists in Timbuktu and the Sahel more broadly, who ruled that tobacco was permitted.[76] In short, while al-Kunti recognized the Diina's military and political dominance and largely welcomed the stability it brought to the commercially important delta region, he did not affirm all of Lobbo's claims as caliph—that is, that he was the one supreme religious and juridical as well as political authority.

Al-Kunti died in 1826, after which the Diina maintained loose control over Timbuktu via an aligned pasha. But crisis returned in 1833 when the pasha supported Arma and Tuareg forces in rebellion. This prompted another conquest of Timbuktu by the Diina's troops along with punitive seizure of elites' property. Al-Kunti's son Mukhtar al-Saghir responded to the crisis by mediating a truce between the Diina and Tuareg. Writing to Lobbo, al-Saghir emphasized that the ongoing conflict was destroying the commercial prosperity of the region and that peace and prosperity would not be possible in the Niger bend without the cooperation of the Tuaregs. This, he insisted, would require Lobbo to accommodate Tuareg requirements of relative autonomy from the laws of the Diina. Lobbo took this advice, and the conflict ceased until the 1840s, when renewed fighting between the Diina's forces and the Kel Tadamakkat, Arma, and Kunta culminated in Lobbo's implementation of a deadly blockade against Timbuktu in 1844 and 1845. This time, al-Saghir's brother Ahmad al-Bakkay intervened to mediate on behalf of the starving Timbuktu. A new arrangement saw Timbuktu paying tribute to the Diina but without a military garrison and with more autonomy over the collection and enforcement of tax.[77]

Ongoing conflicts among the Diina, Islamic scholars outside of the Diina, and Tuareg confederations point to constraints on centralizing political, legal, and spiritual authority across the diverse and interdependent communities and livelihoods in the Middle Niger. The delta relied on access to more arid spaces for pastoral production and trade, and Ahmad Lobbo sought to secure this access by incorporating the southern Sahara into the boundaries of the Diina. But the homogenizing structure and vision of the Diina repeatedly worked at cross-purposes with the reproduction of ties between the delta and the desert. Lobbo adjusted, but the Diina's revolutionary vision of political Islam was consistently seen as a threat by northern religious, commercial, and pastoralist elites.

These conflicts only grew with the fall of the Diina to a competing jihadist movement led by the Tukulör leader Umar Tal. Tal's forces invaded the region in 1862 as the Diina faced ongoing succession conflicts following Lobbo's death in 1845. After years of study and Islamic pilgrimage in the 1830s and 1840s, Tal had gained a following in the Senegambia, which he mobilized toward the goal of conquering and converting the region's Mandinka and Bambara states and establishing a Tukulör Empire. He began his campaigns at the same time that the French military sought to expand its control along the Senegal River (on the map, Sénégal). This threat turned Tal's attention further to the east, with the goal of establishing an Islamic state based in the Middle Niger and further from French interests.[78] In the mid-1850s, Tal conquered Kaarta and subsequently began preparations for a further push east into Segu.

Tal's forces advanced toward Segu in 1859, armed with weapons they had seized from successful attacks on French garrisons. The Diina's ruler, Ahmad III, attempted to undermine Tal's justifications for jihad by asserting that Segu had become a Muslim tributary state of the Diina and that its ruler had converted. When Tal rejected this claim, the Diina joined forces with Segu, which fell in 1861. Tal then launched a controversial campaign against Hamdallahi and the Diina in 1862, arguing that its support for Segu proved it was not a legitimate Islamic state.[79] After initial military victories, including the capture and execution of Ahmad III, the Tukulör struggled to consolidate their political control.[80] By early 1863, the Kunta leader al-Bakkay and members of Ahmad III's family had begun plans for a revolt, which broke out in June and in February 1864. Tal was driven from Hamdallahi and killed. At the same time, revolts were underway in Segu and in the important commercial town of Sinsani.[81]

Tal's imperial project was compromised by the devastation it delivered to the Middle Niger's economy. War and rebellion broke down links between the desert and savanna, isolating agricultural producers from the caravan trade and the commercial towns. More so than Ahmad Lobbo and his successors, Tal and his successors resisted demands for relative autonomy from important merchant interests, and the military campaigns against them provoked armed rebellion along with massive displacement and economic losses. Many merchants ultimately left the towns along the Niger that had served as key nodes connecting desert-side production with the economies of the delta and savanna. In addition to armed resistance, populations simply withdrew from the productive activities on which the state depended. "They produced less, exchanged less, and therefore deprived the new state of a significant income. . . . [M]any farmers hid their granaries deep in the bush to protect their surpluses form Umarian appropriation."[82] David Robinson distinguishes Tal's "imperial jihad" from the "revolutionary jihad" of Ahmad Lobbo: "Umar did not mobilize the indigenous inhabitants of the 'east' [i.e., the inland delta and Segu]. . . . Rather, he recruited thousands of outsiders, like himself, to conquer and colonize." Tal's designs for the Middle Niger were based on his earlier successes to the west, but in this area, the Tukulör had found accommodations with desert-side populations and merchants.[83] Pushed east by French expansion, the movement struggled to reproduce this model through military force alone. When the French themselves turned their ambitions toward the Middle Niger in the early 1880s, their ultimate defeat of the Tukulör relied on collaboration with the existing anti-Tukulör resistance.[84]

The absence of centralized, territorial states in Africa has often been attributed to a lack of capacity and assumed to be a liability to prosperity and security. For example, in Jeffrey Herbst's influential *States and Power in Africa*, he argues that state building on the continent, from ancient times to the present, has been hindered by "inhospitable territories" and "low densities of people." Precolonial African states were decentralized and had "confused" and overlapping systems of sovereignty because of geographical and demographic constraints that rulers had not overcome by the time of European colonization.[85] Herbst's argument reflects common assumptions in political theory about the relationship among security, political order, and space—specifically that security is an effect of political order and that political order requires the spatial encompassment and subordination of other forms of social authority, legitimacy, and meaning making.[86]

In the Middle Niger, where ecology and climate made mobility central to securing livelihoods, order has been secured in relation to different ways of organizing space and of negotiating relationships of identity, belonging, and authority. Whereas the centralization of political authority in the modern state has been associated with the homogenization of space through territorialization, here we find evidence of political centralization depending on recognition of and accommodations with the particularities of place through various forms of subsidiarity. Features of order that state-centric theories of security commonly associate with disorder—including decentralized, nonexclusive spheres of authority and distributed capacities for violence—had benefits for collective security. These characteristics relate to a broader context of interdependence among diverse and dispersed populations whose collective resilience in an uncertain environment depends on capacities for mobility and exchange.

The latter forms of political order were rendered unrecognizable as such by Eurocentric imaginaries of order and anarchy as they developed in relation to colonial and imperial conquest. The following chapter traces how imperial expansion in Africa produced new theories of sovereignty and its relationship to territory, according to which African sovereignty did not need to be recognized internationally because it was not territorial. These innovations shaped emerging conceptions of modern international order, which defined international ordering as primarily a project of managing territorial space, and situated "modernized" territorial administration as a precondition for international security.

TWO

Internationalizing Africa

In 1805, the British government sponsored Mungo Park, who had gained celebrity as the first European to reach the Niger River, on a second expedition to the Niger. Park's first solo trip, which reached the river in 1796, had been funded by a private organization, the Africa Association, which aimed to promote British commercial interests under the guise of scientific exploration and discovery. By the second trip, in the context of the Napoleonic Wars and conflict between France and Britain in Egypt and Senegal, the association had won state support for their mission. This time, Park would lead a small military column, aiming to reach the fabled Timbuktu and to map the river's entire course, which Park had come to believe connected with the Congo. The trip would lay the foundation for the British to establish trading posts and preempt France's growing imperial ambitions in West Africa. For one of the leaders of the Africa Association, Joseph Banks, Britain's ultimate goal should have been to claim "either by conquest or Treaty the whole of the Coast of Africa."[1]

Reflecting this context of imperial competition, Park's second expedition was a militarized one, consisting of thirty-three soldiers and another eight British civilians. Traveling with such a large contingent and with weapons and scientific implements proved deadly both for members of the expedition and ultimately for many of the people that Park encountered leading up to his own death in November 1805. Just four months into the expedition, the majority of its members had succumbed to disease. Rather than turn back, a paranoid Park decided to continue by boat with four soldiers, three slaves, and a guide, avoiding contact with communities along the river and shooting at anyone who tried to approach. As the guide, Amadi Fatouma, would later report, this diminished but heavily armed crew thus proceeded from Segu into Hausaland, violently evading customary tolls and requirements to exchange goods and information with local authorities. Fatouma himself was threatened with violence when he protested against the crew's indiscriminate killing, and when he left the expedition in Hausa territory, he was arrested. After his release, Fatouma learned from a sole surviving slave that the rest of the group had drowned near the village of Bussa, where the river narrowed into rapids. A large group had been waiting for Park and his crew, who had tried to escape capture by jumping into the river.[2] In some accounts, this group was attempting to help Park safely navigate the difficult passage but was attacked and then responded in kind.[3]

If the latter account is true—that Park died while shooting at those trying to assist him—it was a darkly fitting end. In contrast to his more successful solo trip, in which Park had little option but to defer to the expertise and hospitality of his hosts, the disastrous military expedition was characterized by repeated failures to heed the advice of experienced guides. Park's contrasting expeditions to the Niger preview shifts in Europeans' relationships with Africans as imperialist interests in the continent increased. For most of the nineteenth century, imperialists, like Banks, found only inconsistent political and financial support for colonial expansion in Africa. Instead, commercial opportunities were understood to depend on alliances with African rulers and traders, who connected European trading houses with resources and markets that were otherwise too costly to access directly. Toward the end of the nineteenth century, however, European politics was increasingly influenced by special interests advocating direct colonization in Africa.

Direct colonization and empire building not only challenged existing practices of diplomacy and trade in Africa but also conflicted with emerging liberal theories of sovereignty and international law. As Europeans began to imagine the international as a planetary system rather than a continental "society of states," the correspondence between territory and political subjectivity that had defined theories of internationalism and national self-determination in the European context was consistently challenged. As an imperial project, encompassing Africa within a modern international order would ideally incorporate African spaces without giving political standing to

African peoples. This shaped a model of international order in which that order was primarily defined in relation to the management of territorial space, and international subjectivity was made contingent on judgements of territorial competency.

Imperial Expansion and the Berlin Conference on West Africa

In the decades following Park's death, British and French explorers continued their efforts to map the course of the Niger and to reach the fabled city of Timbuktu and the untapped wealth that the city had come to represent in the European imagination. Prior to Park's first voyage, the French had mistakenly believed that the Senegal River connected to the Niger and, therefore, that whatever European power could establish themselves on the upper Senegal would eventually be in a position to dominate European trade with Timbuktu and beyond. Toward this end, French traders and officials made repeated attempts over the eighteenth century to establish permanent trading posts and forts upriver. For some advocates of French expansion, British sponsorship of Mungo Park and of subsequent Niger expeditions amounted to "attacks" on French rights to these areas.[4]

Private organizations and the French government responded by sponsoring their own expeditions. The Geography Society (Société de Géographie) was a principal advocate for commercial expansion to the Niger, and in 1824, it announced a prize, funded in part by the French Ministries of Marine, War, and Interior, for the first French national to reach Timbuktu. René Caillié took the prize, reaching the city in 1828. On his return, Caillié argued that France should establish a fort in Bamako, from which it would be able to control trade along the Niger as well as gold mines to its west.[5] When the French conquest of Algeria began in 1830, ambitions to occupy Bamako only grew. A fort at Bamako would mean not just access to the Niger but also the possibility of connecting France's claims in Algeria to those in Senegal and thus establishing France as the dominant imperial power in North and West Africa.

More than fifty years would pass before the French occupied Bamako, and the event would mark a consequential escalation in Anglo-French competition in West Africa. In the 1850s, efforts to establish French forts further inland in Senegal led to a series of military confrontations, most significantly with Umar Tal's forces. Neither side had the military capacity or political will to sustain hostilities, and through the 1860s and into the 1870s, French colonial officers maintained diplomatic relations with Tal's Tukulör Empire. Tal would protect French trade as long as the French did not seek to extend their military or political control east of the Senegal River. In the late 1870s, French strategy toward the Tukulör Empire began to shift. The empire had been weakened by rebellions and internal political conflicts (chapter 1). In addition, political support for imperial expansion was on the rise in France in the wake of the Franco-Prussian War. In this context, plans for expansion toward the Niger, which had previously been denied funding, found new political life.

In 1879, a proposal to build a railway connecting Senegal to the Niger River at Bamako was approved by the French government, and a military command was established to oversee the project. Government support for the railroad hinged on expectations of peaceful commercial expansion, including by gaining the approval of the Tukulör Empire. But the Ministries of the Marine and Colonies saw the railway project as a vehicle for military and political control. The railway would need to be secured by French forces, which meant that its construction would be preceded by the establishment of military forts along its route—in violation of French commitments to Umar Tal.[6] By 1882, the project had largely abandoned its diplomatic efforts and was proceeding through military conquest. In 1883, French forces occupied Bamako.

Colonial officers justified the shift from a diplomatic and commercial mission to one of military conquest by arguing that French interests were directly threatened by British and Tukulör ambitions and that the window of opportunity for France to establish itself on the Niger was closing. In response, Britain moved to constrain French claims in the Congo. As part of its efforts to secure its position on the Niger, the French government sponsored Pierre de Brazza on an expedition to the Congo basin in 1879. The Congo mission was intended to provide an alternative access route to the Niger from the south. Britain hoped to close off opportunities for further French expansion by negotiating a treaty with Portugal, which had the longest standing European presence at the mouth of the Congo. The treaty negotiations were completed in 1884, and the resulting deal would recognize significant territorial claims by Portugal and grant both powers shared authority over navigation on the river.

The Anglo-Portuguese treaty prompted backlash from European states and the United States.[7] Along with French policies on the upper Niger, the treaty signaled to other states that a new race to make territorial claims in Africa might be developing. Indeed, this is precisely how the British government explained its actions to the Manchester Chamber of Commerce, which opposed the treaty as a threat to existing commercial agreements between its members and sovereign polities along the Congo. "The fact is evident that the natives are gradually losing their control and that the markets are falling into the hands of stronger races. . . . The state of things which [the chamber] desires to retain is passing away. . . . [I]t must be prepared to recognize the contingency of the disappearance of native rule and of the eventual subjection of the tribes to the rule of Powers whose policy might not be consistently friendly to the maintenance and development of British commercial interests."[8] In this context, Prince Otto von Bismarck, who was himself under pressure from proimperialist constituencies in Germany, proposed an international conference with the goal of influencing how this anticipated expansion of European claims on the continent would develop.

In public discourse, the Berlin Conference on West Africa was characterized as a novel effort by the European powers to extend norms of international law and diplomacy that were developing under the Concert of Europe system to the African continent. As *The Economist* reported on its opening day, "The Conference . . . represents the first time that Europe as an informal group has assumed jurisdiction over a large, uncivilized area."[9] Bismarck's framing of the conference suggested as much. He proposed that the Congo and Niger Rivers (and, in the future, all rivers in Africa) should be regulated according to the international regimes that had been developed to ensure free navigation and commerce on international rivers in Europe and the Americas.[10] The prospect of collectively regulating imperial expansion in Africa was appealing as a means of constraining any single state's ability to restrict access to newly accessible African markets and of mitigating risks of imperial competition escalating into a European war.

In practice, however, the conference demonstrated the European powers' hesitancy to accept legal or diplomatic constraints on imperial expansion. Rather than asserting a collective jurisdiction over "uncivilized" areas in Africa writ large, European powers were concerned with preserving Africa's position beyond the boundaries of international law and society, where commercial and political interests would face fewer constraints and less scrutiny. As the French minister Jules Ferry put it, "By virtue of what principle are we to make the law of colonies which are just beginning? . . . Does this not bind our own hands in other parts of the world, and give away a little lightly the colonial regime of the future?"[11] These interests kept the scope of the conference geographically limited. The first two agenda items concerned trade and navigation on the lower Niger River and in the Congo River basin, and the third, which addressed the criteria under which European occupations would be recognized by other European states as legitimate or "effective," was limited to future claims in coastal areas. Even in these limited contexts, states were reluctant to approve legal or diplomatic standards that could constrain their future freedom of action.

Bismarck's proposal to extend existing international legal regimes into Africa faced resistance on the grounds that conditions in Africa were too different from those in Europe and the Americas for such legal regimes to apply. Africa and Africans were outside of the boundaries of the "society of states" that constituted the international, and participants doubted whether it was feasible or desirable to extend those boundaries. Britain's Lord Granville wrote to the German diplomat Baron von Plessen in the lead up to the conference: "The Regulation of the Congress of Vienna in 1815 for the navigation of rivers referred exclusively to such as ran through the well-defined territories of civilized States, whereas the Regulation to be made for the navigation of the Congo and Niger will have to deal with rivers whose course lies through the imperfectly known tracts occupied by savage tribes. The problem therefore to be solved is the application of the general principles of the Treaty of Vienna to the very different circumstances that present themselves in Africa."[12] For Britain, extending international jurisdiction to rivers in Africa would require that African populations and polities first be brought under the sovereignty of "civilized States."[13] This would require European powers to significantly expand the scope of their territorial occupations on the continent, and it was not clear that such occupations would benefit commercial or political interests.

The British delegation was especially concerned with rejecting proposals to project international jurisdiction over the lower Niger River, where British trading houses held monopolies. Challenging British dominance on the Niger was one of France's primary objectives for the conference, and its delegates advocated for establishing an international commission to oversee free trade and navigation on the river. Britain argued that conditions along the Niger made international jurisdiction both unnecessary and likely to damage European commercial interests. First, Britain's longstanding presence on the lower Niger meant that it was capable on its own of ensuring that other European powers could freely navigate the river. In this sense, Britain was already the "Niger power" and would act as an agent of the so-called civilized states without the need for an international organization. But the British were also insistent that their status as the Niger power was dependent on their relationships with polities and leaders on the lower Niger. These authorities "jealously maintain their position as middle-men. . . . They are shrewd and have a keen perception of their interests" and would recognize the establishment of a European organization as a threat to their own position.[14] Thus, not only was international jurisdiction unnecessary but asserting European sovereignty would likely jeopardize the very commercial access that an international organization was supposed to protect.

The British contrasted these circumstances with those on the Congo, whose unique conditions made international jurisdiction potentially feasible and beneficial. First, the Congo had "one well defined mouth" (in contrast to the Niger) on which trading houses representing multiple European nations were already established. This made international administration more feasible both logistically and politically. Perhaps more importantly, the "natives" along the Congo were reportedly "docile" and "willing to sign anything."[15] If this was the case, King Leopold's proposal to establish "a native Confederation under European control" could provide a legal basis for applying existing international legal regimes to the governance of the Congo.[16] These arguments, which were ultimately successful, emphasized unique conditions in the Congo that made international jurisdiction potentially beneficial. In Britain's view, such contexts were limited. In most of the continent, European commerce would be secured by individual European powers through their coastal colonies and trading houses and their relationships with authorities in the interior of Africa, where asserting European sovereignty was too costly.

Britain's support for the status quo reflected its sense of its position as the European "[master] of Africa" based on "the simple fact that we were masters of the sea and that we have considerable experience in dealing with native races."[17] But even those who saw more benefit to internationalization were hesitant to define the legal basis on which international jurisdiction could extend beyond the boundaries of the civilized "society of states." This was especially evident in deliberations over the conference's third agenda item concerning the criteria according to which future European occupations would be recognized as "effective."

Negotiations over effective occupation concerned questions about European and African sovereignty, which the conference ultimately left unresolved. As indicated by the absence of African leaders in Berlin, the conference did not consider that establishing international jurisdiction would involve recognizing African leaders as part of the international society of states. However, they also did not want to categorically deny recognition of African sovereignty. Though imperial expansion regularly proceeded by violating Africans' regimes of political authority, it also depended on those regimes logistically and politically. In addition to material dependency, legal and political recognition of African sovereignty was important to Europeans' own territorial and commercial claims vis-à-vis one another, which were primarily based on treaties with African rulers.

The initial proposal concerning effective occupation, formulated by France and Germany as an attempt to invalidate British territorial claims on the Niger, would require that European powers establish jurisdiction with an administrative presence sufficient to maintain peace and secure commerce and navigation. Otherwise, territorial claims need not be recognized by other European powers, and they could pursue occupation themselves. But by the start of the conference, even Germany and France saw these standards as too burdensome and detrimental to their own territorial ambitions.[18] The French ambassador, for example, rejected language that occupying powers must "establish and maintain . . . a sufficient jurisdiction" because "in certain regions the existing institutions would suffice" and should "be merely preserved."[19] Like Britain, France was interested to affirm that, in some contexts, European commercial interests would be better served by recognizing Africans' authority rather than invalidating it.

However, deliberations on effective occupation remained focused on the criteria according to which other European powers would recognize occupation, not on defining the political standing of African rulers. Consideration of what might make occupation legitimate vis-à-vis Africans was carefully avoided by all but the American delegate John Kasson. Kasson pointed out that the clearest international legal standard for occupation concerned the consent of the population in the occupied territory. "Modern international law follows closely a line which leads to the recognition of the right of native tribes to dispose freely of themselves and of their hereditary title. . . . [M]y government would gladly adhere to a more extended rule, to be based on a principle which should aim at the voluntary consent of the natives whose country is taken possession of, in all cases where they had not provoked the aggression."[20] Even leaving open a significant loophole for "aggression," which would presumably give latitude to justify occupation by conquest where consent was not granted, discussing standards of recognition for African sovereignty was off the table. Kasson's proposal was dismissed, with the session's leader responding that this "touched on a delicate question, upon which the conference hesitated to express an opinion."[21]

Avoiding such delicate questions, the conference left the legal status of African authorities ambiguous. In the end, the final agreement made little change to existing practices. The signatories merely agreed to "accompany [an act of possession] with a notification thereof, addressed to the other Signatory Powers . . . in order to enable them, if need be, to make good any claims of their own."[22] In other words, "effective" occupation simply meant occupation that was recognized by other European powers. The conference as a whole declined to define any consistent or generalizable standards for imperial expansion. The General Act of the Berlin Conference placed very few obligations on signatories, and these obligations only concerned signatories' conduct toward one another. It thus reaffirmed the boundaries of the international as differentiating a civilized "society of states" from its outsides. African spaces and populations remained outside of international jurisdiction as objects on which the subjects of international society might jointly act, not according to law but based on expediency and situational shared interests.

Debates about African sovereignty and European rights to occupation continued after the conference, as I elaborate below. But in practice, European colonizers continued to treat most of Africa as frontier space, beyond the boundaries of international law. Over the next fifteen years, Africa would be partitioned among European states through a combination of military conquest and European negotiations over territorial boundaries. In the latter negotiations, colonial officers and diplomats increasingly rejected treaties with Africans as grounds for excluding other European powers from a territory, appealing instead to standards for "effective occupation," which had been rejected at Berlin. As a German newspaper opined in 1894, "The days of academical African treaties, such as were concluded up to 1890, are past; to have any effect, the Power must have a solid position in the regions in dispute. All appeals to older treaties (affecting territories) with undefined frontiers are of no avail. This the moment for action."[23] This shift reflected growing support for national imperialism in Europe, especially in France and Germany.

Governments that had previously been reluctant to devote military resources to colonial conquest saw political benefit in doing so.

International legal theories of African sovereignty shifted in response to the reality of military conquest. By the turn of the century, the international legal consensus that Kasson cited, which would require recognizing Africans' "right . . . to dispose freely of themselves," had given way to theories that Africans could make no claims to sovereignty because they were uncivilized.[24] While, in 1885, the main imperial powers in Africa were asserting that the protection of African institutions was beneficial for European peace and prosperity, a decade later, diplomats, jurists, and publicists insisted that civilizational progress would be threatened if Europeans did not claim sovereignty over the continent. This shift indicated a changing geographical imaginary of the international. The preservation of (some) African institutions imagined at the conference was tied to Africa's exteriority to the space of the international. The argument that Africa must instead be brought under European sovereignty was indicative of the emerging notion that ordering the international had to be a planetary project. Below, I examine how these changing ideas of the international were incorporated into theories of international order, territory, and sovereignty after the Berlin Conference.

Incorporating Partition into International Law

Conference deliberations generated confusing and contradictory theories of European sovereignty in Africa.[25] On the one hand, it was discussed in relation to occupation, suggesting that Europeans were claiming first title to land that was previously unoccupied from the perspective of international law. On the other hand, European powers had demanded recognition of treaties of protection signed with African rulers, which affirmed varying degrees of Africans' authority over internal affairs. Indeed, the presence of existing forms of governance in African territories had been invoked as justification for rejecting proposals that "effective occupation" require the presence of a European administrative structure. This ambiguity over whether or not Africans had recognizable political rights maximized colonizers' freedom of action. Where political authority was needed, it could be claimed, and where it came with burdensome responsibilities, it could be denied.

In 1885, the premier professional organization for jurists engaged in international law, the Institut de droit international, established a commission to study the issue of effective occupation.[26] In his final report, the chair of this commission, Ferdinand Maritz, argued that the international legal standard for occupation should not be based on the presence or absence of property (*res nullius*)—the widely disputed justification for colonization in North America and Australia—but on the presence or absence of territorial sovereignty (*territorium nullius*). Maritz defined sovereignty as necessarily territorial and confined territorial sovereignty to European forms of political order. "All regions are considered to be *territorium nullius* which do not find themselves effectively under the sovereignty or the protectorate of any of the states forming the community of the law of nations," and sovereignty, it was claimed, did not exist among "savage or semi-barbarian peoples" or with "independent tribes."[27] Protectorate treaties with Africans thus had no standing under international law.

A version of this legal theory had been in development prior to the Berlin Conference by an associate of King Leopold's, the British jurist Sir Travers Twiss, who would later write the Constitution of the Congo Free State. Twiss argued that while Africans clearly had regimes of authority over land and property, "the organisation of the native races . . . is still *tribal*, and *territorial* sovereignty, in the sense in which it has superseded *personal* sovereignty in Europe, is still unknown."[28] This absence of territorial sovereignty gave European states rights of occupation, which could coexist with existing rights of personal sovereignty. As Andrew Fitzmaurice summarizes, "What [Europeans] would occupy would not be the land of other peoples, but the void where territorial sovereignty remained unrealized." Unlike Maritz, Twiss argued that even though African rulers did not have international legal standing, treaties were a legitimate basis for determining one European power's right to claim sovereignty over another. Personal sovereignty still granted Africans rights of property, which they could cede to Europeans.[29] Thus, treaties with African rulers (of which Leopold had collected over 450 by the start of the Berlin Conference)[30] could serve as evidence of a given European power's occupation without granting the African signatory standing under international law.[31]

These arguments for denying Africans international legal standing were controversial and were revisited at the Institut de droit international over the coming years. Critics largely affirmed the definition of *territorium nullius* as the standard for legal occupations. Where they disputed Maritz and Twiss was in their judgement of what counted as territorial sovereignty. The anti-imperialist jurist Gaston Jèze, for example, accepted that it was the presence or absence of territorial sovereignty, not property rights or habitation, that determined whether a territory could be occupied. But he insisted that "savage peoples" with political organization met that standard and thus could not be subject to colonization except through a treaty of cession.[32] Existing treaties with African rulers, therefore, were valid under international law, and European signatories should be bound to their terms.

Members of the Institut de droit international did not reach a consensus as to the terms under which African lands and people should be incorporated into the jurisdiction of the international, but their acceptance of the concept of *territorium nullius* helped solidify the terms under which imperialism would be reconciled with modern international law. For liberal imperialists, affirming a distinction between rights to territorial sovereignty and rights to property was crucial for imagining an imperialism that could coexist with a liberal political order in Europe. Enlightenment political theory and Europe's nationalist revolutions had rejected the equation of rights to sovereignty, a matter of public right, with rights to property, a matter of individual right. To collapse the two in the interest of imperial expansion was seen as a direct threat to the gains that liberals had made against absolute monarchy in Europe.[33] Defining imperial occupation as the occupation of territorial sovereignty, not the occupation of land and property, incorporated Enlightenment critiques of empire into theories of the new imperialism. The new imperialism theoretically was about Europeans' rights to administer territory in the interest of international commerce, not to seize property on behalf of a personal sovereign.

This rehabilitation of imperialism through international law ultimately depended on reimagining space outside of Europe as international territory that was either already claimed or not yet claimed by a legitimate sovereign. This conception of territory overlapped with but also unsettled developing legal theories of territory and sovereignty in the European state.[34] Nineteenth-century political theorists were at pains to distinguish state territory from sovereign property. Theories of the relationship among territory, sovereignty, and population, particularly as they developed in the wake of the 1848 revolutions, had served to constrain the power of individual sovereigns by grounding territorial rights in the collective life of the population rather than in the personal sovereign power of the ruler. For example, Georg Jellinek understood territory as "an ontological attribute of the state and part of its personality: not having, but being." Territory was not an object possessed by a sovereign but rather the materialization in space of the collective life that sovereignty made possible. In his famous tripartite definition of the state, consisting of territory, people, and sovereignty, sovereignty was the means through which a people could actualize their "purposes of life," and these purposes naturally materialized in the space of the state—that is, territory.[35]

Theories of territorial sovereignty as a manifestation of Europe's advanced capacities for rational political organization were a convenient means of excluding African regimes of authority from European concepts of sovereignty. But the next step, defining African lands as not-yet-claimed territories, was more problematic if the relationship between territory and national population was an ontological or metaphysical one. On the one hand, recognizing territory in Africa implied that sovereign communities already existed (as anti-imperialist jurists insisted) and that territory could only be ceded, not occupied. On the other hand, if African space was *territorium nullius* and thus could be incorporated under the sovereignty of a European power, how did African territories and populations then relate to the territory and population of the metropole? As one critic of Jellinek put it, "To consider every African village in German East Africa as part of the *essence* of the German Reich" was antithetical to the imperial project.[36]

Political and legal theorists addressed this problem by arguing that territories outside of Europe had a different relationship to sovereignty and population than did European states. Non-European spaces were territorialized through the projection of European sovereignty, not as a materialization of collective political subjectivity. The territories thus were objects of European states' rights without being part of those states or having their own claims to sovereignty. Jellinek described these nonsovereign territories as *Staatsfragmente*, or "state fragments"—a term that calls to mind Robert Jackson's later concept of "quasi-states."[37] Outside of Europe, territory was thus not a metaphysical or ontological attribute of a political community but "just an object of a state right; a right that could take different forms depending on the space in which the state itself was going to operate."[38] Territory in this context defined a jurisdictional space, which did not necessarily correspond to a recognized political community.[39]

Defining African spaces as *territorium nullius* served to both universalize European regimes of sovereignty and rationalize their unequal application across space. As Luigi Nuzzo concludes, "This did not lead to the exclusion of the colony and its inhabitants from the state order, but 'only' to confine them in a different age—an age in which there was no constitution, no separation of powers, nor the uniqueness of the legal subject."[40] The concept of territory homogenized space, imagining that "the world was intended as a place to be politically organized, covered with states by mankind."[41] But if territory conceptualized the international as a single planetary space, this universalization depended on locating spaces in different times.

From Effective Occupation to Effective Administration:
The League of Nations Mandate System

By the early twentieth century, most scholars and publicists in the West viewed the extension of a Euro-American international order over Africa and Asia as an inevitable result of industrialization, the growth of finance capital, and technological advancements in transportation and communication. As Walter Lippmann put it in 1915, "By some means or other the weak states have to be brought within the framework of commercial administration. . . . The pressure to organize the world is enormous."[42] But despite this sense of inevitability, European imperial expansion was also controversial. Evidence from the colonies suggested that the practical and ideological justifications for imperialism were at odds with what was unfolding in practice. The economic benefits of national imperialism were not materializing as promised in many areas, especially in Africa. Ideologically, white supremacist civilizational discourses were challenged by reports of colonial violence, forced labor regimes, rising mortality, and the breakdown of familial and social ties in the colonies.[43] In addition to its disturbing effects in the colonized world, many scholars and publicists argued that national imperialism posed grave threats to Europe. These included the antidemocratic effects of empowering an imperial financial class, the threat of imperial rivalry leading to European war, and the potential for white domination to spark a global race war.[44]

In this context, many internationally minded intellectuals saw the problem of "governing the native" as one central to the development of a planetary international order suited to new conditions of global interdependence.[45] Colonial administration became a new focus area for scholars of history, political science, economics, and law. Most of these studies sought to identify generalizable strategies for colonial administration toward three main objectives: facilitating the rational and efficient use of labor and natu-

ral resources, securing fair access to those resources by the nationals of all
"civilized" states, and promoting the moral and civilizational development
of colonized populations.[46] The political and commercial interests driving
national imperialism, however, worked at cross-purposes with these ends.
Since the colonial order was premised on the claim that colonized populations were not able to govern themselves, the democratic tools developed to
constrain sovereigns and capitalists in the European context were assumed
unavailable.[47] For many imperial reformers, therefore, the most promising
solution for improving colonial administration was to make it accountable to
international oversight.[48]

Reforming imperialism and colonial administration appeared even more
urgent with the outbreak of World War I. Anti-imperialist thinkers persuasively argued that the war was at least partly a result of imperialism and that
world war would be a perpetual threat if the national imperial order persisted. Almost immediately after the start of the war, France and Britain had
mobilized to conquer Germany's colonies, and the question of what would
happen to those territories after the war was central to debates over why the
war was being fought and how a postwar world should be ordered. At the
Paris Peace Conference, the Allied powers deemed it necessary to address
the political concerns of anti-imperialists, not least as an attempt to counter
Vladimir Lenin's vision of a socialist international order rooted in national
self-determination.[49] In addition to pressure from their Labour Party, British
leaders recognized that American cooperation would require that they accept
international control of at least some of the conquered Turkish and German
colonies. For his part, Woodrow Wilson was convinced that the success of
the entire conference and the viability of a League of Nations depended on
rejecting any appearance of colonial annexation by the war's victors.[50]

The alternative to annexation, the League of Nations mandate system,
was pitched to anti-imperialist interests as incorporating reformers' ideas for
trusteeship. In fact, the plan was largely conceived of by proponents of the
British Empire, namely Jan Smuts and members of the Round Table, who
were, like Wilson, concerned with the defense of white civilization and the
preservation of white racial rule.[51] Smuts and his colleagues had envisioned a
mandate system for territories in eastern Europe and the Middle East, where
a future transition to self-government was anticipated, and not in Africa,
where they presumed indefinite white rule.[52] Wilson borrowed heavily from
Smuts's work in his own proposal that former colonies be assigned a man-

datory power who would administer it on behalf of the League of Nations and according to standards defined by the League. He and his advisers saw the system as building on the precedents of the Berlin Conference and the Algeciras Act of 1906, which had "internationalized" the administration of international commerce in Morocco.[53]

At the Paris Peace Conference, the application of the mandates system to Africa faced ongoing resistance from Britain and especially France. The British came to accept the system (and eventually brought the French along) only after successfully negotiating a compromise that created three tiers of mandates. This would shield territories in Africa and the Pacific Islands from the full weight of the proposed international oversight. So-called A mandates covered roughly the territories that Smuts had envisioned under international administration in his initial proposal, and African and Pacific Island territories would be classified as B and C mandates, in which the assigned powers would have more freedom of action.

Though the mandate system's architects were not primarily concerned with imperial reform, the system became a focus point of anti-imperialist and reformist work both intellectually and politically in the interwar period. This was informed by the work of the Permanent Mandates Commission (PMC), which was established to receive and interpret required annual reports from the mandatory powers and advise the League Council on all matters related to the mandates. In practice, the PMC took on a more ambitious role of fact-finding, textual interpretation of the Covenant of the League of Nations and mandate agreements, and defining and evaluating administrative standards.[54] Its work on these standards had broader import for debates on colonial administration and imperialism. Reporting on the conduct of the mandatory powers was effective in mobilizing international public opinion, which could put political pressure on those powers both at home and within the League. Anti-imperialists and imperialist reformers were an interested audience for the PMC's work, and reformers hoped that its standards would eventually be taken up by all colonial administrators or, more hopefully, that it would inaugurate the transition of all dependent territories into a system of international trusteeship.[55] As such, the influence of the mandate system extended beyond the populations and territories formally under its purview, shaping broader legal and political debates about colonies and dependent territories and their relationship to international order.

The mandate system raised difficult questions about the relationship among sovereignty, territory, and population given that the answers should reconcile the continuation of European imperialism with demands that the postwar order recognize and advance norms of national self-determination. The creation of B and C mandates in particular complicated the mandate system's model of trusteeship (which was the term used in Wilson's early drafts before being replaced by "mandate") as an alternative to colonial annexation. In the A mandates, populations were recognized as being on their way to rule through national self-determination, contingent on their development of a national expression deemed acceptable to Europe. Article 22 of the Covenant of the League of Nations referred to the A mandates as "communities" who "have reached a stage of development where their existence as independent nations can be provisionally recognized."[56] If the mandate system was analogized to trusteeship law, legal title—that is, sovereignty—rested temporarily with the mandatory power who was obligated to protect the interests of the trust's beneficiary, the mandate's population, until such time as the beneficiary was capable of assuming that legal title—that is, when it "came of age."

While A-mandate status recognized nations in development, the creation of B and C mandates reflected colonial powers' demand that such recognition *not* be extended to Africans and Pacific Islanders. The Covenant did not use the term "communities" in reference to Africa or the Pacific Islands. It referred generally to mandatory inhabitants as "peoples," but, in defining the areas under B and C mandates, it distinguished the "peoples" of Central Africa from the "territories" of South West Africa and the Pacific Islands.[57] In these contexts, jurists and diplomats argued, the trusteeship analogy was flawed because there was no recognizable collective within the mandate that could act as beneficiary.[58] As Quincy Wright put it, "It is hardly proper to attribute sovereignty to communities which do not exist. Certainly in many of the mandated areas there is no organized community of all the inhabitants." Though the mandate system established an obligation to "develop such communities if possible[,] . . . a possible future sovereignty based on contingent obligations of another to transfer" did not mean that a latent right of sovereignty could already be recognized.[59] In other words, the existence of the beneficiary was only a theoretical possibility, not a legally recognizable reality.

Refusing to recognize B and C mandates' populations as analogous to beneficiaries of a trust made the mandate system more vulnerable to charges that it was just annexation by another name. The PMC and League Council were thus concerned with differentiating the relationship between the mandatory power and mandated population from that of colonizer and colonized. In so doing, the PMC would ultimately center the mandated *territory*, not the population, as the primary object of League administration and oversight. Prioritizing matters of territorial administration and development deferred questions of political subjectivity and self-determination for the mandates' populations to an undefined future horizon.

Among the first issues that the PMC took up were mandated populations' relationship to nationality and mandatory powers' relationship to sovereignty. It determined that neither nationality nor sovereignty, conventionally understood, existed in the mandate system. Regarding nationality, the PMC recommended in just its second meeting that inhabitants of B and C mandates should be defined as "nationals of the territory itself."[60] Importantly, this defined populations' status vis-à-vis the mandate system individually rather than collectively. Nationality described an individual's relationship to geography, not their relationship to a political community.[61] Similarly, the mandatory power's authority was not rooted in a political or legal relationship of sovereignty. The PMC's most direct statements to this effect came in response to South Africa, which repeatedly claimed to exercise sovereignty over South West Africa and ownership over its territory and infrastructure. In 1927, the PMC's vice chairman confronted South Africa's representative with what Susan Pedersen calls the PMC's "clearest exposition of [its] League-centered theory of sovereignty."[62] "The mandates system . . . implied the exclusion of the right of sovereignty of the mandatory Power over the territory it administered . . . the mandatory Power held its powers of administration and legislation, which were necessary for the accomplishment of its duties as a guardian, not in virtue of its sovereignty over the administered territory but in virtue of the mandate conferred upon it."[63] When South Africa continued to contradict this theory of sovereignty in its own legislation, the League Council reinforced it, concluding that "sovereignty, in the traditional sense of the word, does not reside in the mandatory power."[64] The League's judgements on nationality and sovereignty were supported by an emerging consensus among international jurists. Summarizing jurists' debates in his 1930 *Mandates under the League of Nations*, Quincy Wright concluded that "jurists have less and less found it possible to attribute complete sovereignty of a mandated area to a single state" and that "doctrines of collective and of qualified sovereignty have increased in support."[65] If sovereignty could be said to exist at all, it was shared among some combination of the mandatory power, the League and its members, and, for A mandates, the mandated communities, and it was limited by international law.

In Wright's own analysis, the mandate system highlighted a more general and underappreciated feature of modern international order: this order was constituted by the territorial division of the planet but *not* by the universalization of territorial sovereignty. Wright was critical of arguments that territorial sovereignty was either necessary for political organization or law or was a natural or universal mode of human sociality. The territorial division of the world was simply "the most convenient method for organizing government and avoiding conflict between sovereigns," and this convenience did not require European-style territorial states. Indeed, the expansion of European governance across more and more of the globe had pluralized rather than homogenized types of political organization, producing new "federations, confederations, empires, protectorates, suzerainties, commonwealths, unions, and leagues of nations."[66] Territorial divisions typically marked governmental jurisdiction, but governance did not require the assertion of sovereignty. In Wright's view, international lawyers were mistaken to conceptualize the international system as one based on the universalization of the sovereign nation-state. Modern international order was instead based on the universalization of territory, as the most convenient means of organizing international commerce. Due to historical differences and civilizational inequalities those territories would have different relationships to sovereignty. Nonstate and dependent territories, like those of the mandates, related to sovereignty as objects, not subjects.[67]

If there was little disagreement within the PMC and among most international jurists that B and C mandated populations did not already constitute nations, it was less clear whether the mandate system required efforts to develop nations and, if so, what this would mean. Opinions differed on the correct interpretation of the Covenant's language about the "well-being and development of such peoples" as are "not yet able to stand by themselves under the strenuous conditions of the modern world."[68] For some, well-being and development meant conformity with relatively fixed standards of civilization based on the objective of "efficiently [governing] and utilizing their natural and human resources to the full."[69] Arguably, the creation of A, B, and C mandates in the first place supported this interpretation since racialized civilizational criteria were what justified greater political recognition for the A mandates. But others argued that the objectives of well-being and development meant protecting geographical and cultural difference and encouraging its political expression over time—in short, supporting self-determination.

For the PMC, interpreting the Covenant's language of well-being and development—in relation to the potentially contradictory objectives of self-determination and civilizational advancement—was important for its work formulating standards through which to comparatively assess the performance of the mandates over time. Under the leadership of Frederick Lugard, who joined the PMC in 1923, a year after publishing his influential *The Dual Mandate in British Tropical Africa*, the PMC came to define administrative standards in relation to comparative assessments of economic development. Economic development was conceptualized as an administrative goal that reconciled the promotion of civilizational standards with concern for "native" development and eventual self-determination. This was based on the assumption that the economic development of mandated territories would be a precondition for the national development of mandated populations.

For some members of the PMC, the prior determination that B and C mandates' populations lacked a collective political identity had implications for how well-being and development should be defined and assessed. If the inhabitants of the mandates related to the system as individuals, standards for development should be defined universally, and mandatory powers need not be concerned with protecting ways of life that would be threatened by these standards. As Portuguese member of the PMC M. Freire d'Andrade pointed out, even in "civilized countries," "the inexorable law of labor" required people to "accept employment which is very heavy, unhealthy, and often killing!"[70] Death or disease among those less capable of work was not antithetical to but part of civilized life, and the welfare of the less capable should not impede others' capacities to develop a mandated territory, or so the argument went.

Lugard positioned himself against these arguments. He insisted that mandate administration must be oriented toward "the time when the bulk of the population of Tropical Africa will be able to stand alone," even though this time "may not yet be visible on the horizon."[71] Development for the bulk of the population required that native institutions be preserved, in modified forms, and incorporated into colonial and mandatory governance in order to promote the gradual transformation of native society as a whole. Protection of (modified) native institutions and ways of life addressed native well-being, but it was equally a strategy for economic development because it protected native labor. Lugard was explicit about this in PMC sessions: "It must, however, be admitted that these precautions for the welfare and increase of the native population are dictated by a utilitarian move. The natives are regarded as the greatest 'asset' of the country because of their potential value as laborers. The same argument applies to the good treatment and good feeding of a horse or a plough-ox or to the increase of stock."[72] Native well-being and civilizational advancement through economic growth need not be in conflict but were instead mutually enforcing dimensions of the dual mandate.[73] Lugard thus successfully positioned himself as the defender of the Covenant's vision of development while moving ideas of development firmly away from the political realm and into the economic. According to Lugard's philosophy, which aligned with the logic of differentiating A, B, and C mandates, self-determination would be possible for Africans once native society achieved an adequate level of civilization. Civilization depended on effectively harnessing a territory's labor and resources, out of which a nation might someday emerge.

As the PMC progressed in their work to define and develop standards for mandate administration, the primacy of the economic development of mandated territories over the national development of mandates' populations solidified. This had broader effects on the theory and practice of colonial administration more generally. The PMC's ability to gather comparative data on economic conditions across different mandate areas, to conduct inquiries into different mandatory powers' approaches to development and their results, and to call on the experience of scholars and practitioners to advise its work situated it as a respected source of knowledge on colonialism and its modernization. As Antony Anghie shows, this positioned the mandate system and the PMC at the center of a new scientific discourse on underdevelopment and development. The PMC had unprecedented access to data that could be analyzed using innovative new social science methodologies. This generated ever more sophisticated ways to quantify the substance and sources of mandated territories' underdevelopment, from which strategies for development could be formulated and then tested in those same territories.[74]

In its work addressing questions of sovereignty and development in the B and C mandates, the PMC constructed a model of how African (and Pacific) spaces and populations could be integrated into the modern international order. This would be as territories to be developed, not as political communities. If political communities were to materialize in the distant future, this would be a result of the economic development of those territories and their integration into international commerce, not vice versa. Africans' political affinities and interests would then be legible from the perspective of international order to the degree that they aligned with the existing territorial units and with the maintenance of those territories' relationships to a broader international economy. In a political context where the modern international was increasingly conceptualized in relation to the recognition of political rights and personality for national peoples, the definition of B and C mandates as territories first and foremost articulated a different means through which their relationship to the international could be mediated, which deferred questions of political subjectivity to a distant horizon. A technical discourse on territorial development, deployed with reference to new social scientific data and methodologies, simultaneously reproduced and obscured the white supremacist civilizational logics that guided the design of the mandate system and of the League of Nations more generally.

The mandate system's framework helped define the terms of recognition through which colonized territories gained formal independence within the UN system. Decolonization would eventually proceed in line with a theory of sovereignty as territorial competence. Colonial powers would recognize the independence of their former colonies as a handing over of responsibilities for territorial administration. Newly independent states were held to standards of state responsibility, meaning they were responsible for securing contracts and property relations that had been established under colonialism.[75] Where postcolonial leaders challenged this notion of responsibility—for example, by nationalizing control of natural resources—the principle of nonintervention at the core of international sovereignty was often set aside.

This model, however, was contested by both colonizers and colonized through the mid-twentieth century. By the end of the 1920s, the idea that an objective of colonial administration should be the economic development of colonized territories was widely accepted. But the notion that territorial development would, at least theoretically in the distant future, produce new, territorially defined nations with international political subjectivity was not. In the next section, I briefly introduce how contestations over the relationship between territorial development and international political subjectivity shaped decolonization in French West Africa and, more specifically, in the French Soudan (Mali), which is the focus of the next chapter.

Territorial Development, Decolonization, and the Office du Niger in Mali

After World War I, colonial administrators in French West Africa were facing both poor productivity and persistent rebellion, especially in the Sahel regions of the French Soudan. Military conquest and counterinsurgency campaigns in the Sahel had combined with a drying climate to cause large population displacements and famine. French administrators believed that the colony's viability would depend on increasing population density to support intensive agriculture. A principal barrier to this goal was the Sahel's aridity, and colonial planners had different theories about the causes of this aridity and whether and how it might be overcome. Though geological research suggested that the aridity of the Sahel and Sahara was related to long-term climatic trends, colonial forestry and agricultural planners argued that land use, especially by nomadic pastoralists, was causing desiccation and that this process could be reversed if different practices and technologies were adopted.[76] In 1924, a forestry mission to French West Africa determined that agriculture was being threatened by deforestation and other poor land-use practices and warned that time was running out to reverse this trend.[77]

To address the threat of desiccation and improve productivity, colonial planners argued that the metropole must invest in programs aimed at transforming land-use practices in the Sahel and introducing modern agricultural techniques, especially the plow and irrigation infrastructure. Development plans for the Sahel were part of a broader shift in French colonial policy, developed in the late 1920s, toward "native colonization," or *colonisation indigène*. *Colonisation indigène* was premised on the theory that African peasants could follow a developmental trajectory analogous to that of French peasants—an idea popularized by "administrator-ethnographers" serving in French West Africa.[78] The promise of *colonisation indigène* was that, with the right agricultural techniques and land-use policies, Africans could rapidly achieve agricultural productivity on par with that in Europe. This would provide the material grounds for broader civilizational development, through which Africans would take on greater responsibility for administering African territory.

Politically, this process would not lead to autonomy but rather a closer bond between France and her overseas territories. The arrival point of the civilizing process would be the recognition of civilized Africans as French nationals, with many of the rights and protections of French citizens. *Colonisation indigène* assigned French-educated Africans, the *evolués*, an important role in the French model of development. More than just implementing French policy, they were increasingly asked to produce ethnographic knowledge about the African peasant, family, and society that would inform plans for economic development.[79]

One of the most ambitious development projects conceived as part of the *colonisation indigène* strategy was the Office du Niger, which envisioned a massive irrigation infrastructure supporting intensive agriculture in the inland Niger delta and into the arid regions to its north. The project would resettle families onto individual plots, where they would learn to adopt modern agricultural techniques under the supervision of French managers. Despite significant investment (it received 30 percent of all French funding to the Soudan from the end of World War II to 1959),[80] the project struggled, even at a much smaller scale than the initial proposals. The irrigation scheme and plowing and crop-rotation techniques dictated by management, which were aimed at reproducing practices used in Europe, were ill suited to the ecology and climate of the Sahel. It also did not attract settlers. Administrators forcibly resettled families to the project, used corporal punishment to enforce work requirements, and designed burdensome fee structures to keep them tied to the land.[81] These practices were all legal according to the codes of the *indigénat*, which allowed colonial administrators and, in some cases, any white person to unilaterally impose fines, imprisonment, and corporal punishment on "native" subjects.[82] For all the reformist rhetoric of *colonisation indigénat*, its premise was that African peasants and their ways of life were incompatible with the prosperity of the French Empire and must be urgently transformed. This justified violent practices not unlike those used during military conquest.

Political relationships between the French metropole and the colonies were radically altered by World War II and by the Free French movement. The Free French movement had relied on leadership and fighting forces from Africa (in Chad, Félix Éboué, the only Black governor within the empire, became the first leader of a French territory to break ties with the Vichy government and align with the fledgling Free France), and its propaganda included visions of French republicanism as a multinational and multiracial political project, protecting freedom against global forces of fascism and racism.[83] In 1946, the French Fourth Republic formally replaced its colonial empire with the French

Union, recognizing all inhabitants as citizens but with unequal political rights and representation. The *indigénat* was abolished. This began a period of re-negotiating and contesting the relationship between the economic develop-ment of France's overseas territories and recognition of political rights for those territories and their citizens. Many metropolitan politicians expected that improved standards of living in overseas territories would foster consent for a union that would remain politically unequal, with Paris maintaining sovereignty over dependent peoples who would enjoy limited representation in government and some of the protections of French citizenship.[84]

The French Union (and its successor, the French Community) ultimately broke apart over the question of international recognition for the overseas ter-ritories. In 1956, a compromise was reached in the form of the *loi-cadre*, which introduced a number of political and administrative reforms that devolved power to African territories. African leaders would gain some of the political power they were demanding through control over territorial assemblies while the metropole would bear less responsibility for economic development.[85] But recognition of international political standing for overseas territories separate from France was a nonstarter. For some leaders in the metropole, this would defeat the whole purpose of the French Union: its goal was to strengthen met-ropolitan France's international standing, not dilute it with the interests and demands of Asians and Africans. For West African leaders, international rec-ognition and autonomy over foreign policy became increasingly important in relation to two issues: France's negotiations about a European political and economic community, in which the question of access to African resources and markets figured centrally, and France's war in Algeria. African represen-tatives to the Union had no path to assert influence on either of these issues, both of which represented France's ongoing protection of colonial interests.

By 1958, most anticolonial leaders in French West Africa saw indepen-dence from France as the only path to international recognition, national sovereignty, and protection from colonialism. This left newly independent states with economic challenges that leaders had earlier hoped could be avoided through a federation with France. As the caucus of representatives from overseas territories stated in a 1948 policy declaration, "The modern world has no room for small economic entities whose independence will be a myth if they are not adequately equipped and if they do not participate in a broader 'union.' . . . The temptation of narrow nationalisms represents a grave danger."[86] Ten years later, these leaders saw few options but to accept a bargain whereby international sovereignty would be pinned to "small economic entities" that remained financially dependent.

For Mali, this dilemma was immediately put into relief in negotiations over the future of the Office du Niger. The political party that came to power with independence, the US-RDA (Union soudanaise–Rassemblement démocratique africain), was led by *evolués* whose education had been shaped by *colonisation indigène* and who had endorsed much of the French agenda for economic development based on modernized agriculture. This included a favorable view of the Office du Niger, whose workers US-RDA members had helped to unionize beginning in 1954. The party was critical of the office's exploitative labor practices but saw the project as a whole, as expressed in the party paper *L'Essor* in 1957, as "one of the rare achievements of French engineering, a matter of pride for Soudan, a prospect for the future for all of Africa."[87] At the time of independence, the government's first four-year plan designated more than half of its agricultural investments to the Office du Niger. But the office depended on large capital investments and ongoing technical assistance. This gave France significant leverage in their bilateral negotiations over the terms of independence, which notably allowed a continued presence for French troops using northern Mali as part of their Algerian operations. When Mali cut ties with France and introduced its own currency in 1962, it had secured alternative international funding for the Office du Niger from the Soviet Union, China, and the European Development Fund.[88]

The US-RDA's attachments to the Office du Niger represented a further political bind, as or more significant than continued financial dependence on foreign capital. The party's leadership endorsed much of the diagnosis of economic weakness that had been produced by colonial administrator-ethnographers since the 1920s, and it saw territorial development along these lines as necessary and urgent for the nation to maintain its sovereignty within a hierarchical international system. This put the state on a collision course with populations across the new nation but especially in the Sahel and southern Sahara.

Imperial expansion in Africa and competition to dominate trade on the Niger and Congo Rivers were central to the transformation of the modern international order from a continental "society of states" to a planetary system of territories. Projects to incorporate African spaces into an imperial international order defined international political subjectivity as rooted in a relationship to territory, whose rational administration would be the key to security and prosperity in an era of rapidly increasing global interdependence. "Modernized" territorial administration was thus held up as a precondition for security in "underdeveloped" parts of the globe and thus for the security of international order in general. This model of international political subjectivity as contingent on territorial development laid the groundwork for UN recognition of decolonizing states' independence, which put significant constraints on new states. The next chapter examines how this shaped decolonization in Mali and the development of what would come to be known as "the northern problem."

THREE

Territorializing the Desert to Secure the Nation

In Mali at the time of independence, the centrality of territorial competence to the recognition of postcolonial sovereignty made the desert a particularly contested space. From the perspective of both Bamako and Paris, the landscape of the desert and its inhabitants represented the opposite of well-ordered territory, which different actors saw as presenting different political opportunities and threats. For France, the perceived emptiness of the desert represented the opportunity to maintain a foothold even as colonized territories gained their independence. For the Malian government, the vulnerability of the desert to French control and the population's perceived resistance to inclusion in Mali made it a threat. For political entrepreneurs in northern Mali, the distinctiveness of the desert and its ways of life represented the possibility of autonomy and greater self-determination based on arguments about racial, ethnic, and cultural difference. Violent contestation over these projects would prompt renegotiations of relationships among space, authority, and population in Mali's arid regions, which are ongoing today.

These dimensions of decolonization in Mali point to what Pinar Bilgin terms "the international in security," meaning the ways in which conceptions of and positionality vis-à-vis hierarchies in international order shape "discourses of danger." Bilgin argues that attention to discourses of danger produced in postcolonial contexts illuminates the particular "dynamic relationship between the domestic and international" that shape conceptions of security for "those caught up in hierarchies that were built and sustained during the age of colonialism and beyond."[1] In this case, "domestic" problematizations of northern Mali need to be understood in relation to the ways in which international hierarchy and its dangers for those toward the bottom have been constituted through notions of territorial competency. Postcolonial governments in Mali, as well as the Tuareg nationalist movement that developed in the decades following independence, understood their security in the postwar international order to be contingent on their capacity to perform territorial stateness. As we will see, this situated ideas and practices of spatial ordering that are resistant to territorialization as incompatible with security, regardless of how those ideas and practices relate to collective security in those spaces themselves.

Decolonization and the Saharan Frontier

The postwar international order was grounded in representations of the planet as a closed space, constituted by contiguous territorial units. The United Nations Charter centered the defense of states' "territorial integrity" as the foundation of international peace and security. The charter's endorsement of the territorial integrity of colonies, classified as non-self-governing territories, was less explicit but also implied. Article 73 called for the "progressive development of their free political institutions, according to the circumstances of each territory and its peoples and their varying stages of advancement." This territorial status quo, however, was less settled in the planet's arid zones. For some, arid zones represented a last frontier space, *territorium nullius*, defined by the absence of territorial competencies. Sparsely populated or unpopulated deserts were figured as no-man's-lands that had yet to be made productive. Thanks to the advances of science and technology, it was thought that the twentieth century would finally see deserts become rationally territorialized and integrated into modern economic and administrative systems. Questions of sovereignty would thus ideally reflect capacities and willingness to develop these spaces. While it was becoming more and more difficult by the 1950s to justify the exclusion of colonized peoples from the governance of their territories, the remoteness of deserts from mostly urban anticolonial struggles along with the assumed technical demands of their modernization made these spaces exceptional.[2]

For the French, modernist dreams of territorializing the desert were central to postwar efforts to maintain their status as an African power despite the end of formal colonial rule. In 1946, the constitution of the Fourth Republic

established the French Union, which recognized inhabitants of overseas territories as French citizens, entitled to (unequal) representation in government.
These steps toward establishing a transcontinental and multiracial union reflected political aspirations and solidarities of the Free French movement,
which had been headquartered in Brazzaville and in which Africans had
played a decisive role. But for the Union's first decade, metropolitan politicians repeatedly resisted the devolution of decision-making power to Africans. Initially, the metropole's hope was that Africans would accept ongoing
political inequality if they saw movement toward equality in standards of
living. As the costs of the latter became clearer, however, that calculus reversed. By 1956, metropolitan politicians saw increased autonomy for African leaders over their own territories as a means of lessening the metropole's
responsibilities for infrastructure and economic development.[3]

As France's authority in its African territories became less certain, proposals were developed to construct a new French territory in the Sahara Desert,
which was seen as removed from anticolonial political mobilizations centered
in urban areas. Not only was the Sahara assumed to be distant from the politics of decolonization, its perceived emptiness and economic backwardness
would seem to justify ongoing European control as only states with the most
advanced technical capacities could transform the desert into a productive
space. It was hoped that European financing and technical know-how would
turn the Sahara into a main source of oil and gas for France and western
Europe. The first proposal to establish a French Saharan Africa, with the
same administrative status as French West Africa and French Equatorial
Africa, was brought to the French National Assembly in 1952—the same
year that France began issuing permits for gas and oil prospecting. Gas and
oil fields were discovered in Algeria in 1954 and 1956, and proposals for a
French Sahara were brought to the Assembly of the French Union five times
between 1955 and 1956. After the start of the Algerian War in 1954, the
status of the Sahara was at the heart of France's war aims, and France's attempts to treat southern Algeria separately from the North was a consistent
barrier to negotiations with the National Liberation Front (FLN).[4]

The fate of the Sahara was also important to France's standing in Europe
as states negotiated the formation of a European economic and political community over the 1950s. Plans for European integration centered access to
African resources and markets as one of the main benefits of joining a European common market. Advocates of "Eurafrica" argued that joint European

investments in exploiting African raw materials, especially energy resources in the Sahara, was the way in which Europe could regain its status as a global power and compete with the Soviet Union and United States.[5] In addition to raw materials and hopes for energy independence, the Sahara offered a crucial military asset: remote space for nuclear testing. As one of the main champions of Eurafrica argued at a conference in 1955, geopolitics in the late twentieth century would be shaped by global powers' capacities to exploit vast arid spaces: the Soviet Union was exploiting Siberia, China and India would develop the deserts of Central Asia, and the United States controlled the vast American West. Europe could only compete by harnessing the potential of the Sahara.[6] Pierre Nord, a former intelligence officer in the Free French movement, summarized the theory in a book the same year: "Only Eurafrica is a complete economic, military and political solution. . . . Economically, Eurafrica may very rapidly become a power equal to the USSR and the US, between which it will ensure the equilibrium."[7]

For African leaders, France's Saharan ambitions were not remote from but rather very relevant to the political trajectories of decolonization. Pretensions to redraw territorial borders within the French Union in ways that would reduce the territorial extent of at least some of its African members signified the perpetuation of colonial relations. These colonial overtones were further accentuated by France's deliberations about Eurafrica. France did not include African representatives in these negotiations—in violation of the French Union's premise that overseas territories were integral to the republic.[8] African representatives, like Leopold Senghor and Sourou Migan Apithy, suggested that if a Eurafrica plan was constructed without African participation and approval, Africans would withdraw from the French Union altogether. As Senghor argued in the National Assembly, Africans would "refuse to be the wedding presents or the china" in the integration of Europe.[9]

In part due to opposition from African representatives, proposals to create a French Sahara were repeatedly voted down until, in 1956, a new organization was proposed with more limited authority, the Organisation commune des régions sahariennes (OCRS). The design of OCRS attempted to sidestep political controversy by constraining its authorities to issues of economic development and technical assistance and leaving its territorial boundaries undefined.[10] It was introduced to the French National Assembly by the West African minister Félix Houphouët-Boigny and pitched as an investment in the French-African solidarity that was replacing the colonialism of old. But metropolitan politicians continued to reference territorial ambitions in the Sahara, especially in relation to the war in Algeria. Moreover, only months after the creation of the OCRS, the government created the new Ministry for Saharan Affairs, led by Max Lejeune, who had previously been commanding French troops in Algeria.[11] Across the region, OCRS and France's ongoing war in Algeria were seen as threats to African independence and freedom from colonialism.

The creation of OCRS was perceived as especially threatening by the dominant political party in the French Soudan/Mali, US-RDA. Mali's border with southern Algeria made its Saharan territories of particular interest to France. Both the French military and the FLN maintained bases in northern Mali. Further, the party saw nomadic elites in the North as hostile to US-RDA's anticolonial struggle. Antipathy between the US-RDA party, on the one hand, and nomadic elites, on the other, real and perceived, was influenced by racialized political conflicts over the status of slaves and dependent peoples, which became a major issue shaping party politics and the dominance of US-RDA over its pro-French rival, the Parti soudan progressiste (PSP).

As discussed in chapter 1, nomadic society in the Middle Niger and southern Sahara was structured around relationships of protection and dependency. The French colonial administration, in violation of colonial anti-slavery policies, supported the continuation of nomadic elites' ownership of slaves until the mid 1940s, when they gradually considered reforms. When the French first attempted to conquer the Niger bend, they assumed that they could undermine the military power of the Iwellemedan confederation by organizing the settled populations in the river valley against their nomadic overlords, thereby closing off nomads' access to food and pasture.[12] But settled communities instead largely supported Iwellemedan resistance to the French. French strategy adapted, and their conquest ultimately depended on mobilizing other Tuareg and Arab federations against the Iwellemedan and their allies. French control over the Niger bend and southern Sahara then continued to rely on relationships with these federations and the reproduction of their relationships of protection and dependence, though in altered forms.

In their collaboration with nomadic elites, French colonial officers projected European frameworks of white supremacy and anti-Black racism onto existing racial discourses of whiteness and Blackness in the Sahel. From the seventeenth century on, discourses of political authority and legitimacy in

the Sahel increasingly based authority and legitimacy on genealogical connections to Islam and the Arab world. These genealogies were understood
to make elites racially distinct from the non-Islamic Africans to the south
of the desert's edge. Elite pastoralists adopted a racial identity of whiteness,
referring to themselves as *bidân*, which signified a higher status than Black
(*sudan*) Africans based on their privileged connection to Islam.[13] The French
interpreted and then reinforced privileges associated with whiteness in line
with their own ideologies of race as a biological and phenotypical category.
Notably, *bidân* were omitted from military conscription and forced labor and
assisted the French in their often-violent enforcement of labor and conscription policies against servile populations.[14]

After World War II, when the French Soudan saw the introduction of
the franchise and electoral politics, the status of slaves in the Niger bend
(termed *bellah*, a Songhai term, by the French) was in flux. *Bellah* were increasingly mobilizing for emancipation and land rights, and French administrators sought reform as well, recognizing that the continuation of slavery
undermined claims about their commitment to colonial reform. As Bruce S.
Hall puts it, conflict between *bellah* and Tuareg elites was thus "a ready-made
issue for the anti-colonial political forces" of the US-RDA.[15] Party activists
mobilized *bellah* and other servile populations in the Niger bend and framed
the anticolonial struggle as one not only against French rule but also the
racialized "feudal" structures of Tuareg society. The success of this electoral
strategy reinforced some Tuareg elites' expectations that political autonomy
from France posed a threat to their way of life.

In this context, proposals to separate the Niger bend and southern Sahara
from the rest of the French Soudan found support among some Tuareg and
Arab leaders, and this support was actively cultivated by colonial officers.[16]
When OCRS was established in 1957, French military officers facilitated a
campaign by a former *qadi* of Timbuktu, Mohamed Mahmoud ould Cheick,
to mobilize northern elites in support of continued French rule in the Sahara.
Ould Cheick collected petitions to send to Charles de Gaulle on behalf of
chiefs, religious leaders, and merchants, asserting that "our interests and aspirations could not validly be defended as long as we are attached to a territory
represented and inevitably controlled by a black majority whose ethnicity, interests, and aspirations are not the same as ours. This is why we request your
high equitable intervention to be separated politically and administratively
from French Sudan as soon as possible and to integrate our country and its

Boucle area of Niger into the French Sahara which we are forming part historically and ethnically."[17] French officers continued to support these efforts at least until Mali's independence. After independence, Malian intelligence reports continued to warn of efforts by the French to encourage secessionist aspirations in northern Mali.[18]

For US-RDA and Mali's first president, Modibo Keita, Mali's territorial integrity and thus its status as an independent sovereign state were threatened by populations in its arid northern regions and more specifically by elites' backward feudal systems of political and social authority.[19] They held that under the influence of the French, Tuareg and Arab societies had adopted white supremacist ideologies and systems of social control, which the state would now have to dismantle. This was necessary not only to achieve the social equality within Mali that was championed by US-RDA but also to secure the state in relation to the threat of neocolonialism within a hierarchical international system.

Territorializing the Desert to Secure the Nation

Modibo Keita and US-RDA's suspicions of northern elites overlapped with their own modernist dreams of territorializing the desert.[20] They adopted the widespread view of nomadic pastoralism as fundamentally harmful to land and resources. Taking this into account, one of the destructive effects of colonial rule had been the French romanticizing of nomadic life, which had allowed feudal social relations and related land misuse to continue. Beyond an orientalist fascination with the Tuareg, the French had been indifferent to the well-being and development of populations or resources in the Niger bend and failed to invest in economic or social modernization. The upside of this state of affairs, however, was that introducing state-directed social and economic development should quickly produce significant returns. In US-RDA's first five-year economic plan, it forecasted a growth rate of 11 percent based on increasing productivity in the primary sector. A significant portion of this growth was expected to come from economic transformation in the Sahel: increased cattle exports by rationalizing pastoral production with more sedentary ranching techniques and controlling trade and decreased food imports by teaching nomads to grow and eat their own food.[21]

The Malian government's optimism about transforming arid zones from economic wastelands to engines of growth was au courant. Not only was mastery over the desert expected to be a source of economic strength, it was also associated with international influence and prestige: political discourses of desert transformation situated them as globally relevant "technopolitical zones" that were a foundation for new "geopolitical ties."[22] In 1958, Modibo Keita led a delegation to Israel, where they toured kibbutzim and observed the state's supposed successes "making the desert bloom."[23] The example of Israel influenced Keita's ideas and rhetoric about nation building through the valorization of agricultural labor.[24] On his return, Keita praised Israel's model of economic modernization at a US-RDA conference: "[Israel's] economic takeoff is most of all the result of belief. Belief in the ideal of the resurrection of a country, of the rehabilitation of a persecuted and shattered people willing to regain its unity, which it has already gained by rallying around that which binds: the soil."[25] In the Malian context, Keita similarly envisioned an economic takeoff being driven by a rejuvenation of Malians' connections to the land and to the material and moral rewards of working it.[26]

A principal barrier to implementing the state's social and economic program was the difficulty of controlling the circulation of people, animals, and goods over a vast area. In many parts of the state, connections to a fixed agricultural landscape, on which US-RDA hoped to build the Malian national identity and economy, were at odds with existing patterns of mobility, which were themselves foundational to material well-being and to individual and collective identities. Young people left the villages where they were supposed to contribute to agricultural collectives to earn higher pay in Senegal, Côte d'Ivoire, or France. Merchants and pastoralists traded animals and goods with little regard for newly established national boundaries and state customs policies. If nomads participated in new gardening and agricultural schemes at all, they did so only inconsistently as it aligned with transhumance patterns.

As US-RDA fell farther away from its economic goals, it stepped up efforts to restrict movement. In 1962, new restrictions on migration were introduced, and the state asserted its control over cross-border trade by replacing the CFA franc with the Malian franc.[27] Resistance to these policies was met with violence and repression. The introduction of the Malian franc prompted large protests from the merchant community in Bamako, leading to many arrests. Protestors were charged with conspiracy against the state and seventy-seven were sentenced to prison terms and forced labor.[28] Migration controls were enforced by party vigilantes known for their violence against young would-be migrants.[29] In late 1962, a mass exodus of residents from the Niger bend, apparently to avoid taxes, prompted a military response to prevent their migration. Clashes reportedly left fifty civilians dead.[30]

In 1963, rebellion in the Adagh, the northernmost part of Mali bordering Algeria, precipitated a sweeping military campaign in that region followed by more concerted efforts by the state to sedentarize nomads and defeat "feudal mentalities" with state education.[31] The rebellion was led by members of the Ifoghas clan, which had been a privileged intermediary of the French under colonial rule. Support for the rebellion among the Ifoghas and other Kel Adagh was uneven, and when violence broke out, some chiefs attempted to intervene with the rebels on behalf of the Malian government. However, the Malian army's repression of the rebellion targeted all Kel Adagh as well as their herds. The entire Adagh was declared a *zone interdite*, meaning that anyone in the area "would be considered a rebel and shot on sight." This proved impractical and was revised to create "regrouping zones" within the Adagh, where the civilian population could be concentrated, which doubled as reeducation camps.[32] After the rebels' surrender in 1964, those who remained in the Adagh (many migrated to Algeria) faced continued sedentarization policies under military rule and food insecurity due to the loss of their herds.

The rebellion created a justification for the US-RDA-led government to militarily respond to a threat that had preoccupied it since at least 1957.[33] Its desert regions and inhabitants made Mali's territorial integrity vulnerable, which meant that its claims to sovereignty and independence were vulnerable. In a speech at Chatham House in 1961, Modibo Keita summarized this sense of vulnerability with reference to the crisis in the Congo, which had unfolded during Mali's transition to independence: "With a frontier of 1500 miles running along the border of Algeria (a country in open revolt), and with common frontiers with the French-speaking African countries at a time when relations between France and the Republic of Mali were bad, and when Mali had neither security forces nor police and consequently when subversion was all too possible—suffice it to say that this country had quite understandably in its first preoccupation the securing of its own identity and the prevention of a recurrence of the regrettable drama of the Congo."[34] Like the Congo, Keita saw Mali as having a large, presumably resource-rich zone, remote from the capital, that had geopolitical importance to the Cold War conflict between the East and West. Events in the Congo made it clear that where perceived Cold War interests were involved, Mali could not count on the UN to defend its charter's principles of territorial integrity in a new African state.[35] Mali's vulnerability would thus ultimately be addressed in its arid zones, which could either remain a permanent threat or become an engine of development if its resources could be harnessed effectively.[36]

After the fall of the Keita government to a military coup in 1968, perceptions of the Sahara and Sahel and its economic prospects were transformed by drought. The 1950s and 1960s had been a period of particularly high rainfall, which had buffered Sahelian populations from the full effects of changes to transhumance and mobility. With the droughts of the 1970s and 1980s, modernist dreams of making the Sahara bloom faded from view.

Imagining Azawad: Nationalism in Exile

When the Sahel entered a period of lower rainfall in the late 1960s, strategies for adaptation were limited by constraints on movement and reduced grazing lands due to the expansion of agriculture. Populations in the Adagh were especially vulnerable because their herds had already been devastated by state repression in 1963 and 1964, and they had not yet recovered.[37] This made the effects of an extreme dry period from 1972 to 1973 even more catastrophic. It led to a mass exodus of people and herds south, toward the Niger River valley, which further strained already-depleted pasture, water, and food supplies. Acute food shortages forced pastoralists to kill or sell their herds to avoid starvation. Continued widespread drought impeded typical restocking strategies, like herd splitting, and pastoralism collapsed, especially for the Kel Adagh. Refugees fled to Algeria or Libya or to camps in Mali and Niger. The 1972–1973 crisis had been less devastating to populations in the Niger bend, but the influx of displaced people from the North along with a continued period of low rainfall meant the region was even more vulnerable when another severe drought struck in 1982.[38] This produced another wave of displacement from the Niger bend to the Maghreb and to refugee camps.

Emergency relief was slow and inadequate. Aid groups faced restrictions on their travel and access to refugee camps and relied on the state to distribute aid—some amount of which was redirected for personal sale.[39] Tuareg and Arab families in particular lacked access to food aid. In 1974, reporting by aid groups found that children of nomadic families faced much higher rates of malnutrition than their sedentary counterparts: 3–7 percent of the latter were malnourished, while for nomadic children, the rate was an alarming 10–17 percent.[40] For some, this was evidence of the state's continued perception of Tuareg communities as a threat. In *Le Monde*, the journalist Philippe Decraene accused the Malian government of using its control over humanitarian aid as a "final solution to the Tuareg problem."[41] Regardless of the political interests and intents shaping aid distribution, perceptions of abandonment by the state in the midst of a crisis of apocalyptic proportions for nomadic ways life had momentous political effects. Displaced Tuareg, many of whom had also experienced state violence and repression following the rebellion of 1963, organized politically around the idea that Tuareg communities could never be secure within the Malian state.

The Tuareg nationalist movement that would lead a rebellion in 1990 developed out of experiences of exile in the Maghreb and, to a lesser extent, in Europe. Displaced Tuareg youth refashioned cultural and political identities in relation to their experiences of loss, oppression, and precarity.[42] Known as *ishumar*, a Tamashek variation of the French term for "unemployed," young Tuareg adopted mobile urban lifestyles, following precarious wage labor. *Ishumar* social gatherings were spaces in which Tuareg from different clans, social statuses, and regions analyzed the radical changes affecting life in the Sahel. In music and poetry, which was shared at parties and circulated on cassettes, *ishumar* developed historical and political interpretations of Tuareg's position in the modern world and called for social and political change. Baz Lecocq summarizes the message of *ishumar* lyrics and poetry as follows: "We, the Tuareg people have suffered under oppression and droughts since African independence in the 1960s. Independence left our country divided between various nation-states. Since then, we have moved away from kin and country to the Maghreb. We need to reunite and liberate our country so that we can become prosperous again." By the mid-1970s, like-minded *ishumar* began organizing what they termed the *tanekra*, or "uprising," toward the goal of armed rebellion to establish a Tuareg nation-state. These plans got a boost in 1979 when Muammar Qaddafi invited *ishumar* to join his Popular Front for the Liberation of the Greater Arab Central Sahara and receive military training. When this force was disbanded in 1981, former members were redeployed to Lebanon and to Chad.[43] Veterans of these deployments would become leaders of the military wing of the *tanekra*.

The political project of *tanekra* as it developed through the 1970s and 1980s was premised on critiques not only of colonial and postcolonial states but also of Tuareg society. These critiques developed among the *ishumar* but also among young Tuareg studying in the Maghreb and in Europe, who had a different experience of exile. The latter *évolués* advanced a view of Tuareg society as having been weakened by hierarchies and class divisions that were exploited by the state.[44] Divisions according to clan and status had prevented Tuareg from organizing politically in a way that could be effective in the modern state system: they had failed to organize themselves as a nation. Without a nation-state defined by Tuareg interests and identities, they would persist in a state of permanent vulnerability. The political consciousness that *évolués* and *ishumar* developed away from home ultimately situated them in opposition to the previous generation of authorities—the chiefs who served as intermediaries between the state and the population.[45] The experience of exile fostered new senses of solidarity both among Tuareg and between Tuareg and other marginalized or stateless people. Members of the *tanekra* movement saw their struggle as similar to that of other nationalist and secessionist movements of minoritized peoples without claims to a national state.

The *tanekra* movement drew on discourses of nationalism both in explaining the crisis facing Tuareg populations and in prescribing how a better future could be secured. If traditional frameworks of Tuareg identity, which emphasized clan and lineage, were a source of division, shared attachments to a homeland, the desert, seemed to offer ground for a unified and modernized political identity and one that could make internationally recognizable claims to a state. In 1976, a meeting of members of the *tanekra* movement in Algiers adopted the name Mouvement de libération de l'Azawad, defining the object that the movement sought to liberate as that of a territorial homeland: Azawad.[46] Representing Azawad as a national homeland (*akal n temust* in Tamashek) was a new way of conceptualizing Tuareg political identity in relation to space, or *akal*.[47] As discussed in chapter 1, in Tamashek, *akal* historically referred to a space of belonging, meaning a space in which one can reside in security and without needing special protection. Unlike the political territory of the state, *akal* did not describe mutually exclusive spaces. Boundaries among *akal* were flexible and overlapping, and relationships to those spaces were mediated through clan and kinship and in relation to changing environmental and political conditions. Geographies of *akal* were intertwined with relationships of protection and dependency: it was through these relationships that one was assured security or needed to negotiate security in a given space.

Translating *akal* onto the geography of the territorial nation-state was thus not just a challenge to the territorial legitimacy of Mali but also to the geographies of authority that had grounded relationships within and among Tuareg clan and kinship structures. Centering a single, shared *akal*, the homeland of Azawad, as the object that mediated political belonging would weaken the political mediation of lineage. In this sense, the nationalism of the *tanekra* movement mirrored that of the Malian state, in which the means of forging a new and more modern political identity was to cultivate shared attachments to the land. For both, the concept of a homeland was the means of modernizing elements of Tuareg society seen as backward and of overcoming ethnic and tribal identities that had been exploited by the colonizers.

The Rebellion

The *tanekra* movement's radical vision of an egalitarian territorial nationalism was successful in mobilizing the rebellion, which was launched in June 1990 under the name of the Mouvement populaire de libération de l'Azawad (MPLA), but it did not survive the process of negotiating a peace. When military victories put the movement in a position to make political demands to the government of Mali and to an international audience, political leaders pushed for autonomy, not secession. This reflected leaders' sensitivity to international opposition to secession movements, especially within the Organization of African Unity, as well as rapidly changing political conditions in Mali.[48] Negotiations with the state, which stretched on for nearly five years, situated armed groups as intermediaries not between the state and the "imagined community" of Azawad but among the state and multiple ethnic, clan, and kinship-based formations.

The course of the rebellion was shaped by a democratization movement based in southern Mali that also began in 1990. On March 22, 1991, Malian security forces fired on a large protest march in Bamako, killing up to 150 protesters. On March 26, Moussa Traoré was deposed in a coup d'état. The coup leaders, led by then–lieutenant colonel Amadou Toumani Touré, established a transitional administration toward the creation of a multiparty democracy. In this context, political leaders of the rebellion framed their own movement as having contributed to—catalyzed even—the fall of the authoritarian Traoré government. From this position, the movement could frame its demands as aligned with, rather than in opposition to, the political future of Mali as a whole. The transitional government included two representatives from the rebel movement.[49]

The shift from demands for independence to federalism and autonomy within Mali reflected and then exacerbated divisions between the military and political components of the movement. While the former was dominated by *ishumar*, the latter was led by *évolués*.[50] When the first ceasefire agreement with the government was signed in 1991, its apparent compromise on independence fueled skepticism that the *évolués* were going their own way and abandoning the base of the movement. As negotiations with the state continued, the rebel movement began to fracture based on disagreements over its goals (independence versus autonomy) and based on different groups' interests in negotiating with the state directly.[51] Divisions within the rebellion became entangled with questions of clan, status, and privileged access to the state. Once the state was interested in negotiating, rebel leaders took on a role of intermediary among the state, their fighters, and the communities they claimed to represent. This role both overlapped and competed with the influence that chiefs had long held in their position as intermediaries. Access to the leaders of the rebellion thus became a means through which traditional leaders could reassert their influence as intermediaries with the state, and prominence in the rebellion could translate into influence within—or against—traditional clan structures.

In April 1992, a committee formed to collectively represent the now-multiple armed groups, the Coordination des mouvements et fronts unifiés de l'Azawad (MFUA), who signed an agreement, known as the National Pact, with the transitional government. The key components of the National Pact concerned the integration of rebels into military and civilian government roles and of refugees back into their communities; increased funding for development; administrative redistricting in the northern regions (Timbuktu, Gao, and Kidal), which would give more authority to interregional, regional, and local elected leaders; and the demilitarization of the North and establishment of local policing units.[52]

The peace depended heavily on the successful disarmament of combatants and their integration into government roles. This was a fraught process both between rebels and the military and among rebels themselves. Because of an International Monetary Fund–imposed structural-adjustment program that prevented state hiring, the disarmament and integration process was the only means of accessing state employment at the time. This made the selection of candidates for integration, which was managed among the rebel groups themselves, of particularly high stakes. It also shaped opposition to the peace process among the public given that people who had taken up arms against the state were now eligible for positions that were closed off to everyone else. As the disarmament and integration process faltered, violence in northern Mali worsened through 1993 and 1994. Fighting escalated among armed groups, and civilians who were presumed to support particular factions were targeted by both rebels and the Malian army. The widespread availability of weapons also encouraged opportunistic predation, including armed thefts of vehicles and animals. In 1994, amidst increasingly generalized insecurity in the Niger bend, the Mouvement patriotique Ganda Koy (MPGK; hereafter, Ganda Koy) was created with a stated mission of protecting sedentary populations from Tuareg and Arab violence. Its forces were led by a captain in the Malian army, Abdoulaye Hamadahamane Maiga, who officially deserted but maintained ties with sympathetic military leadership.[53]

With the creation of Ganda Koy, northern Mali was at risk of becoming entirely militarized, with social and economic life mediated exclusively by armed groups and civilian populations vulnerable to attack based on racial, ethnic, and clan identities. As this possibility became clearer, especially in the wake of several shocking massacres, the center of gravity of the peace process shifted from the MFUA and its demands on the state to locally based negotiations focused on securing daily life.[54] Community leaders, especially traditional chiefs, seized the initiative to facilitate negotiations that included, but were not led by, members of armed groups. These meetings established frameworks for broader agreements to be reached among the leadership of armed groups and ultimately with the state.

Peace Building and Decentralization: Recovering Geographies of Interdependence?

Local peace building was rooted in recognition and protection of social and economic interdependence. While the conflict had disrupted these relationships, many communities also relied on longstanding ties of reciprocity and *arkawal* (chapter 1) between villages and pastoralists to cope with violence and insecurity. In their study of "*les liens sociaux au nord du Mali*," based on interviews conducted between 1998 and 2002, Charles Grémont et al. record numerous accounts of these ties. A villager from Hamakulaji, for example, recalled the assistance offered them by their Tuareg neighbors, the Shamanamas. "I remember that during the rebellion, when everyone was afraid, [the Shamanamas] came to get our animals and bring them to pasture. They took them all with the herders to show them the way and told them they had nothing to fear. Between them and us there is something very strong."[55] When violence worsened in 1994, these connections became more difficult to sustain but also offered a foundation from which to redirect the interests of combatants to the security needs of their communities.

The first major success in local peace building was achieved in Bourem in the region of Gao. In Bourem, pastoralists and cultivators had largely maintained their ties with one another even as violence was worsening. After the creation of Ganda Koy and its installation in Bourem, however, pastoralists' continued access to the river and neighboring villages was threatened. At great personal risk, Tuareg leaders drew on their relationships with villagers and the Bourem mayor, Hafizu Adhere Touré, to establish contact with Ganda Koy members.[56] Despite opposition from their leadership, the Ganda Koy in Bourem agreed to hear the pastoralists' concerns. This led to two meetings in November 1994 among pastoralists, villagers, and Ganda Koy to address resource access and security. The meetings produced the Bourem Pact, in which Ganda Koy and village chiefs agreed to protect pastoralists' access to water, pasture, and markets, and the pastoralists agreed to protect villagers from animal theft and inform them of any threatening rebel activity.[57] A committee was established to oversee compliance with the agreement.

The Bourem Pact paved the way for rebel groups—who were also seeking an offramp from the conflict as conditions deteriorated—to negotiate their own agreements. Ganda Koy's role signaled a disavowal of earlier racialized rhetoric against Tuaregs and Arabs, which had included advocating the elimination of all nomads from the Niger bend and prompted an overture from one of the Azawad movements, the Front populaire pour la libération de l'Azawad (FPLA), to meet.[58] Agreements between the FPLA and Ganda Koy and then among multiple armed groups used the Bourem Pact as a framework for confidence building and oversight. Because not all rebel groups were participants within the National Pact framework, the Bourem Pact and its oversight committee, which had credibility across clan and ethnic lines, was an alternative structure under which such agreements could be monitored and enforced.[59]

Dozens of similar meetings took place across northern Mali in 1995 and 1996.[60] Like in Bourem, these meetings brought together communities based on existing relationships of social and economic interdependence, typically including those who shared the same weekly market. Significantly, the geographies of these meetings, which reflected economic complementarity between the river valley and more arid spaces, were not congruent with existing administrative boundaries created by the French, which treated the river as a natural boundary.[61] As such, one effect of these meetings was to reinforce the importance and influence of traditional chiefs, whose relationships with each other and with their constituents corresponded to geographies of economic and social interdependence in ways that state administrative roles did not. These meetings addressed the security challenges that were preventing communities from trading and accessing resources and markets. The revival of these relationships not only helped rebuild trust that had been lost due to conflict but also helped reestablish social and economic ties that had deteriorated well before the rebellion, during the crisis of the droughts.[62]

The local peace-building movement that grew in northern Mali was not initiated or led by the state, but it was enabled by President Alpha Oumar Konaré's efforts to demilitarize the conflict. As violence worsened in 1994 and support for Ganda Koy grew in southern Mali, the government resisted calls to increase its military response.[63] Military units that were accused of abuses were withdrawn from the North, and other units were confined to their garrisons.[64] Publicly, Konaré consistently made the case that the solution to the crisis in the North was one and the same with the solution to economic, social, and political marginalization across Mali: democratization through decentralization. This reframed the government's willingness to meet rebels' demands for increased autonomy and local control over development and security not as rewarding them with a "special status" (the language of the National Pact) but rather as pursuing democratic reforms that would extend to the whole country and from which all Malians would benefit.[65] The strategy of assimilating the issues in the North with the broader process of democratization through decentralization was supported by a particular framing of Malian national identity, which emphasized Mali's history of interdependence among diverse cultures and ethnolinguistic groups.[66] In contrast to US-RDA, which had often equated Malian culture with that of Mande peoples, Konaré's national narrative was one in which the peoples and cultures of the North epitomized Mali's national strengths, specifically its heritage as a commercial and intellectual crossroads specialized in cross-cultural exchange and diplomacy.[67]

The peace-building meetings succeeded in building enough trust among members of the various armed groups that they were willing to disarm. At the end of 1995, cantonment began with combatants turning over weapons to be considered for integration into government roles. On March 27, 1996, three thousand collected weapons were symbolically burned in the Flame of Peace in Timbuktu.

Decentralization as Territorialization

Peace-building meetings in the North had dovetailed with government efforts to promote its plan for decentralization with civil society across the country. Just months before the Bourem meetings, the government launched an initiative of nationwide "concertations," bringing together local political party representatives, government administrators, chiefs and religious leaders, and civil society groups to promote the government's plans for decentralization.[68] In the wake of the celebrated role that civil society, including chiefs and customary authorities, had played in the peace process, many observers expected the Malian decentralization process to empower these same actors as well as the broader cultural heritage that they were seen to represent. As the UN resident coordinator observed in 1996,

> There appears to be a real consensus in Mali for decentralization; this has been influenced by the rebellion, which made evident the need of the northern populations to take greater charge of their destiny. It now seems to be well accepted that the diffusion of power, into civil society, in fact strengthens and stabilizes the nation. . . . In the reconciliation process it seems that, particularly at the top and at the grass roots, the actors have been able to tap into the deep reserve of social capital which surely exists in Mali, and which is one of the country's great strengths.[69]

But decentralization policies were not only informed by the peace-building process or designed to respond to postconflict conditions. They were also a response to the requirements of structural-adjustment agreements, according to which the Konaré government needed to reduce state expenditure in line with lender-defined ideas of "good governance."[70] The latter priorities ultimately worked at cross-purposes with visions of decentralization as a means of local empowerment.

Based on the state's narrative of decentralization as a policy of local control, many interpreted it as an endorsement by the state of traditional systems of resource management, which had been disrupted by the colonial and then postcolonial state.[71] The government's celebration of local and traditional authorities' roles in the peace-building process supported this view. As noted above, the geographies of these meetings reflected longstanding relationships of social and economic interdependence among communities in northern Mali. These did not correspond to existing state administrative jurisdictions, which, following colonial policies, separated "sedentary" and "nomadic" people and treated the river as a natural boundary rather than a shared space. The meetings had reasserted the authority of chieftaincies as the institutions best situated to address issues of intercommunal resource management and conflict resolution.

The decentralization policy promised to replace out-of-touch state administrative structures with ones responsive to local conditions. Specifically, the law required the replacement of the old "arrondissements" with new "communes," or municipalities, whose borders would be determined by local communities themselves. However, the criteria that jurisdictions were supposed to meet were determined by policymakers in Bamako, which fell in line with the policy preferences of the International Monetary Fund (IMF) and World Bank and immediately proved out of step with many communities' conceptions of their localities. Municipalities were supposed to have a minimum population of ten thousand and be "economically viable" while also forming socially cohesive units—for example, through common kinship ties, clan, or ethnicity.[72] In practice, in many areas of Mali, an economically viable municipality of ten thousand or more would be one in which multiple kinship, lineage, and/or ethnic identities were represented. Indeed, as discussed in chapter 1, economic viability in arid spaces depends on the interdependence of groups specializing in different modes of production, which correspond with constructions of ethnic difference.

Among economic viability, population, and social cohesion, the latter was prioritized. This aligned with local populations' perception of decentralization as a means through which identity groups, often associated with existing chieftaincies, would be given access to state resources and representation in state government. In the end, 57.7 percent of the new municipalities had fewer than ten thousand inhabitants, and 20 percent had fewer than five thousand.[73] In some cases, the new municipalities achieved their goal of recognizing and granting administrative standing to existing localities according to familiar and longstanding understandings of social and political belonging as mediated through kinship, clan, or ethnicity. But especially in northern Mali, with its low population densities, even smaller municipalities could consist of a dozen or more villages or nomadic fractions, only one of which would be recognized as the administrative seat of the mayor and council of representatives.[74]

Though the concept of economic viability was set aside for the purposes of creating municipalities, the decentralization law was based on the premise that municipalities were contiguous sociopolitical *and* economic units. Municipalities' claims to legitimacy, based on elections of a council of representatives and a mayor, grounded claims of authority over land and resources in its territorial jurisdiction. In many areas, this represented a significant change in the relationships among social identity, political authority, economic decision-making, and space. This was made more fraught by plans to formalize land and resource tenure by codifying private-property rights. Decentralization laws empowered local authorities to recognize customary rights to land and resources, subject to the terms of future tenure laws. Anticipation that decentralization would ultimately determine the authority to formalize customary rights into private-property rights, which could then be alienated from existing users of land and resources, raised the stakes of defining jurisdictional boundaries and accessing elected positions. This contributed to resource-related conflicts as well as perceptions that democratization was worsening political corruption and rent seeking.[75] Electoral politics generally privileged farming interests over pastoral ones, resulting in decisions on land and resource tenure that expanded farmland and enclosed and privatized grazing lands.[76]

This design of municipal jurisdictions contrasts with the spatial logics that were used to address issues of access to markets and resources in the context of local peace building. In the latter processes, the premise of negotiation and decision-making was the recognition of a space and its resource base as shared among multiple communities, each of whom depended on the reproduction of that space as a shared one. The creation of municipalities as bordered and contiguous sociopolitical and economic units instead defined land and resources as internal to particular jurisdictions. This did not, of course, prevent negotiations over access between a jurisdiction and adjacent ones, but it framed those negotiations in a very different way—namely, in relation to ownership backed up by electoral legitimacy.[77] Moreover, these negotiations involved new elected officials, whose relationships to existing chiefs was not defined in the law. This created a new layer of often-contentious (and monetized) negotiations between elected officials and chiefs, who saw themselves and were often seen by local communities as the proper custodians of land and resource tenure.[78]

In interviews with refugees and displaced persons from northern Mali in 2014, democratization and decentralization were cited as factors behind the rebellion and proliferation of armed groups that began in 2012 (chapter 4).[79] This was primarily attributed to the weakening of traditional authorities and the influence of party politics, which made local administrators accountable to the party rather than the local community. Perceptions of favoritism and corruption undermined faith in local authorities' ability to resolve disputes and ensure justice. For example, an educator from the region of Gao explained that the creation of the communes gave rise to jurisdictional confusion and conflict between already existing village councils and the newly elected municipal representatives. "Each wants to impose his own power. Before, everyone knew a single chief; now, there are many."[80] According to a pastoralist and trader from Ménaka, peace would only return with "the depoliticization of the administration," which he said had been politicized with the introduction of democracy. Local authority had become entangled with national party politics, with positions being decided based on party connections and educational credentials rather than familiarity with local issues and concerns. "Before the *chef de canton* was just the *chef de canton*. Now he wears two boubous. . . . This is the problem. . . . As long as it's like this we will never have peace. Never."[81]

Decentralization promoted a politics of spatial enclosure that was at odds with and, in many cases, undermined familiar mechanisms for securing collective livelihoods. The enclosure of space and the assertion by the state that these spaces mediate sociopolitical and economic identities and rights produced different vectors to assert power and authority in relation to different claims about spatial belonging and exclusion.[82] This process has contributed to the ongoing marginalization of pastoral ways of life and the communities that depend on them. The declining viability of pastoralism was one of the conditions shaping the resurgence of violence in northern Mali that culminated in a multipronged rebellion in 2012, which is the focus of the next chapter. As the 2012 crisis has become an entrenched conflict across multiple

states in the Sahel, armed groups' propaganda has directly appealed to grievances about spatial enclosure and state control over free circulation.[83]

Constructions of and contestations over the arid spaces of the Sahara and
Sahel shaped the trajectory of decolonization in the French Soudan/Mali
from the 1950s to the early 2000s, producing what came to be known as
"the northern problem." To France, the Sahara represented a frontier zone
in which it could rehabilitate its position as a global power. For anticolonial
leaders in Mali, this made its arid regions a principal site in the struggle
against neocolonialism. Asserting Mali's sovereignty as "territorial competence" in the Sahel and Sahara would mean sedentarizing nomads and dis-
mantling "feudal" tribal structures. These policies, which exacerbated the
effects of drought, contributed to a mass exodus of pastoralists in the decades
following independence. In exile, young Tuaregs developed their own nationalist critique of desert ways of life, concluding that they could only be secure
through claiming their own territorial nation-state.

In the wake of armed rebellion, Mali's transition to democracy promised
to rejuvenate postcolonial state building through political and administrative
decentralization. Conceptualized as a technical process of mapping and politically recognizing already-existing localities, in practice, decentralization
produced highly contested changes to existing political and socioeconomic
geographies. Decentralization was premised on the homogenization of state
territory, which short-circuited possibilities for a pluralistic reimagining of
the state that could respond more creatively to Mali's diversity as it materializes in different logics and practices of space. This contributed to the
reproduction of rural populations', especially pastoralists', alienation from
the state's and international organizations' imaginaries of democracy and
development.

The next chapter examines how the post-2001 securitization of the Sahel
as a potential "next Afghanistan" intersected with postconflict political and
economic changes in northern Mali. While the peace process of the 1990s
had promised increased state and donor investments in northern Mali, in the
early 2000s, economic growth was primarily driven by a resurgence in trans-
Saharan commerce, both licit and illicit. The profitability of this trade in
Mali was enabled by the state through its recognition of nonstate authorities

and support for their extralegal activities. At the same time, Mali partnered with US and European militaries to expand surveillance of its northern regions and increase its capacities for border control. The Malian government thus situated itself as dependent on two sources of foreign capital that were tied to contradictory models of "development": rents from the trans-Saharan trade and Western aid, which came with demands for Mali to crack down on the very actors and networks that enabled those rents. The conflict between these two models had increasingly destabilizing effects leading up to the 2012 crisis.

FOUR

Geopolitics and the Malian Crisis

In the early 2000s, the Sahel and Sahara were recognized by a range of actors as a region of growing geopolitical importance. This was most prominently shaped by the US-led "war on terror," which constructed the region as an "ungoverned space" and a potential "next Afghanistan."[1] According to the geopolitical reasoning guiding the ungoverned-spaces diagnosis, the security of a status quo international order could be managed through territorial containment, specifically by monitoring and managing the geographical boundaries between "controlled" and "uncontrolled" spaces and, ideally, by expanding the former while shrinking the latter. An idealized spatial segregation between ordered and disordered space was projected onto the geography of Mali (and the Sahel more broadly), with the seat of government in Bamako and southern Mali more generally representing a relatively secured space and security risks increasing as one moved north toward the desert, where population density and public and private infrastructure—the signifiers of "development"—declined.

At the same time, the Sahel and Sahara were being shaped by a resurgence in trade, made possible by improved security due to the end of conflicts in Algeria, Mali, and Niger and by technologies that made desert transit cheaper and less risky. Expertise in navigating the desert and connections to transnational commercial networks became increasingly profitable in the early 2000s, which shaped the renegotiation of relationships between northern communities and the institutions of the state in the wake of the rebellion and the implementation of democratization and decentralization policies.

In this context, access to and control over trade and mobility in the Sahel and Sahara were becoming more valuable to—and more contested among—state and nonstate actors. These developments in the political economy of the region and its relationship to local and regional security conditions were at odds with and largely illegible within the United States' and its allies' diagnoses of the Sahel as an "ungoverned space."

The geopolitical significance of the Sahel in the early 2000s can thus be understood as, adopting Amy Niang's reformulation of geopolitics, "the outcome of different projections of space that collide in political fields that do not always overlap or make sense together."[2] On the one hand, according to the spatial logics of the war on terror, the region's apparent geographical remoteness signified threat and thus an opportunity to reorder space in line with US and allied ambitions to expand the reach of their military and surveillance capabilities. On the other hand, the region's geography signified opportunity and value in relation to the political and logistical requirements of different forms of transnational trade. This positioned northern Mali as a site of collision among competing projects to reorder space in line with different and contradictory readings of geographical remoteness and its political and economic significance.

Remoteness and Danger: Producing the Sahara-Sahel as an "Ungoverned Space"

In a meeting at the US Africa Command (AFRICOM) headquarters, a military planner showed me a map of the "Greater Indian Ocean Region" to explain how US military strategy in Africa fit into a global view of US security interests.[3] He described the map as depicting one part of an "arc of instability," which stretched from the Horn of Africa through the Middle East and Central Asia and into the Pacific. US security interests, he explained, depended on protecting the "global commons" from the disruptions that could come from this arc of instability. Specifically, the map depicted shipping routes and their densities along with "planned" and "potential" hydrocarbon areas." The "pivot" of this arc, he said, was the Horn of Africa. This explained the significance of the command's permanent basing locations in Djibouti and at Manda Bay Airfield in Kenya, which protect shipping routes and provide logistical support to US military operations in the Middle East.

This geography of an arc of instability and its relationship to the security of a global commons, meaning the infrastructure that sustains international commerce, were popularized in the aftermath of the 9/11 al-Qaeda attacks as "The Pentagon's New Map."[4] However, this mapping of global space and US security interests began to be promoted within the Department of Defense (DOD) a decade earlier as part of a campaign to repurpose the Cold War strategy of containment for a post-Soviet future. In post–Cold War military planning, DOD leadership argued for maintaining a global US military posture in response not to a particular threat but to what they described as the inherent uncertainty of the post–Cold War global security environment. Given conditions of uncertainty, an overall strategy of containment was still necessary, but the object to contain would be uncertainty and volatility itself rather than a specific, known threat.

In the absence of a specific threatening actor, this strategy aimed to define threats in relation to a spatial mapping of political and socioeconomic conditions, predicting where uncertainty was likely to translate into instability. The resulting geographies of threat maintained features of Cold War security strategy in that it divided the world into two broad zones: the areas of the world that were well integrated into a US-led liberal economic and collective security system and the areas that were outside of this system. This mapping of the post–Cold War environment was first laid out in a 1992 *Defense Planning Guidance* draft, which argued that the US victory in the Cold War had created a "democratic 'zone of peace.'" Future US military posture, the draft asserted, should be aimed at the protection and expansion of that zone of peace. The draft introduced a new "strategic concept" that would become increasingly central to US military planning: "shaping the future security environment."[5]

"Shaping" was framed as a response to the uncertain nature of the post–Cold War security environment. In this context, strategy could not be based on predictions about the future but should instead "help shape the future."[6] The draft, which was leaked to the *New York Times*, generated controversy at the time, but its core ideas were adopted in subsequent strategic reviews and updates to military doctrine, even with a change in presidential administration and party. In the military's first major strategic review since the end of the Cold War, the 1997 *Quadrennial Defense Review* (*QDR*), the concept of "shaping the future security environment" was central. The review introduced a strategy of "shape-respond-prepare," in which US military posture would be designed to "shape the international environment and to be better able to respond to a variety of smaller-scale contingencies and asymmetric threats."[7] In practice, shaping called for the US military to maintain a limited but global forward posture that could be rapidly scaled up in response to events.

The strategic approach of shaping produced both change and continuity in the geographies of US military presence around the globe. It envisioned shaping as a risk-mitigation strategy that could be used in areas of the world where the United States did not see a direct threat to its interests and thus could not justify significant investments but where the environment was deemed volatile or uncertain. For example, in post–Cold War reviews of US foreign policy in Africa, policymakers concluded that the United States had very little strategic interest there.[8] At the same time, the continent represented the kind of volatile or unstable environment in which uncertain future threats were likely to emerge, and the 1997 *QDR* cited "failing and failed states" in Africa as a context where shaping could mitigate the emergence of threats to US interests.[9] An early example of shaping strategy was the African Crisis Response Initiative (ACRI), created in 1996, which was envisioned as a standby crisis-response force made up of African units trained by US forces. The goal of the ACRI was to establish relationships with African militaries that would enable the US military to have a limited but sustained presence on the continent as well as long-term access to bases and other logistical support. This was seen as a very low-cost (the ACRI's annual budget was only $15 million) means of monitoring uncertain conditions on the continent while establishing the capacity to respond militarily to threats if and when they emerge.[10]

The 2001 al-Qaeda attacks on the United States increased political support, within and outside of the DOD, for maintaining a global military posture oriented toward shaping. The attacks also further defined the geographical reasoning that would guide shaping posture. Shaping was described as a means of "preventing the next Afghanistan" by identifying spaces that shared the characteristics that had enabled al-Qaeda to operate out of Afghanistan and establishing access for the US military to operate in them.[11] Military planners described these environments as "ungoverned spaces," which was promoted as a new "threat paradigm" that should be integrated into strategic planning and guide decisions about military posture.[12]

As a threat paradigm, the concept of ungoverned spaces was used as a predictive and prescriptive tool. Based on a distant reading of space, specifically the presence or absence of state capacities as well as demographic characteristics, a geography of containment could be tailored to the priority threat of al-Qaeda and Islamist terrorism. The threat paradigm of ungoverned spaces attributed threat less to the characteristics or components of space—for example, its ecologies, peoples, histories, and entanglements with other spaces—than to its contours, meaning the degree to which its boundaries were encompassed within institutions and systems identified with security, specifically the territorial state and an international-market economy. This determined the kinds of information that were seen as relevant for interpreting security conditions and guiding interventions to affect those conditions.

A lack of comprehensive information is, to some degree, intrinsic to the nature of the threat as it is imagined through the lens of ungoverned spaces. It is remoteness, specifically the presumed distance from the ordering effects of state government and of economic development and from the legibility they provide, that makes these spaces threatening. What signifies threat is therefore an absence. If the condition being diagnosed is one of *lack*, more information about what is actually present need not be sought. In applying the concept of ungoverned spaces to diagnose specific environments as threatening, policymakers cited the absence of information about these places as itself a signifier of risk.[13] A lack of information thus paradoxically increased confidence that the concept of ungoverned spaces was applicable to a given space.

In a 2001 hearing on the terrorist threat in Africa, for example, Susan Rice highlighted a lack of "sufficient personnel and expertise to understand as well as we need to what is going on in a number of these societies" and commented, "I cannot begin to tell you how ill-equipped we are from an intelligence collection point of view in Africa." However, she also asserted that "terrorist networks are exploiting Africa thoroughly," and "these are the swamps we must drain . . . for the cold, hard reason that to do otherwise, we are going to place our national security at further and more permanent risk." Confidence that "Africa's porous borders" and "weak law enforcement" constitute a terrorism threat did not require the kind of context-specific knowledge or expertise that policymakers, like Rice, readily admitted was lacking.[14] Instead, a bird's-eye view of landscape, demography, and cultural affinities could be mapped onto an existing threat paradigm of ungoverned spaces to produce an assessment of risks posed to the United States.

As Wolfram Lacher highlights, the presumed illegibility of ungoverned spaces also "provided an almost indefinite scope for newly produced information about an area," which could then be leveraged by various actors to produce threat diagnoses aligned with their interests.[15] The "Sahara-Sahel" region was produced as a threatening potential "next Afghanistan" within US military strategy in this context.[16] This was shaped in large part by concerns within the US European Command—which had operational authority over most of the African continent before the creation of AFRICOM in 2007—that it would be marginalized in the context of a global war on terror centered on the Middle East and Central Asia.[17] Leadership was therefore concerned with identifying an area within its jurisdiction that could be prioritized for counterterrorism interventions. Command leadership saw the Sahara-Sahel as a region that could be persuasively analogized to Afghanistan. Two main characteristics identified the region as threatening: its landscape and its demographic characteristics, including that the majority of its population practiced Islam. Spatially, the Sahara was described as "vast and trackless," needing a radical increase in surveillance.[18] Demographically, poverty and high fertility were read as inherently destabilizing and were directly compared to demographic indicators in 1990s Afghanistan.[19] While the "moderation" of West African Islamic practice was consistently praised in security assessments, the presence of foreign-funded mosques and Islamic schools was characterized as a vector through which the contagion of Islamic terrorism could easily spread.[20]

The post-9/11 threat paradigm of ungoverned spaces thus consolidated the initially controversial proposal by DOD leadership that the US military must maintain a global forward posture, even in the absence of any specific global threat, to manage and shape conditions of uncertainty. When al-Qaeda and Islamist terrorism emerged as the principal object of US national security policy, shaping strategy was not narrowed in relation to the specific locations in which al-Qaeda operated. Instead, it justified bolstering the existing diffuse-force posture based on the expectation that a "next Afghanistan" could emerge in ungoverned spaces that could be used as "safe havens" by terrorists or other hostile actors. Either spaces were encompassed within security-providing institutions and systems or they were not, and the more remote spaces were from these enclosures, the greater the threats they posed. In response to threat conditions shaped by remoteness, US policy to manage threat centered on producing proximity by maintaining access for US personnel and surveillance capacities in and near ungoverned spaces.

In the Sahel, this strategy guided the creation of the Pan-Sahel Initiative

(PSI) in 2002, which provided training and equipment to Mali, Niger, Chad, and Mauritania while enabling the United States to ramp up its own surveillance in the region. In 2005, the PSI was expanded into the counterterrorism-focused Operation Enduring Freedom Trans-Sahara (later renamed Operation Juniper Shield) alongside the Trans-Saharan Counter-Terrorism Partnership, which funded State Department, US Agency for International Development (USAID), and DOD counterterrorism programming. These operations and programs were presented as capacity-building interventions to help states better control their own territories and borders and to boost populations' resilience against the influence or recruitment strategies of extremist groups. But the level of investment in these programs fell far short of what would be required to significantly affect state or military capacity, as AFRICOM personnel readily acknowledged. Instead, their primary purpose was to maintain relationships with African militaries and governments that allowed small but durable deployments of US forces and assets.[21] As an example, a military planner pointed to US efforts to help the Nigerien military control its borders. He described the program as a "drop in the bucket": to actually secure the border would require a much bigger investment as well as cooperation with other powers, like China, which would require "the US to stop being the hegemon."[22] Instead, border-control programs build relationships with African militaries, which are the foundation for continued US access. As another respondent put it, "If something comes up, it's having the relationships so that if you need to move a flexible force in then you could."[23]

While shaping is partly aimed at enabling a rapid response to threat, strategists also emphasized its role in influencing how threats develop in the first place. Access to remote spaces translates into "shaping the future threat environment" by altering others' expectations of how events are likely to unfold in those spaces. The physical presence of US forces, whether they are participating in a joint exercise with African troops or building a school, is presumed to shape expectations and thus behavior. First, shaping should deter "hostile actors" who would exploit these spaces for violent or criminal ends. If the United States is seen as having the will and capacity to operate in areas that would otherwise be assumed remote from US interests, this will affect the behavior of those actors. In short, "the bad guys are watching what we're doing through proxies."[24] Second, shaping should reassure the local population of the presence of "good guys" and thus reduce the influence of criminal or terrorist groups. Some AFRICOM personnel expressed confidence that, in Africa, the presence of Americans was inherently reassuring because it represented competence, progress, and/or development that was otherwise lacking. Similarly, shaping should reassure partner governments and militaries such that the United States becomes and/or remains their "security partner of choice."[25] This should assure long-term access for US personnel and infrastructure, including through the sale and transfer of US-made weapons systems, through which recipients continue to rely on US support for training and maintenance. Overall, shaping aims to limit security risks associated with geographical remoteness by engineering low-cost and low-risk proximity. This reflects the US military's assessment of its own strategic advantages relative to potential rivals, which rest primarily in its capacities to read and influence geographical space, including at long range, through superior surveillance technologies and logistical capacities and an extensive and growing basing infrastructure.

But this imaginary of geography and the means of influencing and controlling it radically flattens space and its relationship to security conditions. Assumptions about the effects that US presence will have on various actors—hostile actors, populations, and governments—presume that these actors similarly interpret physical access to space as translatable to control over that space. This fails to account for spatial dimensions of both time and scale; in short, it fails to account for *place* as a ground through which meaning, expectations, and behavior materialize in space. Temporally, associating physical presence with control discounts how relationships to place are shaped by history and memory and thus by socially and culturally specific understandings of how space relates to power and authority. In relation to scale, using physical presence in space as a proxy for influence or control relies on territorial distance and proximity at least roughly correlating with social or political distance and proximity. As I elaborate below, this cartographical reading of space renders the Sahel's relationships to processes and conditions at other spatial scales illegible.

Remoteness and Connectivity: Security and Development in a Globalized Sahel and Sahara

In 2002, when US military planners were beginning to identify the Sahara-Sahel as a potential next Afghanistan, the region was benefitting from a period of improving security and economic prosperity. Political violence in Algeria, Mali, and Niger had come to an end. One small and hardcore group from the Algerian Civil War, the Groupe salafiste pour la prédication et le combat (GSPC), was present in southern Algeria and northern Mali but with little capacity. The end of widespread violence enabled increased trade across the Sahel and Sahara. This growth was also enabled by more widespread access to 4x4 vehicles, satellite phones, and GPS, which made Saharan trade less risky and easier to navigate with less expertise. In the early 2000s, Saharan routes began to be utilized for the narcotics trade. This was a result of increasing demand in Europe alongside more aggressive enforcement measures to restrict smuggling through the Mediterranean. Saharan routes were desirable for the global narcotics trade due to the existence of longstanding trading networks there that could reliably transport goods to Europe and western Asia, as well as its relative distance from—and illegibility to—European counternarcotic enforcement.

The resurgence of Saharan trade in the early 2000s, as a route for narcotics but also for a variety of commodities, reflects the Sahel's and Sahara's position as spaces of regional and global connection rather than disconnection. As we have seen, life in the Sahel and Sahara has been shaped by the requirements of mobility and exchange. The reproduction of life in particular locales is dependent on its connections and interactions with places elsewhere. This shapes a geography in which physical proximity does not necessarily correlate with connection or influence. Given the importance of mobility and access to extended social networks, places are defined less by their location than by their connections.[26] A place at a great distance may be "closer" than an adjacent one.

Judith Scheele's ethnographic research in the Malian town of al-Khalil is illustrative. Al-Khalil is a settlement near the Algerian border made up of family compounds with well-secured garages that provide a stopping and connection point for traders of all kinds of goods. There, traders can restock fuel and supplies, collect information, and negotiate deals. Al-Khalil is important because of its location—its simultaneous remoteness and proximity to the Mali-Algeria border—and in spite of it: traders will go well out of their way to stop there so that they can access its logistical, informational, and social networks. In relation to these networks, the town itself is not so much a node as is each compound within it. Locals refer to each garage as "a state in itself."[27] Each has closer ties to family and business associates hundreds of miles away than they do to the compound next door.

Al-Khalil thus cannot be understood in isolation but only as part of multiple overlapping wholes, which is highlighted by Scheele's account of the crucial role that women play in these networks. Women are "conspicuously absent from Al-Khalil," but it is women who maintain the residences and households "at either end of, and at intervals along, the smuggling trail; they hold family networks together and they forge new alliances."[28] A view of al-Khalil alone suggests that its smuggling economy is entirely male. However, this would be to misunderstand why al-Khalil is important to these men: it is less the services and information offered by the other men who are present than the networks in which each garage is embedded—networks maintained and cultivated by people who are not visible in al-Khalil itself.

The same is true of the relationship between al-Khalil and the state. Taken on its own, al-Khalil is antithetical to the state. It is an example of the state's absence and failure. Indeed, Scheele recounts how residents boast of their success in driving out the Malian civil servants who had been appointed to the town.[29] However, al-Khalil is also evidence of the state's effectiveness, or, put another way, it is itself a state effect. It would not exist without the state practices that make the Algeria-Mali border both efficacious—in terms of the price differentials it creates, the costs (in terms of risk and/or fees) incurred by crossing it, and the disparities in standards of living and wages on either side—and porous. Al-Khalil thus puts into relief relationships and processes that are occluded by the geographical imaginary of the territorial state. That imaginary reads geographical remoteness as a signifier of social, political, and economic remoteness. Here, characteristics of remoteness produce conditions for connectivity.

As al-Khalil begins to show, characteristics of remoteness in the Sahel and the Sahara, specifically low densities of population and of public and private infrastructure, do not produce isolation but rather constitute the terms of the region's integration into national, regional, and global political and economic systems and relationships. In the early 2000s, this remoteness became profitable in new ways based on its changing value to the circulation of criminalized commodities, such as cocaine, cannabis, untaxed cigarettes, and arms. The leveraging of this remoteness in relation to changing trafficking interests began to transform political and economic order in northern Mali. One of the most significant developments has been the monetization and militarization of control over desert transit.

As discussed in chapter 1, access to space in arid zones is typically oriented around terms of *inclusion* rather than *exclusion*. Particular communities have priority access to space and to resource patches within it, but this is not understood as a right to exclude others. It is rather a prerogative to regulate access and often to collect a fee or promise of reciprocal access to other spaces and resources. Political and economic influence and prestige are associated with priority access to wider spaces, and this has historically been correlated with hierarchical relationships of protection and dependency over less mobile populations. A former Tuareg fighter interviewed by Francesco Strazzari puts it this way:

> One couldn't say that the Sahara is a no-man's land. We just have a different sense of space. In our culture, the land is given in common to the whole community. No one has the right to keep me out, nor deny the authorization to graze my cattle. Nevertheless, it is my duty to ask permission to do so. It is the same with the right of passage, which is a tribute paid to the locals so that they grant you protection on their territory. Indeed, it is not a right; it is a matter of respect and recognition. It's about the acknowledgment of local leaderships.[30]

The principle of rights of passage, or the offer of tribute in recognition of another's authority in a place, shapes understandings of legitimate and illegitimate movement and trade through the Sahel and Sahara. Outsiders are expected to seek permission in order to safely transit through particular areas, and failure to do so can legitimate actions to interdict transit, including violently, according to norms of *razzia* (chapter 1).[31] With the resurgence of high-profit trade through the Sahara, the stakes of asserting this authority became much higher in some areas. At the same time, the cost of entry into trading and smuggling activities was falling due to GPS, satellite phones, and the availability of 4x4 vehicles. This made it more logistically feasible to transit the desert without the approval and accompaniment of local guides and deference to local authorities. Overall, these trends facilitated the entry of new traders, including from families of historically lower social standing, into commercial activities that had previously been dominated by groups with higher status.[32]

These developments in relationships of political and economic power, mobility, and trade in northern Mali were also affected by decentralization policies, which began to be implemented in the late 1990s (chapter 3). These policies created new local jurisdictions, which would elect mayors and representatives to the national government. The creation of new jurisdictions and elected positions altered the politics of land and resource tenure in many parts of Mali. Whereas local tenure issues and questions of mobility were traditionally managed by customary authorities, this could be challenged by new elected officials, who could recruit support from national political parties and the state. Elected municipal officials served as intermediaries between their communities and the state, including as access points to development funding and foreign aid. This positioned them as powerful resource brokers, whose relationships with customary leaders could empower or marginalize those leaders depending on how both parties negotiated the relationship. In some parts of northern Mali, notably in Kidal and Ménaka, conflict between traditional authorities and younger challengers, many of whom had exercised political power in the context of the rebellion, was contentious and violent.[33]

These changes in municipal governance and in trade overlapped with the ongoing renegotiation of political relationships that had begun with the rebellion. The possibility to earn a quick fortune through trafficking represented an additional challenge to social and political hierarchies and their relationship to traditions of nobility and dependency. In this context, access to the narcotics trade could be leveraged into broader political and economic influence. Individuals involved in the trade supported local businesses and became influential in local politics, using their resources to influence elections. Under Mali's decentralization policies, which allow communities to establish new municipalities if they reach a certain population threshold, some traffickers were able to establish new municipal jurisdictions, through which they could negotiate political protection in exchange for funneling trafficking rents to state officials.[34]

In addition to the trafficking of commodities, northern Mali became home to another industry with access to extraordinary amounts of foreign capital in the early 2000s: hostage taking. The GSPC—which had installed itself near the Mali-Algeria border after refusing the amnesty deal that ended the Algerian Civil War—carried out its first major hostage operation in 2003 when it abducted thirty-two European tourists in the desert. This represented a departure from the GSPC's usual practices, and several theories emerged to explain it. One proposed that the abduction was a false flag operation organized by Algerian security forces to take advantage of the "global war on terror" and the interest it had generated in the Sahara and thus recruit Western support for its own interests in the region.[35] If this was the origin of the operation, it was successful. At Algeria's urging (President Abdelaziz Bouteflika was among the first foreign leaders to visit President George Bush in Washington, DC, after the 9/11 attacks), the GSPC had already been added to the Federal Bureau of Investigation's list of international terrorist groups in 2002, and the 2003 kidnapping was used as justification to expand US counterterrorism operations in the Sahel, with Algeria as a key ally and beneficiary of intelligence sharing. It is also possible that the incident was simply opportunistic on the part of the GSPC. The captured European tourists had been traveling without the customary use of local guides, and the abduction could thus be justified as a means of compensation according to some interpretations of *razzia*.[36] Whatever the origin, the incident proved that an extraordinary amount of foreign capital could be gained through hostage taking and, it turned out, backchannel negotiations with very willing European governments and their brokers.

The government of Mali, under President Amadou Toumani Touré (ATT), elected in 2002, became a key intermediary in these ransom negotiations as hostage taking in the desert became more common. It is widely understood that ATT had an arrangement with the GSPC (which changed its name to al-Qaeda in the Islamic Maghreb [AQIM] in 2006) such that they could use northern Mali as a place to hold hostages and negotiate their release as long as they did not abduct tourists in Mali itself.[37] Whatever this arrangement may have been, the operation of hostage taking and ransom negotiations in Mali generated significant rents for the state and for the negotiators themselves. The ATT government was also involved in protecting and profiting from narcotics trafficking in northern Mali.[38] In addition to being a source of rents for the state, its involvement in trafficking was a means through which it attempted to influence the political landscape by protecting some groups' access to trafficking over others. Specifically, the state favored the growing political and economic influence of historical "vassals"—including Tilemsi Arabs and *imghad* Tuareg—over the noble Kunta and Ifoghas.[39] This culminated in state mobilization of armed militias, which targeted some trafficking activities while protecting others.

In this context, political order in Mali could be characterized by what Thomas Hüsken and Georg Klute term "heterarchy," shaped by rivalries among different "big men" whose power and influence are related to their position as intermediaries among multiple sources of capital and different systems of authority. Heterarchy describes "the mutable as well as unstable intertwining of state and nonstate orders and the plurality of different power groups" that order relationships of influence and the governance and distribution of resources.[40] Within this heterarchical order, individuals were able to accumulate outsized influence by positioning themselves as nodal points connecting multiple groups and interests, including state officials, traffickers, NGO leaders, foreign donors, and hostage takers and negotiators.[41]

Conditions in northern Mali in the 2000s were thus not defined by an *absence* of government but by the multiplication of overlapping projects of governance toward different ends, which were sometimes compatible and sometimes not.[42] For example, from the perspective of the ATT government, the production of northern Mali as a space conducive to criminalized economic activity was not at odds with the reproduction of his government's influence in those spaces or with its position as the internationally recognized sovereign. Indeed, as I discuss further below, the perceived weakness of the Malian state increased the government's access to foreign security aid. On the other hand, the prevalence of trafficking represented an opportunity for northern elites to assert more autonomy from the state to the extent that trafficking profits made local officials less dependent on access to development funding and aid distributed by the state.

Trafficking and hostage taking had uneven effects on collective security in northern Mali, but these effects became more consistently negative as trafficking became more militarized in the late 2000s. Initially, the broader resurgence of trade, of which trafficking was one part, was a means through which pastoralists could cope with threats to their livelihoods. For many pastoralists in northern Mali, peace and democratization in the late 1990s did not bring the hoped-for economic benefits as decentralization policies encouraged land privatization, and agriculture-centric aid projects continued to enclose historical grazing lands. As pastoralism declined and as life became increasingly monetized, long-distance trade became more important to livelihoods in northern Mali, especially for communities that relied on pastoralism and transhumance. Trade represented not just a supplemental source of income but also a livelihood with social and cultural resonance with nomadic traditions and identities, which made use of pastoralists' expertise in desert navigation and access to extended social networks.

The political and economic developments just described, however, also strained the social and material infrastructures facilitating desert mobility and increasingly favored those with access to military means. While decentralization reforms had already contributed to sidelining existing institutions for negotiating mobility, competition over trafficking profits further marginalized the authority of those without privileged access to state and military officials and/or connections to armed smugglers. The militarization of trafficking, including through the ATT government's support of militia groups, promoted the territorialization of fixed areas and routes over which traffickers claimed exclusive access. This threatened the livelihoods of pastoralists and other traders who depended on the ability to negotiate mobility.

The Global War on Terror and the Malian Crisis

While the ATT government relied on rents from trafficking and hostage taking, it simultaneously positioned itself as the principal state partner for Western-led security interventions in the Sahel in the context of the war on terror. Rather than self-contradictory, this can be understood as a consistent strategy for leveraging Mali's northern regions—which had long been seen by the state as unproductive—based on their changing significance to multiple sources of foreign capital. In relation to global trafficking interests and their growing dependence on Saharan routes, the state's desert terrain, which previous governments saw as a threat, could be a resource. In relation to US and allied security interests in areas seen as analogous to Afghanistan, Mali was positioned to greatly increase its access to foreign security aid.

The objectives of foreign security aid, however, came into increasingly direct conflict with the state's attempts to manage, and profit from, the militarization and monetization of Saharan trade. Foreign security interventions were based on the assumption that expanding state and military presence across more of northern Mali's territory would produce greater security and stability by encompassing previously disconnected spaces within the security-producing institution of the state. As described above, however, the state was not absent from northern Mali but rather was part of a heterarchical order in which the state's influence was dependent on its recognition of and accommodations to multiple nonstate actors and institutions. Policies for a more assertive state disrupted these already-tenuous accommodations. This was ultimately characterized by some in northern Mali as the abandonment by the state—with the backing of foreign allies—of its commitments under previous peace agreements and thus as grounds to take up arms again.

When he was elected as an independent in 2002, ATT was enormously

popular as the military officer who led the coup against the Traoré dictator-
ship and then handed power over to a democratic transition (chapter 3). His
lack of party affiliation ten years later was also popular in the wake of inter-
party conflict, which had threatened the Third Republic during Konaré's
presidency.[43] ATT united a large coalition of political elites, seeming to rise
above a contentious and divided political culture through his "consensus politics." ATT's charisma and exceptional role in recent Malian history enabled
him to lead a government that, like Konaré's, did not have an effective opposition but without the political climate of party fracturing that had characterized the first years of the republic.

Consensus politics did not remain a stabilizing force, however. While it
was praised by external actors, especially donors, consensus politics became
increasingly unpopular because of its association with state rent seeking and
corruption. The 2007 World Bank country-strategy paper for Mali, for example, reported that "Mali's political structure promotes stable, democratic
institutions. There is a strong tradition of consensus in Malian politics and
the country is considered one of the most politically and socially stable countries in Africa."[44] However, during this period, popular dissatisfaction with
those institutions was high: a 2008 Afrobarometer poll, for instance, found
that 74 percent of Malians agreed with the statement that "the government's
economic policies have hurt most people and only benefited a few," 59 percent believed that public officials were unaccountable to the law, and about
half were not satisfied with how democracy was functioning in Mali.[45] Mali
also had one of the lowest voter-turnout rates among African democracies
throughout the 2000s.[46] ATT's government by consensus increased the power
of the already constitutionally strong executive over the legislature by weakening the role of political parties in the legislative process, without which
effective opposition failed to materialize.[47] Whereas under the Konaré government, it was common to "challenge the government on all points," under
ATT, the legislature "functioned in a context of unanimity, where the voice
of critique simply did not exist."[48]

The viability of consensus politics was closely tied to increasing foreign
aid streams to Mali during ATT's two terms in office.[49] As foreign aid became
tied to donor conditionalities in the 1990s and 2000s, Mali stood out as a
"donor darling" because of its high performance on "good governance" and
policy-performance indicators.[50] In a context of increasing aid flows, cooperation with ATT's consensus politics was desirable because it facilitated access

to these funds; the ATT administration maintained its broad and fragile coalition by redistributing these resources as a means of political compensation. Once the political class had associated themselves with ATT's agenda of increasing foreign aid, none of these actors had an interest in raising issues of aid accountability and effectiveness.[51] The opacity of foreign aid, due to a proliferation of donors and programs, poor data collection, and a lack of resources for adequate policy research and analysis in Mali also made it very difficult for those outside the political class to hold the government accountable.[52] Further, donors themselves benefitted from a political climate that facilitated high levels of aid distribution. Donors found increasing pressures to disperse large amounts of aid in Mali in a climate of aid conditionality given its ideal status as being both extremely poor and a high performer on donor indices tracking governance and economic reforms. Maximizing aid flows by deferring to donors' preferences was thus politically useful for Malian political elites—by enabling government revenues to be more widely dispersed among potential rivals than they otherwise could be—while donors benefitted from being able to report high disbursements to a site that performed well on their evaluative indices.

The political expediency of using foreign aid to curry the political favor of elites undermined implementation of the "development" components of the National Pact (chapter 3). The pact increased Bamako's role in distributing development funds to northern regions, as did external donor requirements that percentages of the budget support they provided be used for northern regions. However, much of these funds were redirected toward political favors and bureaucratic overhead in Bamako. For example, as part of the postrebellion peace plan, outside donors funded a parastatal to lead development investments in the North, the Agence de développement du Nord-Mali (ADN), which was created in March 2005. ADN was widely criticized for a lack of activity in the North; its most visible investments were in a sleek headquarters in Bamako, over two thousand kilometers away from the areas in which the agency was supposed to invest.[53]

ATT's focus on maximizing foreign aid translated into enthusiastic support for US counterterrorism aid to Mali. Mali became a favored US counterterrorism "partner" with the launch of the aforementioned PSI in 2002. Both in public and private (as evident in leaked cables from the US embassy in Bamako), the Malian government was considered to be a model partner in the global war on terror despite being severely constrained by a poorly resourced military.[54] Between 2009 and 2012, Mali was the largest single recipient of resources through the Trans-Saharan Counter-terrorism Partnership, receiving $40.6 million in allocations.[55] As investments to mitigate potential threat increased, however, security conditions deteriorated.

US military personnel began training Malian army units in 2003 as part of PSI. From the outset, this presence raised alarm among some Malians, especially in the context of the US invasion of Iraq and alarmist rhetoric among US military and political leaders characterizing the Sahel as a "breeding ground" for terrorism.[56] Rumors about US military objectives spread widely. For example, a 2005 International Crisis Group report described one rumor about US objectives, which I heard repeated in Niamey in 2014:[57] "One rumour circulating . . . is that the U.S. wants to control Gao and Tessalit in the east because they lie on the meridian line (zero degrees). The story goes that, 'whoever controls that line controls the whole world, because he can either move to the right or to the left.'"[58] More common in my own conversations was the belief that the US military had come to the Sahel to prospect for natural resources on behalf of American companies.[59] These rumors reflected the disconnect between US discourses about the threat of terrorism in the Sahel and local populations' views. US accounts of PSI as a response to terrorism—particularly when this threat was described as one of "ungoverned spaces" that were "breeding grounds" for terrorists—were so out of touch with conditions on the ground that this explanation simply did not seem credible. Additionally, some saw US military presence as likely to attract its enemies to the Sahel and create a terrorist threat where none had existed. As a Malian women's rights activist told the *Christian Science Monitor* in 2009, "We see that around the world, wherever the Americans are, there is a temptation for Al Qaeda to be there."[60]

As relations between some northern communities and the state were already deteriorating in the mid-2000s, some northern leaders took up the discourses of the war on terror in framing the state (in partnership with the United States) as an enemy. David Gutelius, a researcher who lived in Timbuktu during this period, observed the circulation of political pamphlets and radio broadcasts making this case: "As American and other Western authorities have imagined and portrayed northern Mali as a hotbed of potential terrorists, northern leaders, sometimes drawing directly on these media statements, have imagined and portrayed US forces and the Malian military as arrayed against the community."[61] A new rebel group, the Alliance for

Democratic Change (ADC), which had links to traffickers, took control of the towns of Kidal and Ménaka in May 2006 before quickly agreeing to renewed negotiations with the state, mediated by Algeria. This produced the controversial Algiers Accords, to which not all members of the ADC signed on. Sporadic attacks by nonsignatories continued until a ceasefire in 2009. Between 2006 and 2009, the state empowered armed militias that were not under the command and control of the military to carry out attacks against actual or presumed rebels, whom the government characterized as criminals.

To domestic audiences, the government dismissed the violence as banditry, arguing that those posturing as rebels had no legitimate political grievances but were simply interested in producing a "no-man's-land" where they could profit off of illegal activities. To American officials, state agents emphasized that this kind of no-man's-land was a terrorism threat. A November 2007 cable from the Bamako embassy reports that ATT described Ibrahim ag Bahanga, the leader of the rebels who rejected the Algiers Accords, as benefitting terrorists. "President Touré did not specifically link Bahanga to AQIM, he said Bahanga's actions have increased the instability that benefits AQIM. 'Bahanga,' said the President, 'is strengthening banditry, insecurity, the fundamentalists and Algerian Salafists.'"[62] Northern leaders made the same argument about the ATT government—that it was enabling AQIM, as well as militarized trafficking networks, for its own profit. For example, in a May 2008 meeting at the US embassy, a rebel leader and National Assembly representative, Deity ag Simidou, "expressed disappointment with the international community's willingness to take President Touré's descriptions of his efforts to resolve the crisis at face-value and said [rebel leaders] had tried in vain . . . to work with the President to implement the Algiers Accords." He went on to explain that the government was interested in enabling AQIM's continued presence in Mali: "Ag Simidou accused Mali of actively channeling AQIM into traditional Tuareg zones like Tessalit to fuel rumors of Tuareg ties to terrorism. At the micro level, he charged that several Malian officials were working with AQIM to secure a percentage of any eventual ransom payment for the release of the two Austrian hostages." Ag Simidou's ultimate point to embassy officials was that the rebels were "the only military force in northern Mali willing and able to take on AQIM" and that US support to the Malian army was undermining that very force.[63] He argued that if the United States was not willing to arm the rebels themselves, they should cease support to the Malian army or, at the very least, insist on the arrests of government and military officials known to be assisting AQIM.[64]

As represented in these examples, US counterterrorism interests were instrumentalized by all sides between 2006 and 2009 as a means of battling for legitimacy and for US material support. This had limited efficacy because American officials were never convinced of either side's narrative. However, overall, US counterterrorism interests had the effect of strengthening the state's position vis-à-vis challengers. US policy remained focused on strengthening bilateral relationships with the Malian government and military as a means of maintaining its own presence in the region.

Following a decline in rebel violence in 2009, international attention to security in the Sahel only increased. This was partly driven by French interests in the region, which motivated a return to more interventionist policies after a period of relative disengagement. Beginning in the late 1990s, facing international criticism for its actions in Rwanda, the French government sought to reform its Africa policies by pursuing joint goals of "Africanization" and "Europeanization." France would reduce its own military presence in Africa and close military bases, focusing instead on training and equipping African militaries. It would call on European Union (EU) members to increase their capacities to secure EU citizens and assets on the continent, which would free up the French military to contribute to NATO and UN missions elsewhere and signal that France's role as a global power was not confined to Africa. While France maintained a significant military presence in Côte d'Ivoire, where it intervened in 2002, and in Chad, where its longstanding Operation Épervier remained active, the Jacques Chirac, Nicolas Sarkozy, and François Hollande governments publicly supported reducing French forces on the continent and shifting decision-making on Africa policy from the military to the Ministry for Foreign Affairs.[65] These shifts were also influenced by the United States' increased military presence in the Sahel, which was expected to reduce the risks of French withdrawal.[66] If, in the past, France had been wary of US interests in West Africa, seeing this as potential encroachment on its sphere of influence, in the early 2000s, it mostly welcomed US attention to the Sahel and directly benefitted from intelligence sharing.

These plans to reduce France's military presence in Africa were complicated by hostage taking and rebel violence in the mid-2000s, especially as this affected the French company Areva's expansion of uranium-mining operations in Niger.[67] France's initial response followed the government's conception of Africanization and Europeanization. In 2008, the same year a government white paper proposed to close all but two bases in Africa, France established its Plan Sahel, a low-budget initiative to provide counterterrorism training to the militaries of nine states. It also advocated for the European Union to prioritize funding for security initiatives in the Sahel. The EU began developing its own strategy for security and development in the Sahel in 2008. This strategy, which was finalized in 2011, aimed to "redeploy" states' administration and security capabilities in "the contested zones of the Sahel."[68]

The ATT government responded to European states' funding priorities in the Sahel by establishing the Programme spécial pour la paix, la sécurité et le développement du Nord Mali (PSPSDN) in Mali, which was announced in 2010. The majority of the funding for the €50 million PSPSDN came from France, the EU, and Canada. The program would create eleven Secure Development and Governance Centers at strategic locations in the North, each of which would house state security forces while also providing government services.[69] The plans were initially met with enthusiasm in the targeted communities, but this was short lived as it became clear that the program's priority was to install state security forces.[70]

One of the most vocal critics of the PSPSDN was a network of northern leaders who had organized themselves, following a meeting in Kidal in late 2009, in response to declining security conditions: the Advocacy Network of Peace, Security and Development in Northern Mali. The network's assessment of northern communities' vulnerabilities anticipated the risks and limitations of a program like the PSPSDN. In its founding manifesto, the group emphasized that Mali's northern regions had become an object of diverse outside interests, related to natural resource prospecting, global counterterrorism strategies, clandestine immigration, and trafficking of all kinds. In this context, the network's stated objective was to "find an adequate solution in a peaceful and republican framework" in order to "prevent the pillage of our resources, the instrumentalization of our region toward nontransparent ends, [and] serious attacks on the environment and on populations' lives."[71] The group called for action on six priority areas: reforming governance in line with the "specificities" of the North, especially to enable participation by nomadic populations; expanding employment opportunities for youth outside of trafficking; promoting human rights; shoring up local conflict-resolution mechanisms by supporting the moral authority of chiefs; promoting economic, social, and environmental development; and developing northern infrastructure. In their view, the convergence of new and diverse interests in the North and their effects on local populations' livelihoods and security increased the urgency of addressing longstanding issues of political representation and self-government. The PSPSDN instead prioritized the expansion of state security infrastructure, envisioned as a technical, rather than political, intervention based on the assumption that security dividends would come from a combination of improved territorial control and government-service delivery.

As reflected by the Advocacy Network, attributing insecurity to a lack of state-service delivery or control over territory was out of step with many northerners' perceptions of security conditions and their relationship to the state. This remained the case even after the 2012 crisis, according to interviews and survey research. In a 2013 survey of nine hundred internally displaced persons in Mali, for example, respondents prioritized political solutions to the conflict over an increase in state development or security interventions. In response to the question, "In your opinion, what solutions do you recommend for solving this crisis?" the highest percentage, 41 percent, said good governance and fighting corruption, while the second highest, 22 percent, prioritized dialogue and reconciliation. Only 2 percent selected financial investment in the North, and only 3 percent named increased military presence.[72]

Interviews with forty-three refugees and internally displaced persons in 2014 similarly contradicted the hypothesis that instability in the North was primarily correlated with levels of "development" or state-service delivery. Indeed, every displaced person interviewed reported that livelihoods in their communities were stable or improving in the years before the crisis, though many reported increased criminal activity (e.g., needing to lock up motor-bikes) beginning around 2006.[73] Respondents from the northern cities of Gao, Timbuktu, and Kidal in particular reported that incomes and access to both daily necessities and consumer items were generally increasing in the ten years leading up to the 2012 crisis. Respondents primarily linked "development," or the lack of it, to declining security conditions as it related to perceptions of injustice—specifically the sense that political elites were misusing resources that were meant for "development," that particular communities (especially Tuareg elites in Kidal) were receiving a disproportionate amount of aid and investment, and that northerners themselves were excluded from the Bamako-trained political and professional classes that had the most influence over development funding.

For many, the PSPSDN accentuated the latter perceptions of injustice in relation to state investment. For example, initial plans for disbursements of PSPSDN funds appeared to favor Kidal over the other northern regions, and building contracts were given to companies from Bamako rather than to firms based in the North.[74] In the broader context of the ATT government's relationships to northern elites, the PSPSDN could have served as another tool through which the state could attempt to pick winners and losers amidst broader transformations of political and economic relationships in northern Mali. Ultimately, it was too short lived to have this effect. The program was abandoned with the launch of another rebellion on January 17, 2012, by the National Movement of Azawad.[75] The group's leadership included many members of the Advocacy Network of Peace, Security and Development in Northern Mali.

International security interventions aimed at strengthening the Malian state against the threat of terrorism were oriented toward conditions of lack. While this was predominantly described in relation to the absence of the state, the diagnosis of "ungoverned spaces" went beyond that, reproducing an imaginary of Mali's arid spaces as, for all intents and purposes, empty not just of state order or economic development but of history, culture, politics, and ecology.

Equating order with the projection of authority over territorial space makes it difficult to recognize how security conditions materialize in relation to events and processes that intersect multiple spatial scales. In this case, characteristics of geographical remoteness were misread as signifiers of disconnection and threat. But relative remoteness and Sahelian populations' expertise in negotiating it have contributed instead to an increasing density of global connections in the Sahel and Sahara, including in relation to the criminalization of various types of mobility and the opportunities for profit that this creates. These geopolitical dynamics are changing the ways in which populations relate to and reproduce spaces in the Sahel and Sahara. In particular, capacities for and the risks and benefits associated with mobility are changing as authority over space and resources becomes increasingly monetized and militarized. It is these changes in the social and political relationships regulating mobility, rather than the mere presence or absence of state administration, that are likely to have the most significant effects on security for populations in the Sahel.

Conclusion

On July 6, 2024, the heads of state of Mali, Burkina Faso, and Niger announced plans to expand their Alliance of Sahel States (AES)—initially established as a defense pact in September 2023—into a political confederation. When the alliance was first created, Niger's new military government, which had taken power in a coup d'état, was being threatened by the Economic Community of West African States (ECOWAS) with military intervention to restore the ousted civilian government. Mali's Assimi Goïta, who came to power in a 2021 coup, and Ibrahim Traoré of Burkina Faso, who led a 2022 coup, announced that their states would take up arms to defend their fellow junta leader if necessary. The following January, all three states announced their withdrawal from ECOWAS. The transformation of the AES into a confederation signals the three states' commitment to remaining outside of ECOWAS, which they accuse of being beholden to Western interests. The July summit's final communiqué promised diplomatic, economic, and military cooperation to fight terrorism, improve economic development, and secure the free circulation of goods and people across their territories.

In their speeches at the summit, Goïta, Traoré, and Niger's junta leader Abdourahamane Tiani continued a line of argument that has won them a great deal of popular support in their home states and across the region: the alliance is protecting African sovereignty, which their predecessors and ECOWAS failed to do, and leading a final break from France and its imperialist allies. In Traoré's words, for example, "Imperialists view Africa as their dominion, believing they own our people, lands, and resources. Since the illusory independence granted to African nations in the 1960s, they've installed local proxies to maintain their control. We refer to these proxies as 'house slaves'—individuals whose sole aspiration is to emulate and serve their masters."[1] According to the junta leaders, the West's imperialist interests explain why—after more than a decade of French counterterrorism operations, a UN-led stabilization mission, and US and European training and intelligence gathering—jihadist groups have only proliferated. These missions were never really about the security and well-being of Sahelian populations, they argue, but rather justified a permanent foreign military presence to protect Western interests in mineral and energy resources.

For the AES states, defending African sovereignty means, first and foremost, reasserting control over their territories by expelling Western troops and defeating rebel and jihadist groups. The defense of territorial sovereignty has justified escalating military campaigns and, in Mali's case, the decision to terminate an internationally brokered peace process that had been in place since 2015. Following the withdrawal of the UN Multidimensional Integrated Stabilization Mission in Mali in 2023, with the help of the Wagner mercenary group, the Malian army reopened hostilities with groups party to that agreement in order to reclaim the town of Kidal, which had been secured by UN and French troops instead of the Malian army since 2014. Many Malians saw this as an insult to national sovereignty, and the purported reassertion of Mali's sovereignty and territorial integrity in Kidal has come to symbolize the raison d'état of AES's military regimes, as indicated in the final communiqué of the July 6 summit.[2] Freed from internationally imposed political constraints, the AES states intend to reassert their territorial sovereignty by taking more aggressive military action against rebel and jihadist groups with support from foreign partners who, they argue, respect African sovereignty more than the imperialist West.

As of June 2025, escalating military campaigns have had little success in weakening armed groups. In July 2024, for example, Tuareg separatists won a decisive victory in a multiday battle near the Algerian border, killing more than eighty Wagner troops, including a commander, and dozens of Malian troops.[3] In central Mali, Burkina Faso, and western Niger, attacks by the jihadist network Support Group for Islam and Muslims (known by its Arabic acronym JNIM) are on the rise. So are attacks on civilians accused of sympathizing with jihadist and rebel groups. Human rights groups and journalists have documented repeated cases of civilian massacres carried out by the Malian and Burkinabe armies, Wagner, and state-supported militias.[4] Arabic-, Tamashek-, and especially Fulani-speaking communities have been disproportionately targeted: according to the organization Armed Conflict Location and Event Data, Fulani—who are about 10 percent of the Burkinabe population and 14 percent of the Malian population—made up half of civilian-conflict deaths in those states in 2022.[5]

The targeting of these populations reflects ongoing stigmatization of pastoralists as being aligned with rebels and jihadists. As these communities have become increasingly vulnerable to violence and displacement, jihadist groups have focused recruitment efforts on them. These groups' arguments about the illegitimacy and immorality of the state center long-standing pastoralist grievances concerning land-use policies and privatization, border controls, and overall sedentarist biases.[6] For their part, the AES regimes have so far not signaled interest in addressing these grievances. Significantly, the final communiqué released at the July 6 summit excluded any mention of pastoralism from its statement of development priorities, which included agriculture, mining, and communication and transportation infrastructure.[7] Overall, the military governments of the AES have outlined a vision of security and development for the Sahel that emphasizes territorial control as the basis for defending their sovereignty. As it has in the past, this appears to correlate with an escalation of violence and displacement in these states' more arid zones.

This book has argued that this model of sovereignty as territorial control is not, as the AES regimes suggest, a path of escape from imperialist hierarchies in modern international order but rather actually constitutive of them. That international security came to be defined as a problem of ordering territories and not, for example, as a problem of relations among peoples reflects nineteenth- and twentieth-century imperial interests in encompassing non-Western lands and resources within the space of the international while excluding non-Western peoples from international political subjectivity. The requirement for political communities to have a particular relationship to territory still disciplines the kinds of political subjectivities that are recognized as legitimate international actors. I have argued that this subverts self-determination in contexts where collective identities and ways of life are not congruent with the territorial division of the planet. Moreover, spaces and populations that resist territorial control have been produced as global security threats, which justifies intervention, including the use of violence, to transform political and social relations in ways that have often rendered them less, rather than more, secure.

By focusing on the case of the Middle Niger / Mali, the book has shown how the pursuit of security and development through territorialization has impeded the capacities of many communities in the Sahel to secure themselves, their livelihoods, and their social and cultural identities. In the Sahel, security and development have historically not been rooted in territorialization. Its arid ecology has shaped strategies for security and prosperity oriented toward mobility and the reproduction of flexible geographies of social and political authority. This corresponds to conditions of climatic variability and unpredictable scarcity, where livelihoods depend on exchange connecting groups across long distances who specialize in different production strategies. Relationships of interdependence across these distances and production strategies distribute the risk of ecological uncertainty and contingency. As I showed in chapter 1, these characteristics of the Sahel are not antithetical to political order but rather have been central to projects of state building and empire. They have shaped particular ways of problematizing and responding to the political and ethical questions concerning the problem of living together across difference and diversity.

Iwellemedan hegemony in the Niger bend, reproduced via an expansive network of intermediaries, illustrated nonterritorial spatial logics of political centralization and expansion. The capacity to expand the spatial reach of political authority and influence corresponded not with the subordination and internalization of other social formations but with recognition of coexisting frameworks of authority, both political and nonpolitical. This reflected the power and prestige of groups specialized in mobility, specifically elite nomadic pastoralists, commercial diasporas, and Islamic clerics and scholars, who maintained relative autonomy from political authorities. We also see evidence of these requirements for political centralization in the state-building project of the Diina in the inland Niger delta and its relationship to political and religious authorities in Timbuktu and the Niger bend. The delta relied on access to more arid spaces to the north for pastoral production and trade, and the Diina (and the Tukulör state that succeeded it) sought to encompass these areas within their boundaries. But the homogenizing structure and vision of the Diina and Tukulör states repeatedly worked at cross-purposes with existing infrastructures for securing commerce in the region, which corresponded with forms of political and religious pluralism. Repeated military campaigns to conquer the Niger bend had devastating effects on the region's economy by disrupting the links between the desert and savanna.

Chapter 2 showed how, from the late nineteenth to the mid-twentieth centuries, a diversity of forms of political authority and order across the planet was transformed into an international system where all polities are (ideally) territories. Imperial expansion on the African continent was central to this process. Interests in controlling trade on the Niger and Congo Rivers came to situate African spaces and populations as central problems for the ordering of a new international system, beginning with the Berlin Conference on West Africa. The conference paved the way for the military partition of the continent, which was justified post facto by declaring Africa *territorium nullius*: African rulers did not exercise *territorial* sovereignty and therefore lacked international political personality. This theory of territorial sovereignty was further refined in the context of international debates over colonial reform—notably, in the League of Nations mandate system. The mandate system developed standards for international trusteeship, which defined territorial development as the objective of colonial administration and as a path through which colonized peoples could one day achieve national self-determination. This informed the doctrine of sovereign recognition that would structure decolonization under the UN. Sovereignty for newly independent states would be contingent on their willingness and capacity to administer their territories as such.

Chapter 3 examined how the equation of international sovereignty with capacities for territorial administration shaped decolonization in Mali. At independence, the Malian government perceived nomadic Arabic- and Tamashek-speaking populations as a problem not only in relation to domestic state building but also based on its understanding of international hierarchy and the threat of neocolonialism. French politicians were actively pursuing the creation of a new Saharan territory, which would require partitioning Algeria and Mali, based on familiar claims that the desert was, for all intents and purposes, empty and thus not relevant to the question of African independence. In this context, perceived ungovernability in the North, based on the difficulty of encompassing it within the territorial infrastructures of the state, presented a threat to Malian sovereignty on two fronts: on the one hand, populations in the North themselves might threaten the state by rebelling, and, on the other hand, the ungovernability of the North made Malian sovereignty vulnerable to international intervention.

In the wake of droughts, failed development schemes, and rebellion, however, different ways of thinking about state building and development, particularly in arid contexts, gained more attention in the 1990s. Scholars and practitioners with expertise on arid regions highlighted the importance of social and political institutions that facilitated mobility and showed how efforts to territorialize these spaces threatened pastoral livelihoods and the arid ecologies on which they depend. Interest in participatory development and in decentralization reforms in Africa created openings to recognize greater diversity in the ways in which different communities experience and produce the spaces they inhabit. In northern Mali, local peace-building initiatives focused on rebuilding socioeconomic and political institutions and practices that connect pastoral, agricultural, and riverine producers. Democratization and decentralization reforms promised to better account for Mali's historical, cultural, and ecological diversity in redefining political constituencies and their different relationships to the state. I have argued that these openings toward more pluralist conceptions of security and development in Mali, however, narrowed considerably in relation to IMF and World Bank policy prescriptions and the interests of an entrenched political class in Bamako. In practice, democratization and decentralization in Mali largely focused on creating new territorial jurisdictions and privatizing land and resources.

In the early 2000s, the Sahel's relationship to a hierarchical international order shifted significantly as conditions of perceived deficiency or lack were redefined as international security threats rather than development and humanitarian concerns. Chapter 4 showed how international intervention to prevent the Sahel's "ungoverned spaces" from becoming the "next Afghanistan" contributed to the political and security crisis that began in Mali in 2012. One effect of the securitization of the Sahel is that critical thinking about territorial state building and development and its relationship to arid ecologies and ways of life largely disappeared from the work of major international donors and organizations. To the extent that pastoral livelihoods are a focus of international initiatives in the Sahel, this is mostly with the objective of making rural-subsistence practices more "resilient" in order to lessen the appeal of jihadist groups, migration, or narcotics trafficking. In this context, pastoral livelihoods do not offer a perspective from which the territorial model of the international state system might be seen in a new light but are rather approached through instrumental means of reinforcing the stability of that system through strategies of territorial containment.

But the spatial ideas and practices that shape ways of life in the Sahel are not just elements of rural-subsistence strategies. They also point to distinct archives of knowledge and practice that speak to the core problematics of international order: how to live together under conditions of diversity, interdependence, and uncertainty. These archives have been neglected in political science and IR research on international security. I have argued that this partly reflects problematic assumptions about space, order, and security that are at the foundation of modern political theory—that security is an effect of political order and that political order requires the encompassment and subordination of other forms of social authority, legitimacy, and meaning making. Dropping the equation of political order with territorial control can shift our view of the relationship between space and security from one of vertical control, where spatial *exclusion* is a key mechanism of security and a signifier of competent authority, to one of mutual constitution, where security is a collective project of reproducing the material and social conditions of cohabitation. This would take the security effects of diverse spatial logics and practices as an empirical question rather than a theoretical given.

Toward these ends, theorizing security from the perspective of the Sahel is generative for rethinking relationships among space, ecology, population, and political order. If a territorial model of order theorizes security as containment, examples from the Sahel model security as connection. Security in this context depends on mobility and circulation, which depend on maintaining relationships of reciprocity. The importance of reproducing these relationships across diverse spaces and populations shapes understandings of identity and ethics that center engagements with difference and the role of the stranger and are oriented toward mediating the inclusion of outsiders rather than their exclusion. This corresponds with distinct geographies of political identity, belonging, and authority in which relationships to space are not mutually exclusive. Territorial geographies of political order presume to secure an "inside" space by maintaining its separation from an "outside": political authority is legitimated through its reproduction of the boundaries between inside and outside, and these boundaries define political identity and belonging. Where political order is secured in relation to mobility, rather than territory, authority is legitimated instead through capacities to traverse boundaries between the inside and outside. Political identity and belonging are not fixed in space but mediate practices of negotiating and adjusting relationships to space. This allows for a responsiveness to dynamic ecological conditions that is closed off where geographies of identity and authority are static.

The latter ways of conceptualizing and negotiating relationships among political order, subjectivity, and space ground a very different geography of the international than that of the modern territorial state system. I have argued that recognizing this diversity is crucial for understanding and responding to changing global security conditions. By expanding and pluralizing conceptions of how political order and security relate to the production of space, ordering strategies that have been misread as signifiers of *dis*order become recognizable as such. This is important analytically for developing more accurate empirical and theoretical accounts of global security conditions and their relationship to political order. More urgently, delinking the theory and practice of security from the political project of territorial control will be necessary for mitigating ongoing harms of international security interventions, which have repeatedly exacerbated violence, displacement, and political marginalization in the spaces they purport to secure.

Notes

Introduction

1. Gregory Mann, *From Empires to NGOs in the West African Sahel* (Cambridge: Cambridge University Press, 2014), 4.

2. Nicholas Schmidle, "The Saharan Conundrum," *New York Times Magazine*, February 13, 2009, https://www.nytimes.com/2009/02/15/magazine/15Africa-t.html.

3. Stuart Hall, "Who Needs 'Identity'?," in *Questions of Cultural Identity*, ed. Hall and Paul Du Gay (London: Sage, 1996), 4–5; Pinar Bilgin, *The International in Security, Security in the International* (London: Routledge, 2016), 4–5. On Africa's position as a constitutive outside in theories of international order, see Siba N. Grovogui, *Beyond Eurocentrism and Anarchy: Memories of International Order and Institutions* (New York: Palgrave Macmillan, 2006), 1–23; Zubairu Wai, "Africa in/and International Relations: An Introduction," in *Recentering Africa in International Relations: Beyond Lack, Peripherality, and Failure*, ed. Marta Iñiguez de Heredia and Wai (New York: Palgrave MacMillan, 2019).

4. Nisha Shah, "The Territorial Trap of the Territorial Trap: Global Transformation and the Problem of the State's Two Territories," *International Political Sociology* 6, no. 1 (2012): 67; John Agnew, "The Territorial Trap: The Geographical Assumptions of International Relations Theory," *Review of International Political Economy* 1, no. 1 (1994). More recent discussions of the territorial trap in IR research include Orit Gazit, "A Simmelian Approach to Space in World Politics," *International Theory* 10, no. 2 (2018); Amy Niang, "Space and the Geopolitical," *Millennium: Journal of International Studies* 51, no. 1 (2023).

5. Agnew, "Territorial Trap," 55.

6. Shah, "Territorial Trap," 57. For a recent review of these limitations in IR research, see Daniel Lambach, "Space, Scale, and Global Politics: Towards a Critical Approach to Space in International Relations," *Review of International Studies* 48, no. 2 (2022).

7. Henri Lefebvre, *State, Space, World: Selected Essays*, ed. Neil Brenner and Stuart Elden, trans. Gerald Moore, Brenner, and Elden (Minneapolis: University of Minnesota Press, 2009), loc. 2226 of 4274, Kindle.

8. Neil Brenner and Stuart Elden, "Henri Lefebvre on State, Space, Territory," *International Political Sociology* 3, no. 4 (2009): 359.

9. Quoted in Brenner and Elden, "Henri Lefebvre," 358.

10. Brenner and Elden, "Henri Lefebvre," 353.

11. Beate Jahn, "IR and the State of Nature: The Cultural Origins of a Ruling Ideology," *Review of International Studies* 25, no. 3 (1999): 417–18.

12. Naeem Inayatullah and David L. Blaney, *International Relations and the Problem of Difference* (New York: Routledge, 2004), 56. See also Johannes Fabian, *Time and the Other: How Anthropology Constructs Its Object* (New York: Columbia University Press, 1983).

13. In this way, Eurocentrism's embrace of linear, evolutionary time is paradoxically also a dualist metaphysics that opposes the body to reason and nature to society. Anibal Quijano and Michael Ennis, "Coloniality of Power, Eurocentrism, and Latin America," *Nepantla: Views from the South* 1, no. 3 (2000): 554–56.

14. Jordan Branch, "'Colonial Reflection' and Territoriality: The Peripheral Origins of Sovereign Statehood," *European Journal of International Relations* 18, no. 2 (2010); Kerry Goettlich, "The Colonial Origins of Modern Territoriality: Property Surveying in the Thirteen Colonies," *American Political Science Review* 116, no. 3 (2022); Karem Nisancioglu, "Racial Sovereignty," *European Journal of International Relations* 26, no. 1 (2020).

15. Branch, "'Colonial Reflection' and Territoriality," 284, 285. See also Goettlich, "Colonial Origins."

16. Nisancioglu, "Racial Sovereignty," 41.

17. This paragraph is a near reproduction of Casey McNeill, "Deterritorialized Threats and the 'Territorial Trap': The Geographical Imaginaries of Piracy in the Gulf of Aden," *Alternatives: Global, Local, Political* 48, no. 2 (2023): 173.

18. Branch, "'Colonial Reflection' and Territoriality."

19. Shah, "Territorial Trap," 57–76, 61–62.

20. Brian Schmidt, *The Political Discourse of Anarchy: A Disciplinary History of International Relations* (Albany: State University of New York Press, 1998), chap. 3.

21. John H. Herz, "Rise and Demise of the Territorial State," *World Politics* 9, no. 4 (1957): 482. Italics added.

22. Herz, "Rise and Demise," 482. See also Siba N. Grovogui, "Regimes of Sovereignty: International Morality and the African Condition," *European Journal of International Relations* 8, no. 3 (2002).

23. Grovogui, *Beyond Eurocentrism and Anarchy*, chap. 1.

24. Stephen Ellis, "Climate Variability and Complex Ecosystem Dynamics: Implications for Pastoral Development," in *Living with Uncertainty: New Directions in Pastoral Development in Africa*, ed. Ian Scoones (London: Intermediate Technology Publications, 1995), 38.

25. Ian Scoones, "New Directions in Pastoral Development in Africa," in *Living with Uncertainty: New Directions in Pastoral Development in Africa*, ed. Scoones (London: Intermediate Technology Publications, 1995), 1–2.

26. Maryam Niamir-Fuller, "Managing Mobility in African Rangelands," in *Property Rights, Risk and Livestock Development in Africa*, ed. Nancy McCarthy et al. (Washington, DC: International Food Policy Research Institute, 1999), 105–6.

27. Greg Perrier, "New Directions in Range Management Planning in Africa," in *Living with Uncertainty: New Directions in Pastoral Development in Africa*, ed. Ian Scoones (London: Intermediate Technology Publications, 1995), 54–55.

28. Amy Niang, "Ransoming, Compensatory Violence, and Humanitarianism in the Sahel," *Alternatives: Global, Local, Political* 39, no. 4 (2014): 238.

29. Niang, "Ransoming"; Louise E. Sweet, "Camel Raiding of North Arabian Bedouin: A Mechanism of Ecological Adaptation," *American Anthropologist* 67, no. 5 (1965).

30. Niang, "Ransoming," 235.

31. Elias N. Saad, *Social History of Timbuktu: The Role of Muslim Scholars and Notables, 1400–1900* (Cambridge: Cambridge University Press, 1983), 45–46; Richard L. Roberts, *Warriors, Merchants, and Slaves: The State and the Economy in the Middle Niger Valley, 1700–1914* (Stanford: Stanford University Press, 1987), 95–100; Mauro Nobili, *Sultan, Caliph and the Renewer of the Faith: Ahmad Lobbo, the Tarikh al-Fattish and the Making of an Islamic State in West Africa* (Cambridge: Cambridge University Press, 2020), 168–80.

32. L. O. Sanneh, *Beyond Jihad: The Pacifist Tradition in West African Islam* (Oxford: Oxford University Press, 2016).

33. Ousmane Kane, *Beyond Timbuktu: An Intellectual History of Muslim West Africa* (Cambridge, MA: Harvard University Press, 2016), 44–45.

34. Saad, *Social History of Timbuktu*, 34–41, 45–46. Sources on Sunni Ali's conflict with Timbuktu's scholars may be exaggerated, however, because they sought to contrast Askia Muhammad's Islamic authority with the backwardness of his predecessor. See Michael A. Gomez, "Timbuktu under Imperial Songhay: A Reconsideration of Autonomy," *Journal of African History* 31, no. 1 (1990); Bruce S. Hall, "Arguing Sovereignty in Songhay," *Afriques: Débats, methods et terraines d'histoire* 4 (2013).

35. Saad, *Social History of Timbuktu*, 49.

36. Rudolph T. Ware, *The Walking Qur'an: Islamic Education, Embodied Knowledge, and History in West Africa* (Chapel Hill: University of North Carolina Press, 2014), 83–84.

37. Charles Grémont, "Villages and Crossroads: Changing Territorialities among the Tuareg of Northern Mali," in *Saharan Frontiers: Space and Mobility in Northwest Africa*, ed. James McDougall and Judith Scheele (Bloomington: Indiana University Press, 2012), 134.

38. Judith Scheele, "Northwest African Perspectives on the Concept of the State," *HAU: Journal of Ethnographic Theory* 12, no. 3 (2022): 739, 738–39.

39. Eric Cofie Timpong-Jones et al., "Transhumance Pastoralism in West Africa—

Its Importance, Policies and Challenges," *African Journal of Range and Forage Science* 40, no. 1 (2023): 115.

40. Judith Scheele, *Smugglers and Saints of the Sahara: Regional Connectivity in the Twentieth Century* (Cambridge: Cambridge University Press, 2012).

41. Scheele, *Smugglers and Saints.*

42. Siba N. Grovogui, "Dunes Shift, Humans Adapt: Political Transformations and Military Coups in the African Sahel," *CODESRIA Bulletin* 1 (2024).

43. Amy Niang, *The Postcolonial African State in Transition: Stateness and Modes of Sovereignty* (Lanham: Rowman and Littlefield, 2018), 43.

44. Scheele, "Northwest African Perspectives," 736; Niang, *Postcolonial African State,* 187.

45. See, e.g., Dida Badi and Georg Klute, "Jihadi Governance in Northern Mali: Socio-political Orders in Contest," in *Local Self-Governance and Varieties of Statehood: Tensions and Cooperation,* ed. Dieter Neubert, Hans-Joachim Lauth, and Christoph Mohamad-Klotzbach (Cham: Springer, 2022); Morten Bøås and Francesco Strazzari, "Governance, Fragility and Insurgency in the Sahel: A Hybrid Political Order in the Making," *International Spectator* 55, no. 4 (2020); Francesco Strazzari and G. Zanoletti, "North Africa: Organized Crime, the Sahel-Sahara Region and State (Un)making," in *Handbook of Organized Crime and Politics,* ed. Felia Allum and Stan Gilmour (Northampton, MA: Edward Elgar, 2019); Thomas Hüsken and Georg Klute, "Political Orders in the Making: Emerging Forms of Political Organization from Libya to Northern Mali," *African Security* 8, no. 4 (2015); Bruce Whitehouse and Francesco Strazzari, "Introduction: Rethinking Challenges to State Sovereignty in Mali and Northwest Africa," *African Security* 8, no. 4 (2015).

46. Carole L. Crumley, "Heterarchy and the Analysis of Complex Societies," *Archeological Papers of the American Anthropological Association* 6, no. 1 (1995): 3.

47. Badi and Klute, "Jihadi Governance," 162.

48. Tor A. Benjaminsen and Boubacar Ba, "Why Do Pastoralists in Mali Join Jihadist Groups? A Political Ecological Explanation," *Journal of Peasant Studies* 46, no. 1 (2019): 10–11; Tor A. Benjaminsen and Boubacar Ba, "A Moral Economy of Pastoralists? Understanding the 'Jihadist' Insurgency in Mali," *Political Geography* 113, no. 3 (2024): 4.

49. Badi and Klute, "Jihadi Governance," 168.

50. Luca Raineri and Francesco Strazzari, "State, Secession, and Jihad: The Micropolitical Economy of Conflict in Northern Mali," *African Security* 8, no. 4 (2015): 261.

51. Benjaminsen and Ba, "Pastoralists in Mali," 10–11; Benjaminsen and Ba, "Moral Economy of Pastoralists," 4–5.

52. Strazzari and Zanoletti, "North Africa," 301; Amy Niang, "Stateness and Borderness in Mediation: Productions and Contestations of Space in the Sahel" (Working Papers Series No. 26, Adaptation and Creativity in Africa: Technologies and Significations in the Making of Order and Disorder, German Research Foundation, Berlin, 2018), 15.

53. Niang, "Stateness and Borderness," 12.

54. Niang, "Space and the Geopolitical," 287, 293.

Chapter 1

1. James L. A. Webb, *Desert Frontier: Ecological and Economic Change along the Western Sahel, 1600–1850* (Madison: University of Wisconsin Press, 1995).

2. Niamir-Fuller, "Managing Mobility"; Maryam Niamir-Fuller, "The Resilience of Pastoral Herding in Sahelian Africa," in *Linking Social and Ecological Systems: Management Practices and Social Mechanisms for Building Resilience*, ed. Fikret Berkes and Carl Folke (Cambridge: Cambridge University Press, 1998); Claude Raynaut et al., *Societies and Nature in the Sahel* (London: Routledge, 1997); Scoones, "New Directions."

3. Niamir-Fuller, "Resilience of Pastoral Herding," 271–73.

4. Stephen Baier, "Economic History and Development: Drought and the Sahellan Economies of Niger," *African Economic History* 1 (1976); Tor A. Benjaminsen and Christian Lund, eds., *Politics, Property and Production in the West African Sahel: Understanding Natural Resources Management* (London: Zed Books, 2001); Paul E. Lovejoy and Stephen Baier, "The Desert-Side Economy of the Central Sudan," *International Journal of African Historical Studies* 8, no. 4 (1975).

5. Maryam Niamir-Fuller and Matthew Turner, "A Review of Recent Literature on Pastoralism and Transhumance in Africa," in *Managing Mobility in African Rangelands: The Legitimization of Transhumance*, ed. Niamir-Fuller (London: Intermediate Technology Publications, 1999), 38–39.

6. Roderick James McIntosh, *The Peoples of the Middle Niger: The Island of Gold* (Malden, MA: Blackwell, 1998), xix.

7. E. Ann McDougall, "The Sahara Reconsidered: Pastoralism, Politics and Salt from the Ninth through the Twelfth Centuries," in "Business Empires in Equatorial Africa," ed. W. G. Clarence-Smith, special issue, *African Economic History*, no. 12 (1983).

8. Roberts, *Warriors, Merchants, and Slaves*, 10.

9. Judith Scheele, "Traders, Saints, and Irrigation: Reflections on Saharan Connectivity," *Journal of African History* 51, no. 3 (2010).

10. Sanneh, *Beyond Jihad*, 92.

11. Saad, *Social History of Timbuktu*, 45–49.

12. Sanneh, *Beyond Jihad*.

13. Roberts, *Warriors, Merchants, and Slaves*, 17.

14. Ware, *Walking Qur'an*, 83.

15. Ware, *Walking Qur'an*, 84.

16. Kane, *Beyond Timbuktu*, chap. 2.

17. George E. Brooks, "A Provisional Historical Schema for Western Africa Based on Seven Climate Periods (ca. 9000 B.C. to the 19th Century)," *Cahiers d'études africaines* 26, nos. 1–2 (1986): 55–59; Sharon Nicholson, "Climatic Variations in the Sahel and Other African Regions during the Past Five Centuries," *Journal of Arid Environments* 1, no. 1 (1978): 9–11; Webb, *Desert Frontier*, 10–14.

18. Webb, *Desert Frontier*, 19–21.

19. Martin A. Klein, "The Impact of the Atlantic Slave Trade on the Societies of the Western Sudan," *Social Science History* 14, no. 2 (1990); Paul E. Lovejoy, "Islam, Slavery, and Political Transformation in West Africa: Constraints on the Trans-Atlantic Slave Trade," *Outre-mers* 89, no. 336 (2002).

20. Klein, "Impact," 234–35.

21. Klein, "Impact," 239–40.

22. Paul E. Lovejoy, *Jihād in West Africa during the Age of Revolutions* (Athens: Ohio University Press, 2016), chap. 5.

23. Sanneh, *Beyond Jihad*, 180, 226.

24. Bruce S. Hall, *A History of Race in Muslim West Africa, 1600–1960* (Cambridge: Cambridge University Press, 2011).

25. Ibrahima Thioub, "Stigmas and Memory of Slavery in West Africa: Skin Color and Blood as Social Fracture Lines," *New Global Studies* 6, no. 3 (2012): 6–7.

26. Thioub, "Stigmas and Memory."

27. Charles Grémont, *Les Touaregs Iwellemmedan, 1647–1896: Un ensemble politique de la boucle du Niger* (Paris: Karthala, 2010), 228; Brooks, "Provisional Historical Schema," 56; Klein, "Impact," 244.

28. Grémont, *Les Touaregs Iwellemmedan*, 182.

29. Nobili, *Sultan*, 9.

30. Saad, *Social History of Timbuktu*, 57.

31. Grémont, *Les Touaregs Iwellemmedan*, 228–31.

32. Richard L. Roberts, "Production and Reproduction of Warrior States: Segu Bambara and Segu Tokolor, c. 1712–1890," *International Journal of African Historical Studies* 13, no. 3 (1980).

33. Roberts, "Production and Reproduction"; Klein, "Impact."

34. Lovejoy, "Islam."

35. Brooks, "Provisional Historical Schema," 57.

36. Baz Lecocq, *Disputed Desert: Decolonisation, Competing Nationalisms and Tuareg Rebellions in Northern Mali* (Leiden: Brill, 2010), 9, 10, 17–18.

37. André Bourgeot, "Pasture in the Malian Gourma: Habitation by Humans and Animals," in *The Future of Pastoral Peoples: Proceedings of a Conference Held in Nairobi, Kenya, 4–8 August 1980*, ed. John G. Galaty et al. (Ottawa: International Development Research Centre, 1981); Baz Lecocq, "This Country Is Your Country: Territory, Borders, and Decentralisation in Tuareg Politics," *Itinerario* 27, no. 1 (2003).

38. Lecocq, "This Country," 60. See also Bourgeot, "Pasture," 166.

39. Lecocq, "This Country," 60, 61.

40. Grémont, *Les Touaregs Iwellemmedan*, 209, 257–60, 398.

41. Grémont, *Les Touaregs Iwellemmedan*.

42. Grémont, *Les Touaregs Iwellemmedan*, 324–26, 328, 345.

43. Grémont, *Les Touaregs Iwellemmedan*, 305–6.

44. Grémont, *Les Touaregs Iwellemmedan*, 374. The original reads, "Fidélité à un

serment, à quelque chose de tissé ensemble, dont la transgression passe pour porter malheur."

45. Grémont, *Les Touaregs Iwellemmedan*, 375, 374.

46. Grémont, *Les Touaregs Iwellemmedan*, 390–95.

47. Thomas Rid, "Razzia: A Turning Point in Modern Strategy," *Terrorism and Political Violence* 21, no. 4 (2009): 618–19; Sweet, "Camel Raiding."

48. Niang, "Ransoming," 235.

49. Grémont, *Les Touaregs Iwellemmedan*, 390–95.

50. Grémont describes this dynamic in the relationship between the Kel Ekummed and Idnan Tuareg in Gao. See Grémont, *Les Touaregs Iwellemmedan*, 329.

51. Grémont, *Les Touaregs Iwellemmedan*, 393–94.

52. Grémont, *Les Touaregs Iwellemmedan*, 394.

53. Grémont gives an example from the joint defense of the Songhai village of Fafa in the 1880s. The Kel Talatayt (one of the three *tewsiten* of the Kel Ekummed) assembled a large fighting force from across the confederation to defeat a Tuareg confederation from the east that was trying to assert their dominance over Fafa. Grémont's interlocutor reports the Kel Talatayt having assembled a force of one hundred boats to cross the river and confront the enemy. Grémont, *Les Touaregs Iwellemmedan*, 369.

54. Grémont, *Les Touaregs Iwellemmedan*, 281, 282, 284, 284–86, 290.

55. Nobili, *Sultan*, 131; Kane, *Beyond Timbuktu*, 70.

56. Kane, *Beyond Timbuktu*, 70.

57. Richard Moorehead, "Mali," in *Custodians of the Commons: Pastoral Land Tenure in Africa*, ed. Lane Charles (London: Taylor and Francis, 2014), 50–51; Matthew D. Turner, "The Micropolitics of Common Property Management on the Maasina Floodplains of Central Mali," *Canadian Journal of African Studies* 40, no. 1 (2006): 47.

58. Richard Moorehead, "Structural Chaos: Community and State Management of Common Property in Mali" (PhD diss., University of Sussex, 1997), 182.

59. Trond Vedeld, "History, Continuity and Change in Fulani Resource Regimes," in *Politics, Property and Production in the West African Sahel: Understanding Natural Resources Management*, ed. Tor A. Benjaminsen and Christian Lund (London: Zed Books, 2001), 123.

60. Nobili, *Sultan*, 10. On the economy of the Segu state and its connections to the delta and the desert, see Roberts, *Warriors, Merchants, and Slaves*, chap. 2.

61. Vedeld, "History, Continuity and Change," 123–24.

62. Nobili, *Sultan*, 10–11, 129–33.

63. Nobili, *Sultan*, 11.

64. Richard Moorehead, "Structural Chaos," 183; Lorenzo Cotula and Salmana Cissé, "Changes in 'Customary' Resource Tenure Systems in the Inner Niger Delta, Mali," *Journal of Legal Pluralism and Unofficial Law* 38, no. 52 (2006): 10.

65. Moorehead, "Structural Chaos," 183.

66. Pascal Legrosse, "Les règles d'accès des troupeaux Peuls aux paturages du

delta: Central du Niger (Mali)," in *Managing Mobility in African Rangelands: The Legitimization of Transhumance*, ed. Maryam Niamir-Fuller (London: Intermediate Technology Publications, 1999), 89–95.

67. Cotula and Cissé, "Changes," 11.

68. Legrosse, "Les règles"; Matthew D. Turner, "The Role of Social Networks, Indefinite Boundaries and Political Bargaining in Maintaining the Ecological and Economic Resilience of the Transhumance Systems of Sudano-Sahelian West Africa," in *Managing Mobility in African Rangelands: The Legitimization of Transhumance*, ed. Maryam Niamir-Fuller (London: Intermediate Technology Publications, 1999).

69. Niamir-Fuller and Turner, "Review of Recent Literature," 41.

70. Vedeld, "History, Continuity and Change," 125; Marion Johnson, "The Economic Foundations of an Islamic Theocracy—the Case of Masina," *Journal of African History* 17, no. 4 (1976): 483–88.

71. William A. Brown, "The Caliphate of Hamdullahi" (PhD diss., University of Wisconsin, 1969), 61–63.

72. Quoted in Ghislaine Lydon, *On Trans-Saharan Trails* (Cambridge: Cambridge University Press, 2009), 116.

73. Roberts, *Warriors, Merchants, and Slaves*, 68.

74. Nobili, *Sultan*, 161–68.

75. Nobili, *Sultan*, 155–60.

76. Nobili, *Sultan*, 168–69.

77. Nobili, *Sultan*, 173, 178–79.

78. Roberts, *Warriors, Merchants, and Slaves*, 79.

79. David Robinson, *The Holy War of Umar Tal: The Western Sudan in the Mid-Nineteenth Century* (Oxford: Oxford University Press, 1985), 250, 263, 282.

80. B. O. Oloruntimehin, "Resistance Movements in the Tukulor Empire," *Cahiers d'études africaines* 8, no. 29 (1968).

81. D. Robinson, *Holy War*, 305–10, 274, 278–79.

82. Roberts, *Warriors, Merchants, and Slaves*, 107, 96.

83. D. Robinson, *Holy War*, 367, 360.

84. Oloruntimehin, "Resistance Movements," 142–43.

85. Jeffrey Herbst, *States and Power in Africa: Comparative Lessons in Authority and Control* (Princeton: Princeton University Press, 2014), 11, chap. 2.

86. James Ferguson and Akhil Gupta, "Spatializing States: Toward an Ethnography of Neoliberal Governmentality," *American Ethnologist* 29, no. 4 (2002).

Chapter 2

1. Quoted in Dane Kennedy, *Mungo Park's Ghost: The Haunted Hubris of British Explorers in Nineteenth-Century Africa* (Cambridge: Cambridge University Press, 2024), 16.

2. Kennedy, *Mungo Park's Ghost*, 27–30.

3. Charles W. J. Withers, *Majestic River: Mungo Park and the Exploration of the Niger* (Havertown: Birlinn, 2022), 109.

4. William B. Cohen, "Imperial Mirage: The Western Sudan in French Thought and Action," *Journal of the Historical Society of Nigeria* 7, no. 3 (1974): 418, 421.

5. W. Cohen, "Imperial Mirage," 430.

6. A. S. Kanya-Forstner, *The Conquest of Western Sudan: A Study in French Military Imperialism* (Cambridge: Cambridge University Press, 1969), 84–94.

7. S. E. Crowe, *The Berlin West African Conference: 1884–1885* (London: Longmans, Green, 1942), 20.

8. Fitzmaurice to Hutton, May 10, 1884, C. 4023, no. 50, in R. J. Gavin and J. A. Betley, eds., *The Scramble for Africa: Documents on the Berlin West African Conference and Related Subjects, 1884/1885* (Ibadan: Ibadan University Press, 1973), 22.

9. Quoted in William Roger Louis, "The Berlin Congo Conference," in *France and Britain in Africa: Imperial Rivalry and Colonial Rule*, ed. Prosser Gifford and Louis (New Haven: Yale University Press, 1971), 215.

10. "Protocol No. 1," meeting, November 15, 1884, C. 4361, in Gavin and Betley, *Scramble for Africa*, 130. Interest in applying international jurisdiction in Africa had been developing in the years leading up to the conference, led by jurists associated with King Leopold II of Belgium. See Jan Vandersmissen, "The King's Most Eloquent Campaigner: Emile De Laveleye, Leopold II and the Creation of the Congo Free State," *Revue belge d'histoire contemporaine* 41, no. 1 (2011).

11. Jules Ferry, notes on the German proposal, no. 376, in Gavin and Betley, *Scramble for Africa*, 329.

12. Granville to Plesson, October 8, 1884, C. 4205, no. 11, in Gavin and Betley, *Scramble for Africa*, 43.

13. T. V. Lister, minutes on the West African Conference, October 14, 1884, FO 403/46, no. 26, in Gavin and Betley, *Scramble for Africa*, 46.

14. H. P. Anderson, memorandum on the West African Conference, October 14, 1884, FO 403/46, no. 26-2, in Gavin and Betley, *Scramble for Africa*, 48.

15. Anderson, memorandum, October 14, 1884, 48.

16. Anderson, memorandum, October 14, 1884, 49.

17. Quoted in G. N. Uzoigwe, "Spheres of Influence and the Doctrine of the Hinterland in the Partition of Africa," *Journal of African Studies* 3, no. 2 (1976): 199.

18. Crowe, *Berlin West African Conference*, 180–81.

19. *Report of the Commission Charged with the Examination of the Project of Declaration Respecting the New Occupations on the Coasts of Africa*, in Gavin and Betley, *Scramble for Africa*, 248.

20. "Protocol No. 8," sitting, January 31, 1885, in Gavin and Betley, *Scramble for Africa*, 240.

21. "Protocol No. 8," 240.

22. "General Act of the Berlin Conference," in Gavin and Betley, *Scramble for Africa*, 300.

23. Quoted in Boniface I. Obichere, *West African States and European Expansion: The Dahomey-Niger Hinterland, 1885–1898* (New Haven: Yale University Press, 1971), 178.

24. Mark Frank Lindley, *The Acquisition and Government of Backward Territory in International Law: Being a Treatise on the Law and Practice Relating to Colonial Expansion* (New York: Longmans, Green, 1926), 20.

25. J. Fisch, "Africa as Terra Nullius: The Berlin Conference and International Law," in *Bismarck, Europe, and Africa: The Berlin Africa Conference 1884–1885 and the Onset of Partition*, ed. Stig Förster, Wolfgang J. Mommsen, and Ronald Robinson (Oxford: Oxford University Press, 1988), 354–63.

26. Andrew Fitzmaurice, *Sovereignty, Property and Empire* (Cambridge: Cambridge University Press, 2014), 285; Fisch, "Africa as Terra Nullius," 363–64.

27. Quoted in Fitzmaurice, *Sovereignty, Property and Empire*, 285–86.

28. Quoted in Fitzmaurice, *Sovereignty, Property and Empire*, 280.

29. Fitzmaurice, *Sovereignty, Property and Empire*, 239, 287.

30. Adam Hochschild, *King Leopold's Ghost: A Story of Greed, Terror, and Heroism in Colonial Africa* (New York: Harper Collins, 1999), 71.

31. Fitzmaurice, *Sovereignty, Property and Empire*, 287.

32. Fitzmaurice, *Sovereignty, Property and Empire*, 292–96.

33. Fitzmaurice, *Sovereignty, Property and Empire*, chap. 7.

34. Stefan Salomon, "The Construction of Territory in Nineteenth and Early Twentieth Century International Legal Doctrine," *Zeitschrift für öffentliches Recht* 77, no. 1 (2022); Luigi Nuzzo, "Territory, Sovereignty, and the Construction of the Colonial Space," in *International Law and Empire: Historical Explorations*, ed. Martti Koskenniemi, Walter Rech, and Manuel Jiménez Fonseca (Oxford: Oxford University Press, 2017).

35. Quoted in Salomon, "Construction of Territory," 76–77. See also the commentary therein.

36. Quoted in Salomon, "Construction of Territory," 78.

37. Nuzzo, "Territory," 286; Robert H. Jackson, *Quasi-States: Sovereignty, International Relations, and the Third World* (Cambridge: Cambridge University Press, 1990).

38. Nuzzo, "Territory," 287.

39. Salomon, "Construction of Territory," 87.

40. Nuzzo, "Territory," 287.

41. Fisch, "Africa as Terra Nullius," 357.

42. Walter Lippmann, *The Stakes of Diplomacy* (New York: Henry Holt, 1915), 97–98.

43. See, e.g., Edmund Dene Morel, *Red Rubber: The Story of the Rubber Slave Trade Which Flourished on the Congo for Twenty Years, 1890–1910* (Manchester: National Labour Press, 1919); Leonard Woolf, *Empire and Commerce in Africa: A Study in Economic Imperialism* (Westminster: George Allen and Unwin, 1920).

44. John Atkinson Hobson, *Imperialism: A Study* (New York: James Pott, 1902); W. E. B. Du Bois, "The African Roots of War," *The Atlantic*, May 1915.

45. See, e.g., Paul Samuel Reinsch, *Colonial Administration* (New York: Macmillan, 1905); Alleyne Ireland, "On the Need for a Scientific Study of Colonial Administration," *Proceedings of the American Political Science Association* 3, no. 3 (1906). On the im-

perial origins of interwar theories of international order, see Vineet Thakur and Peter C.J. Vale, *South Africa, Race and the Making of International Relations* (London: Rowman and Littlefield, 2020); Robert Vitalis, *White World Order, Black Power Politics: The Birth of American International Relations* (Ithaca: Cornell University Press, 2015).

46. Reinsch, *Colonial Administration*.

47. This was with notable exceptions. Anti-imperialists, like W. E. B. Du Bois, argued that building democratic power among the colonized was the solution to the threats of imperialism. Du Bois, "African Roots of War."

48. See, e.g., Lippmann, *Stakes of Diplomacy*; John Atkinson Hobson, *Towards International Government* (London: Macmillan, 1915); Woolf, *Empire and Commerce*; Edmund Dene Morel, *Africa and the Peace of Europe* (London: National Labour Press, 1917).

49. Adom Getachew, *Worldmaking after Empire* (Princeton: Princeton University Press, 2019), 38–39.

50. Michael Dennis Callahan, *Mandates and Empire: The League of Nations and Africa, 1914–1931* (Brighton: Sussex Academic Press, 2008), 31.

51. On Wilson's and Smuts's co-optation of self-determination in defense of empire and white rule, see Getachew, *Worldmaking after Empire*, chap. 2. On the Round Table and its influence on racialized theories and institutions of international order, see Thakur and Vale, *South Africa*.

52. Callahan, *Mandates and Empire*, 21.

53. William Roger Louis, "African Origins of the Mandates Idea," *International Organization* 19, no. 1 (1965): 24–26.

54. Susan Pedersen, *The Guardians* (Oxford: Oxford University Press, 2015).

55. Callahan, *Mandates and Empire*, 143.

56. Quoted in Quincy Wright, *Mandates under the League of Nations* (1930; repr., New York: Greenwood Press, 1968), 591.

57. Quoted in Wright, *Mandates*, 591.

58. Leonard V. Smith, "Sovereignty under the League of Nations Mandates: The Jurists' Debates," *Journal of the History of International Law* 21, no. 4 (2019): 574.

59. Wright, *Mandates*, 331.

60. Wright, *Mandates*, 461.

61. Individuals could be naturalized into the nationality of the mandatory power on a case-by-case basis, which was a means of ensuring that white settlers could access citizenship rights.

62. Pedersen, *Guardians*, 217.

63. Quoted in Pedersen, *Guardians*, 217.

64. Quoted in Pedersen, *Guardians*, 220.

65. Wright, *Mandates*, 339.

66. Wright, *Mandates*, 269–73, 268, 276. On the geographical diversity of European imperial expansion and its relationship to different legal and political strategies, see L. Benton, *A Search for Sovereignty: Law and Geography in European Empires, 1400–1900* (Cambridge: Cambridge University Press, 2009).

67. Wright, *Mandates*, 284–86, 295.

68. Quoted in Wright, *Mandates*, 591.

69. Wright, *Mandates*, 231.

70. Quoted in Wright, *Mandates*, 254.

71. Quoted in Wright, *Mandates*, 232.

72. Quoted in Antony Anghie, *Imperialism, Sovereignty, and the Making of International Law* (New York: Cambridge University Press, 2007), 166.

73. Pedersen, *Guardians*, 109.

74. Anghie, *Imperialism*, 182–86. See also Siba N. Grovogui, *Sovereigns, Quasi Sovereigns, and Africans: Race and Self-Determination in International Law* (Minneapolis: University of Minnesota Press, 1996).

75. Anghie, *Imperialism*, 210.

76. Diana K. Davis, *The Arid Lands: History, Power, Knowledge* (Cambridge, MA: MIT Press, 2016), 99–125; Monica M. van Beusekom, "From Underpopulation to Overpopulation: French Perceptions of Population, Environment, and Agricultural Development in French Soudan (Mali), 1900–1960," *Environmental History* 4, no. 2 (1999): 204–7.

77. Van Beusekom, "From Underpopulation to Overpopulation," 204.

78. Monica M. van Beusekom, "Individualism, Community, and Cooperatives in the Development Thinking of the Union Soudanaise–RDA, 1946–1960," *African Studies Review* 51, no. 2 (2008): 7–8.

79. Mann, *From Empires to NGOs*.

80. Monica M. van Beusekom, "*Colonisation Indigène*: French Rural Development Ideology at the Office Du Niger, 1920–1940," *International Journal of African Historical Studies* 30, no. 2 (1997): 320.

81. Jean Filipovich, "Destined to Fail: Forced Settlement at the Office Du Niger, 1926–45," *Journal of African History* 42, no. 2 (2001): 247–54; van Beusekom, "*Colonisation Indigène*," 318.

82. The importance of the *indigénat* to French colonial administration made the mandate system's policy on nationality of particular concern. It raised questions about whether populations in Togo and Cameroon could be subject to the same codes even though they were not subjects of France. The commissioners of Togo and Cameroon were engaged in a six-year back-and-forth with the PMC and League over how to designate the nationality of their mandated populations so that the *indigénat* could still be applied. Callahan, *Mandates and Empire*, 112–13.

83. Grovogui, *Beyond Eurocentrism and Anarchy*, chap. 1.

84. Charles de Gaulle, e.g., argued that economic development of the overseas territories must be a precondition for pursuing greater political rights. Amy Niang, "Rehistoricizing the Sovereignty Principle: Stature, Decline, and Anxieties about a Foundational Norm," in *Recentering Africa in International Relations*, ed. Marta Iniguez de Heredia and Zubairu Wai (New York: Palgrave Macmillan, 2019), 132.

85. Frederick Cooper, *Citizenship between Empire and Nation: Remaking France and French Africa, 1945–1960* (Princeton: Princeton University Press, 2014), 219.

86. Quoted in Cooper, *Citizenship*, 190.

87. Van Beusekom, "Individualism, Community, and Cooperatives," 6, 5.

88. Filipovich, "Destined to Fail," 259–260.

Chapter 3

1. Bilgin, *International in Security*, 128, 129.

2. Robert S. G. Fletcher, "Decolonization and the Arid World," in *The Oxford Handbook of the Ends of Empire*, ed. Martin Thomas and Andrew S. Thompson (Oxford: Oxford University Press, 2018).

3. Cooper, *Citizenship*, 219.

4. Berny Sèbe, "In the Shadow of the Algerian War: The United States and the Common Organisation of Saharan Regions (Ocrs), 1957–62," *Journal of Imperial and Commonwealth History* 38, no. 2 (2010): 306–7.

5. Muriam Haleh Davis, "The Sahara as the 'Cornerstone' of Eurafrica: European Integration and Technical Sovereignty Seen from the Desert," *Journal of European Integration History* 23, no. 1 (2017).

6. Peo Hansen and Stefan Jonsson, *Eurafrica: The Untold History of European Integration and Colonialism* (London: Bloomsbury, 2014), 104.

7. Quoted in P. Hansen and Jonsson, *Eurafrica*, 145–46.

8. Cooper, *Citizenship*, 206.

9. Quoted in Cooper, *Citizenship*, 206.

10. Davis, "Sahara as the 'Cornerstone.'"

11. Naffet Keïta, "De l'identitaire au problème de la territorialité: L'OCRS et les sociétés Kel Tamacheq du Mali," in *Hommes et sociétés*, ed. GEMDEV and the University of Mali ([Paris]: Karthala, 2005), 96–97; Sèbe, "In the Shadow," 308.

12. Grémont, *Les Touaregs Iwellemmedan*, 410–11.

13. B. Hall, *History of Race*.

14. Bruce S. Hall, "Bellah Histories of Decolonization, Iklan Paths to Freedom: The Meanings of Race and Slavery in the Late-Colonial Niger Bend (Mali), 1944–1960," *International Journal of African Historical Studies* 44, no. 1 (2011).

15. B. Hall, "Bellah Histories of Decolonization," 76–77.

16. Pierre Boilley, "The Late Colonial State in the AOF and the Nomadic Societies," *Itinerario* 23 (1999): 105–7; Lecocq, *Disputed Desert*, 41–52; Keïta, "De l'identitaire"; B. Hall, *History of Race*, 298–306.

17. Quoted in Boilley, "Late Colonial State," 105–6.

18. Lecocq, *Disputed Desert*, 145–51.

19. Keïta, "De l'identitaire."

20. Lecocq, *Disputed Desert*, chap. 3.

21. Lecocq, *Disputed Desert*, 127–28.

22. Neha Vora and Natalie Koch, "The Political Lives of Deserts," *Annals of the American Association of Geographers* 111, no. 1 (2021): 90.

23. But see Alan George, "'Making the Desert Bloom': A Myth Examined," *Journal of Palestine Studies* 8, no. 2 (1979).

24. Van Beusekom, "Individualism, Community, and Cooperatives," 18.

25. Quoted in Lecocq, *Disputed Desert*, 135.

26. Francis G. Snyder, "The Political Thought of Modibo Keita," *Journal of Modern African Studies* 5, no. 1 (1967); Catherine Bogosian, "The 'Little Farming Soldiers': The Evolution of a Labor Army in Post-colonial Mali," *Mande Studies* 5, no. 1 (2003); Lecocq, *Disputed Desert*, 63–73.

27. Daouda Gary-Tounkara, "Quand les migrants demandent la route, Modibo Keita rétorque: 'Retournez à la terre!' Les 'baragnini' et la désertion du chantier national (1958–1968)," *Mande Studies* 5, no. 1 (2003).

28. Lecocq, *Disputed Desert*, 70–71.

29. Gary-Tounkara, "Quand les migrants," 55–56.

30. Lecocq, *Disputed Desert*, 69–70.

31. Lecocq, *Disputed Desert*, chap. 4.

32. Lecocq, *Disputed Desert*, 157, 177.

33. Keïta, "De l'identitaire."

34. Modibo Keita, "The Foreign Policy of Mali," *International Affairs* 37, no. 4 (1961): 435.

35. Keita, "Foreign Policy of Mali."

36. Adom Getachew's account of an anticolonial right to self-determination also emphasizes the constraints and contradictions of embracing territorial integrity as an integral part of that right, especially in relation to questions of territorial bordering and secession and as applied to settler colonial contexts. Getachew, *Worldmaking after Empire*, 74, 86–87, 102–3. The politics of postcolonial state building in Mali and in the Sahel more broadly highlight that the dilemmas of tying self-determination to territorial integrity extend beyond the territorial definition of "borders" and of "sovereignty" to territorialization itself—i.e., the production of space as territory in the first place.

37. Lecocq, *Disputed Desert*, 197.

38. Charles Grémont et al., *Les liens sociaux au nord du Mali: Entre fleuves et dunes; Récits et témoignages* (Paris: Karthala, 2004), 164.

39. Lecocq, *Disputed Desert*, 199–200.

40. Pierre Boilley, "Les Kel Adagh: Un siècle de dépendances, de la prise de Tombouctou (1893) au pacte national (1992); Étude des évolutions politiques, sociales et économiques d'une population Touarègue (Soudan Français, République du Mali)" (PhD diss., Université Paris-Diderot, 1994), 361.

41. Quoted in Boilley, "Les Kel Adagh," 361.

42. Baz Lecocq, "Unemployed Intellectuals in the Sahara: The Teshumara Nationalist Movement and the Revolutions in Tuareg Society," *International Review of Social History* 49, no. 12 (2004); Boilley, "Les Kel Adagh," 377–84; Lecocq, *Disputed Desert*, 208–18.

43. Lecocq, "Unemployed Intellectuals," 94, 96–98, 103.

44. Lecocq, "Unemployed Intellectuals," 102 and passim.

45. Lecocq, *Disputed Desert*, 223.

46. Lecocq, *Disputed Desert*, 220–22, 233–34.

47. Lecocq, *Disputed Desert*, 220–22.

48. Boilley, "Les Kel Adagh," 449.

49. Robin-Edward Poulton and Ibrahim ag Youssouf, *A Peace of Timbuktu: Democratic Governance, Development and African Peacemaking* (Geneva: United Nations Institute for Disarmament Research, 1998), 60–61.

50. Lecocq, "Unemployed Intellectuals."

51. Boilley, "Les Kel Adagh," 463–84; Lecocq, *Disputed Desert*, 263–69.

52. Poulton and Youssouf, *Peace of Timbuktu*, 64.

53. Poulton and Youssouf, *Peace of Timbuktu*, 117, 71.

54. Poulton and Youssouf, *Peace of Timbuktu*, 72–75.

55. Grémont et al., *Les liens sociaux*, 65–68, 66. Quote translated from French.

56. Grémont et al., *Les liens sociaux*, 68–82.

57. Lecocq, *Disputed Desert*, 299–300.

58. Poulton and Youssouf, *Peace of Timbuktu*, 216.

59. Lecocq, *Disputed Desert*, 301.

60. Susanna D. Wing, *Constructing Democracy in Transitioning Societies of Africa: Constitutionalism and Deliberation in Mali* (New York: Palgrave Macmillan, 2008), 161–66; Kare Lode, *Civil Society Takes Responsibility: Popular Involvement in the Peace Process in Mali* (Oslo: Norwegian Church Aid and PRIO, 1997), https://www.prio.org/publications/7216.

61. Poulton and Youssouf, *Peace of Timbuktu*, 110–12.

62. Grémont et al., *Les liens sociaux*, chap. 4.

63. Some within the United Nations suggested that the failing military integration process could be revived by creating prestigious integrated units that would receive specialized training in desert "peacekeeping," thus making integration more appealing to military officers while also increasing effectiveness against rebel tactics. Poulton and Youssouf, *Peace of Timbuktu*, 104.

64. Lode, *Civil Society Takes Responsibility*, 29–30.

65. Jennifer C. Seely, "A Political Analysis of Decentralisation: Coopting the Tuareg Threat in Mali," *Journal of Modern African Studies* 39, no. 3 (2001).

66. On Mali's democratization process, see Wing, *Constructing Democracy*.

67. On the politics of Malian cultural identity during the Konaré presidency, see Rosa De Jorio, "Narratives of the Nation and Democracy in Mali. A View from Modibo Keita's Memorial," *Cahiers d'études africaines* 43, no. 172 (2003); Cécile Canut, "Construction des discours identitaires au Mali: Ethnicisation et instrumentalisation des Senankuya," *Cahiers d'études africaines* 46, no. 184 (2006).

68. Poulton and Youssouf, *Peace of Timbuktu*, 106–7.

69. Quoted in Poulton and Youssouf, *Peace of Timbuktu*, 237.

70. Charles Grémont, "Comment les Touaregs ont perdu le fleuve: Éclairage sur les pratiques et les représentations foncières dans le cercle de Gao (Mali), 19e–20e siècles," *Patrimonies naturels au Sud: Territoires, identités et stratégies locales*, edited by Marie-Christine Cormier-Salem, Dominique Juhé-Beaulaton, Jean Boutrais, and Bernard Roussel (Montpellier: IRD éditions, 2005), 279.

71. Grémont et al., *Les liens sociaux*, 202.

72. Eric Idelman, *Decentralisation and Boundary Setting in Mali: The Case of Kita District* (London: International Institute for Environment and Development, 2009), https://www.iied.org/12558iied.

73. Idelman, *Decentralisation and Boundary Setting*, 4.

74. Grémont et al., *Les liens sociaux*, 203.

75. For case studies on the relationship between decentralization policies and resource-related conflicts, see Karin Nijenhuis, "Does Decentralisation Serve Everyone? The Struggle for Power in a Malian Village," *European Journal of Development Research* 15, no. 2 (2003); Cotula and Cissé, "Changes"; Sabrina Beeler, *Conflicts between Farmers and Herders in Northwestern Mali* (London: International Institute for Environment and Development, 2006), https://www.iied.org/12533iied; Tor A. Benjaminsen and Boubacar Ba, "Farmer-Herder Conflicts, Pastoral Marginalisation and Corruption: A Case Study from the Inland Niger Delta of Mali," *Geographical Journal* 175, no. 1 (2009).

76. Cotula and Cissé, "Changes," 14–15; Grémont et al., *Les liens sociaux*, 207–8; Benjaminsen and Ba, "Farmer-Herder Conflicts."

77. Georg Klute, "De la chefferie administrative à la parasouveraineté régionale," in *Horizons nomades en Afrique sahélienne*, ed. André Bourgeot (Paris: Karthala, 1999). For analyses of how municipal jurisdictions and electoral competition over them shaped changing understandings of ownership, territory, and clan identity among Tuareg communities, see also Lecocq, "This Country."

78. A 2000 interview by Grémont et al. summarizes one understanding of the relative legitimacy of chiefs and mayors:

> If the mayors take care of [land management,] I think they will sell all of our [shared pastures] and convert them to fields. Village chiefs can't do this because for a very long time they have been the ones who managed the land. We are afraid of the . . . mayors because they are the ones who come and go. In a short time they can sell everything and go and it's not their problem. The chief of the village inherited his power and that is why he has the trust of the population. If he manages for fifty years he is obliged to work well so that his son can replace him and so the people have confidence in him.

Grémont et al., *Les liens sociaux*, 207. Translated from French. On monetized negotiations, see Cotula and Cissé, "Changes"; Benjaminsen and Ba, "Farmer-Herder Conflicts."

79. Based on interviews conducted in Bamako, Mopti, and Sevaré, Mali, and in Niamey, Niger, between January and July 2014. All interviews were conducted in confidentiality, and the names of interviewees are withheld by mutual agreement.

80. Interview with internally displaced person, Bamako, April 6, 2014.

81. Interview with refugee, Niamey, June 24, 2014.

82. Niang, "Stateness and Borderness."

83. Francesco Strazzari, *Azawad and the Rights of Passage: The Role of Illicit Trade in*

the Logic of Armed Group Formation in Northern Mali (Oslo: Norwegian Peacebuilding Resource Center, 2015); Benjaminsen and Ba, "Pastoralists in Mali."

Chapter 4

1. This chapter focuses on US security strategies for the Sahel with minimal attention to French and other European interests. From 2002 to 2011, the Sahel was a relatively low priority for the French and other European allies. Following the end of the Cold War, the French government, facing international criticism for its activities in Rwanda, pursued a policy of partial military withdrawal from Africa beginning in the late 1990s. A strategic shift away from the continent was further influenced by France's contributions to the North Atlantic Treaty Organization (NATO) mission in Afghanistan beginning in 2001, which strained tight military budgets and limited public support for foreign intervention. In this context, France welcomed an increased military presence of the United States in Africa based on expectations that France's reduced presence would be long-term. This shifted with NATO's Libya intervention in 2011 and the 2012 crisis in Mali. In 2013, France reversed course, launching Operation Serval and reinvesting in a large military presence in the Sahel. However, for the 2002–2011 period, the United States was playing the lead role in the international securitization of the Sahel as part of the so-called global war on terror. See Stephen Burgess, "Military Intervention in Africa: French and US Approaches Compared," *Journal of European, Middle Eastern and African Affairs* 1, no. 1 (Spring 2019); T. Chafer, "France in Mali: Towards a New Africa Strategy?," *International Journal of Francophone Studies* 19, no. 2 (2016); C. S. Chivvis, *The French War on Al Qa'ida in Africa* (Cambridge: Cambridge University Press, 2015).

2. Niang, "Space and the Geopolitical," 286.

3. Interview with military planner, Stuttgart, April 24, 2013.

4. Thomas P. M. Barnett, *The Pentagon's New Map: War and Peace in the Twenty-First Century* (New York: Penguin, 2005).

5. National Security Council, *Defense Planning Guidance, FY 1994–1999* ([Washington, DC]: NSC, April 16, 1992), 4, National Archives, www.archives.gov/files/declassification/iscap/pdf/2008-003-docs1-12.pdf.

6. National Security Council, *Defense Planning Guidance*, 4.

7. Office of the Secretary of Defense, *Quadrennial Defense Review Report* (Washington, DC: Department of Defense, 1997), v.

8. Reed Kramer, "National Security Review 30: American Policy toward Africa in the 1990s—Key Findings," *Africa News Service*, March 28, 1993.

9. Office of the Secretary of Defense, *Quadrennial Defense Review Report*, 3.

10. Regarding the budget, see Emmanuel Aning, "African Crisis Response Initiative and the New African Security (Dis)order," *African Journal of Political Science* 6, no. 1 (2001).

11. Interview with member of State Department, Stuttgart, April 24, 2013; interview with military planner, Stuttgart, April 24, 2013.

12. Robert Lamb, *Ungoverned Areas and Threats from Safe Havens* (Washington,

DC: Office of the Under Secretary of Defense for Policy, 2008); Angel Rabasa et al., *Ungoverned Territories: Understanding and Reducing Terrorism Risks* (Washington, DC: RAND, 2007).

13. Wolfram Lacher, "Actually Existing Security: The Political Economy of the Saharan Threat," *Security Dialogue* 39, no. 4 (2008).

14. *Africa and the War on Global Terrorism: Hearing before the House of Representatives Committee on International Relations Subcommittee on Africa*, 107th Congress (2001), 68, 21, 18, http://commdocs.house.gov/committees/intlrel/hfa76191.000/hfa76191_0f.htm.

15. Lacher, "Actually Existing Security," 384.

16. This hyphenated description of the region became prominent in military and security discourses in the early 2000s.

17. Toby Archer and Tihomir Popovic, *The Trans-Saharan Counter-Terrorism Initiative: The US War on Terrorism in Northwest Africa* (Helsinki: Finnish Institute of International Affairs, 2007); Raf Khatchadourian, "Pursuing Terrorists in the Great Desert," *Village Voice*, August 30, 2006; Mike McGovern, *Islamist Terror in the Sahel: Fact or Fiction?*, Africa Report No. 92 (Brussels: International Crisis Group, March 31, 2005).

18. Stewart Powell, "Swamp of Terror in the Sahara," *Air Force Magazine*, November 2004.

19. Lacher, "Actually Existing Security," 396.

20. William B. Farrell and Carla M. Komich, *USAID/DCHA/CMM Assessment: Northern Mali* (Washington, DC: Management Systems International, 2004).

21. Casey McNeill, "'Playing the Away Game': AFRICOM in the Sahara-Sahel," *Political Geography* 58 (May 2017).

22. Interview with military planner, Stuttgart, April 24, 2013.

23. Interview with communications officer, Stuttgart, June 26, 2013.

24. Interview with military planner, Stuttgart, April 24, 2013.

25. Interview with US embassy personnel, Bamako, July 7, 2014.

26. Scheele, *Smugglers and Saints*, 13.

27. Scheele, *Smugglers and Saints*, 6. See also ibid., intro.

28. Judith Scheele, "Garage or Caravanserail: Saharan Connectivity in al-Khalil, Northern Mali," in *Saharan Frontiers: Space and Mobility in Northwest Africa*, ed. James McDougall and Scheele (Bloomington: Indiana University Press, 2012), 227.

29. Scheele, *Smugglers and Saints*, 5.

30. Strazzari, *Azawad*, 2.

31. Amy Niang, "The Political Economy of Ransoming in the Sahel: The History, the Ethics and the Practice," *African Economic History* 42 (2014).

32. Scheele, *Smugglers and Saints*, chap. 3.

33. Lecocq, "This Country."

34. Peter Tinti, *Illicit Trafficking and Instability in Mali: Past, Present, Future* (Geneva: Global Initiative against Transnational Organized Crime, 2014), 12–13.

35. Jeremy Keenan, *The Dark Sahara: America's War on Terror in the Sahara* (New York: Pluto, 2009).

36. Niang, "Political Economy of Ransoming."

37. Interview with community leader, Bamako, March 5, 2014; interview with journalist, Bamako, February 11, 2014; interview with journalist, Bamako, February 12, 2014; interview with journalist, Bamako, May 6, 2014.

38. Interview with researcher, Bamako, February 20, 2014; interview with member of Northern Citizens' Collective (COREN), Bamako, March 27, 2014.

39. Wolfram Lacher, *Organized Crime and Conflict in the Sahel-Sahara Region*, The Carnegie Papers: Middle East (Washington, DC: Carnegie Endowment for International Peace, 2012), 11–14; Tinti, *Illicit Trafficking*, 11–13; Strazzari, *Azawad*.

40. Hüsken and Klute, "Political Orders," 321.

41. Morten Bøås, "Crime, Coping, and Resistance in the Mali-Sahel Periphery," *African Security* 8, no. 4 (2015).

42. See also Bøås and Strazzari, "Governance, Fragility and Insurgency"; Strazzari and Zanoletti, "North Africa"; Badi and Klute, "Jihadi Governance."

43. Leonardo A. Villalón and Abdourahmane Idrissa, "The Tribulations of a Successful Transition: Institutional Dynamics and Elite Rivalry in Mali," in *The Fate of Africa's Democratic Experiments: Elites and Institutions*, ed. Villalón and Peter Von Doepp (Bloomington: Indiana University Press, 2005).

44. Quoted in Nicolas Van de Walle, "Foreign Aid in Dangerous Places: The Donors and Mali's Democracy" (WIDER Working Paper 2012/61, UNU-WIDER, 2012), 2.

45. Van de Walle, "Foreign Aid," 11–12.

46. Jaimie Bleck, "Countries at the Crossroads 2011: Mali," *Freedom House* 11 (2011).

47. Villalón and Idrissa, "Tribulations"; Susanna D. Wing, "Mali: Politics of a Crisis," *African Affairs* 112, no. 448 (2013).

48. Interview with government official, Bamako, February 12, 2014.

49. Hamidou Magassa and Stefan Meyer, "The Impact of Aid Policies on Domestic Democratisation Processes: The Case of Mali" (FRIDE Working Paper 50, Fundacion para las Relaciones Internacionales y el Diálogo Exterior, 2008); interview with researcher, Bamako, April 7, 2014; interview with journalist, Bamako, February 11, 2014.

50. Isaline Bergamaschi, "The Fall of a Donor Darling: The Role of Aid in Mali's Crisis," *Journal of Modern African Studies* 52, no. 3 (2014).

51. Interview with researcher, July 8, 2014.

52. Magassa and Meyer, "Impact of Aid Policies."

53. Van de Walle, "Foreign Aid," 15; Morten Bøås and Liv Elin Torheim, "The Trouble in Mali: Corruption, Collusion, Resistance," *Third World Quarterly* 34, no. 7 (2013).

54. US Embassy Bamako, "Working with the Malians on Sahel Security," cable 08BAMAKO485, May 30, 2008, WikiLeaks, https://search.wikileaks.org/plusd/cables/08BAMAKO485_a.html.

55. Charles M. Johnson Jr. et al., *Combating Terrorism: US Efforts in Northwest Africa*

Would Be Strengthened by Enhanced Program Management (Washington, DC: Government Accountability Office, 2014), https://www.gao.gov/products/gao-14-518.

56. David Gutelius, "Islam in Northern Mali and the War on Terror," *Journal of Contemporary African Studies* 25, no. 1 (2007).

57. Interview with civil society leader, Niamey, May 17, 2012.

58. McGovern, *Islamist Terror*, 35.

59. Interview with journalist, Bamako, March 1, 2014.

60. Scott Baldauf, "Al Qaeda Rises in West Africa," *Christian Science Monitor*, December 27, 2009.

61. Gutelius, "Islam in Northern Mali," 71–72.

62. US Embassy Bamako, "The Deputy Secretary in Mali: Meetings with President Toure and Foreign Minister," cable 07BAMAKO1361, November 28, 2007, WikiLeaks, https://wikileaks.org/plusd/cables/07BAMAKO1361_a.html.

63. US Embassy Bamako, "Of Tuaregs and Terrorists: A Rebel's View of Unrest in the North and AQIM," cable 08BAMAKO0462, May 21, 2008, WikiLeaks, https://search.wikileaks.org/plusd/cables/08BAMAKO462_a.html.

64. This paragraph draws from Casey McNeill, "'*Ça devient le Texas la-bas*': Territoriality and the Diagnosis of Crisis in the Sahel," in *Identités sahéliennes en temps de crise*, ed. Baz Lecocq and Amy Niang (Berlin: Lit Verlag, 2019), 240–41.

65. Chafer, "France in Mali."

66. Chivvis, *French War on Al Qa'ida*, chap. 3.

67. Jeremy Keenan, "Uranium Goes Critical in Niger: Tuareg Rebellions Threaten Sahelian Conflagration," *Review of African Political Economy* 35, no. 117 (2008).

68. European Union External Action Service, *Strategy for Security and Development in the Sahel* ([Brussels]: EEAS, n.d.), accessed February 28, 2025, http://eeas.europa.eu/archives/docs/africa/docs/sahel_strategy_en.pdf.

69. International Crisis Group, *Mali: Avoiding Escalation*, Africa Report No. 189 (Brussels: ICG, July 18, 2012), 6–7.

70. Interview with researcher, Bamako, February 14, 2014; interview with journalist, Bamako, May 6, 2014.

71. Alhabass ag Intalla, *Manifeste pour la creation d'un réseau de plaidoyer en faveur de la paix, de la sécurité et du développement au nord Mali* (Kidal: Assemblée Nationale, November 3, 2009), https://www.eda.admin.ch/content/dam/countries/countries-content/mali/fr/resource_fr_196456.pdf.

72. Abdoulaye Dembele, Jaimie Bleck, and Sidiki Guindo, *Reconstructing the Malian State: Perspectives of Internally Displaced Persons; Results from a Survey Conducted June 2013* (Notre Dame, IN: Helen Kellogg Institute for International Studies, 2014).

73. Interview with journalist, Bamako, July 3, 2014.

74. Baba Ahmed, "Coup de theatre au PSPSDN: Les communautés du Nord à couteaux tirés," *Le combat*, August 24, 2011.

75. The NATO-supported rebellion against the Qaddafi government in Libya

contributed to the outbreak of rebellion in Mali. This precipitated a return to north-ern Mali of former rebels who had been employed by Qaddafi's defense forces. The ATT government appears to have made a severe miscalculation in seeking to estab-lish good relations between the state and these returnees by welcoming them back without disarming them. This may have seemed strategic within ATT's fractious approach to the North: he may have hoped that these armed returnees, welcomed back with a "red carpet," would further marginalize his opponents. Others speculate that ATT sought to foment low-level insurgency in the North to justify staying in power past his two-term limit, which was ending in 2012. Whatever the calculation from the perspective of the ATT government, the return of these former fighters re-sulted in a resurgence of rebel violence targeting military outposts. As military casu-alties increased, the government faced a political backlash and accusations of complicity with traffickers and terrorists. When a seemingly improvisational coup succeeded in ousting ATT from office, multiple armed groups that were already active to varying degrees in the North—connected to the smuggling and hostage in-dustries and to resurgent separatist ambitions—quickly seized territory, facilitated by a temporary alliance among fighters organized under the banners of (secular) inde-pendence for Azawad and the establishment of an Islamic state. On the events lead-ing up to the 2012 crisis and its immediate aftermath, see Baz Lecocq et al., "One Hippopotamus and Eight Blind Analysts: A Multivocal Analysis of the 2012 Political Crisis in the Divided Republic of Mali," *Review of African Political Economy* 40, no. 137 (2013).

Conclusion

1. Quoted in Zeenat Hansrod, "New Sahel Confederation Challenges Regional Order as ECOWAS Seeks Dialogue," *RFI*, July 7, 2024.

2. Présidence de la République du Mali (website), "Premier sommet des chefs d'état de l'alliance des états du sahel Niamey, le 06 juillet 2024, communiqué final," 2024, https://koulouba.ml/premier-sommet-des-chefs-detat-de-lalliance-des-etats-du -sahel-niamey-le-06-juillet-2024-communique-final/.

3. Jan van der Made, "Russian Wagner Group Reports Massive Losses in Mali," *RFI*, July 31, 2024.

4. Human Rights Watch, "Mali: Islamist Armed Groups, Ethnic Militias Commit Atrocities," May 8, 2024, https://www.hrw.org/news/2024/05/08/mali-islamist-armed -groups-ethnic-militias-commit-atrocities; Associated Press, "Mali's Army and Rus-sian Mercenaries Accused of Killing Dozens of Civilians in Kidal Region," July 5, 2024, https://apnews.com/article/mali-violence-army-tuareg-403b4c5a68462b7514f1 4cf26e1da116; Human Rights Watch, "Burkina Faso: Army Massacres 223 Villag-ers," April 25, 2024, https://www.hrw.org/news/2024/04/25/burkina-faso-army-mas sacres-223-villagers.

5. Cited in James Courtright, "Ethnic Killings by West African Armies Are Un-dermining Regional Security," *Foreign Policy*, March 7, 2023, https://foreignpolicy.

com/2023/03/07/mali-burkina-faso-fulani-ethnic-killings-by-west-african-armies
-are-undermining-regional-security/.

6. Benjaminsen and Ba, "Pastoralists in Mali"; Benjaminsen and Ba, "Moral Economy of Pastoralists."

7. Présidence de la République du Mali, "Premier sommet."

Bibliography

Adamson, Fiona B. "Pushing the Boundaries: Can We 'Decolonize' Security Studies." *Journal of Global Security Studies* 5, no. 1 (2020): 129–35.

Adamson, Fiona B. "Spaces of Global Security: Beyond Methodological Nationalism." *Journal of Global Security Studies* 1, no. 1 (2016): 19–35.

Adamson, Fiona B., and Kelly M. Greenhill. "Globality and Entangled Security: Rethinking the Post-1945 Order." *New Global Studies* 15, nos. 2–3 (2021): 165–80.

Adibe, Clement Eme. "Weak States and the Emerging Taxonomy of Security in World Politics." *Futures* 26, no. 5 (1994): 490–505.

Africa and the War on Global Terrorism: Hearing before the House of Representatives Committee on International Relations Subcommittee on Africa. 107th Congress (2001). http://commdocs.house.gov/committees/intlrel/hfa76191.000/hfa76191_0f.htm.

ag Intalla, Alhabass. *Manifeste pour la creation d'un réseau de plaidoyer en faveur de la paix, de la sécurité et du développement au nord Mali.* Kidal: Assemblée Nationale, November 3, 2009. https://www.eda.admin.ch/content/dam/countries/countries-content/mali/fr/resource_fr_196456.pdf.

Agnew, John. "The Territorial Trap: The Geographical Assumptions of International Relations Theory." *Review of International Political Economy* 1, no. 1 (1994): 53–80.

Ahmed, Baba. "Coup de theatre au PSPSDN: Les communautés du Nord à couteaux tirés." *Le combat*, August 24, 2011.

Anghie, Antony. *Imperialism, Sovereignty, and the Making of International Law.* New York: Cambridge University Press, 2007.

Anghie, Antony. "Time Present and Time Past: Globalization, International Financial Institutions, and the Third World." *New York University Journal of International Law* 32, no. 2 (2000): 243–90.

Aning, Emmanuel. "African Crisis Response Initiative and the New African Security (Dis)order." *African Journal of Political Science* 6, no. 1 (2001): 43–67.

Archer, Toby, and Tihomir Popovic. *The Trans-Saharan Counter-Terrorism Initiative: The US War on Terrorism in Northwest Africa.* Helsinki: Finnish Institute of International Affairs, 2007.

Ashworth, Lucian M. "Warriors, Pacifists and Empires: Race and Racism in International Thought before 1914." *International Affairs* 98, no. 1 (2022): 281–301.

Associated Press. "Mali's Army and Russian Mercenaries Accused of Killing Dozens of Civilians in Kidal Region." July 5, 2024. https://apnews.com/article/mali -violence-army-tuareg-403b4c5a68462b7514f14cf26e1da116.

Austen, Ralph A. "Africa in the Global Decolonization Process." In *Trustee for the Human Community: Ralph J. Bunche, the United Nations, and the Decolonization of Africa*, edited by Robert A. Hill and Edmond J. Keller, 161–80. Athens: Ohio University Press, 2010.

Bâ, Amadou Hampaté, and Jacques Daget. *L'empire Peul du Macina (1818–1853).* Paris: Les Nouvelles Editions Africaines, 1975.

Badi, Dida, and Georg Klute. "Jihadi Governance in Northern Mali: Socio-political Orders in Contest." In *Local Self-Governance and Varieties of Statehood: Tensions and Cooperation*, edited by Dieter Neubert, Hans-Joachim Lauth, and Christoph Mohamad-Klotzbach, 157–75. Cham: Springer, 2022.

Bagayoko, Niagalé. "Explaining the Failure of Internationally-Supported Defence and Security Reforms in Sahelian States." *Conflict, Security and Development* 22, no. 3 (2022): 243–69.

Bagayoko, Niagale, Eboe Hutchful, and Robin Luckham. "Hybrid Security Governance in Africa: Rethinking the Foundations of Security, Justice and Legitimate Public Authority." *Conflict, Security and Development* 16, no. 1 (2016): 1–32.

Baier, Stephen. "Ecologically Based Trade and the State in Precolonial West Africa." *Cahiers d'études africaines* 20, no. 77 (1980): 149–54.

Baier, Stephen. "Economic History and Development: Drought and the Sahellan Economies of Niger." *African Economic History* 1 (1976): 1–16.

Baier, Stephen. "Trans-Saharan Trade and the Sahel: Damergu, 1870–1930." *Journal of African History* 18, no. 1 (1977): 37–60.

Baldaro, Edoardo. "Rashomon in the Sahel: Conflict Dynamics of Security Regionalism." *Security Dialogue* 52, no. 3 (2021): 266–83.

Baldaro, Edoardo, and Elisa Lopez Lucia. "Spaces of (In-)security and Intervention: Spatial Competition and the Politics of Regional Organizations in the Sahel." *Territory, Politics, Governance* 12, no. 8 (2024): 1095–113.

Baldauf, Scott. "Al Qaeda Rises in West Africa." *Christian Science Monitor*, December 27, 2009.

Barder, Alexander D. *Global Race War: International Politics and Racial Hierarchy.* New York: Oxford University Press, 2021.

Barkawi, Tarak, and Mark Laffey. "The Postcolonial Moment in Security Studies." *Review of International Studies* 32, no. 2 (2006): 329–52.

Barnett, Thomas P. M. *The Pentagon's New Map: War and Peace in the Twenty-First Century.* New York: Penguin, 2005.

Bartelson, Jens. "The Social Construction of Globality." *International Political Sociology* 4, no. 3 (2010): 219–35.

Bassett, Thomas J. "Cartography and Empire Building in Nineteenth-Century West Africa." *Geographical Review* 84, no. 3 (1994): 316–35.

Beckert, Sven. "American Danger: United States Empire, Eurafrica, and the Territorialization of Industrial Capitalism, 1870–1950." *American Historical Review* 122, no. 4 (2017): 1137–70.

Beeler, Sabrina. *Conflicts between Farmers and Herders in Northwestern Mali.* London: International Institute for Environment and Development, 2006. https://www.iied.org/12533iied.

Beer, George Louis. *African Questions at the Paris Peace Conference: With Papers on Egypt, Mesopotamia, and the Colonial Settlement.* New York: Macmillan, 1923.

Benjaminsen, Tor A. "Natural Resource Management, Paradigm Shifts, and the Decentralization Reform in Mali." *Human Ecology* 25, no. 1 (1997): 121–43.

Benjaminsen, Tor A., and Boubacar Ba. "Farmer-Herder Conflicts, Pastoral Marginalisation and Corruption: A Case Study from the Inland Niger Delta of Mali." *Geographical Journal* 175, no. 1 (2009): 71–81.

Benjaminsen, Tor A., and Boubacar Ba. "Fulani-Dogon Killings in Mali: Farmer-Herder Conflicts as Insurgency and Counterinsurgency." *African Security* 14, no. 1 (2021): 4–26.

Benjaminsen, Tor A., and Boubacar Ba. "A Moral Economy of Pastoralists? Understanding the 'Jihadist' Insurgency in Mali." *Political Geography* 113, no. 3 (2024): 1–10.

Benjaminsen, Tor A., and Boubacar Ba. "Why Do Pastoralists in Mali Join Jihadist Groups? A Political Ecological Explanation." *Journal of Peasant Studies* 46, no. 1 (2019): 1–20.

Benjaminsen, Tor A., and Gunnvor Berge. "Myths of Timbuktu: From African El Dorado to Desertification." *International Journal of Political Economy* 34, no. 1 (2004): 31–59.

Benjaminsen, Tor A., and Pierre Hiernaux. "From Desiccation to Global Climate Change: A History of the Desertification Narrative in the West African Sahel, 1900–2018." *Global Environment* 12, no. 1 (2019): 206–36.

Benjaminsen, Tor A., and Christian Lund, eds. *Politics, Property and Production in the West African Sahel: Understanding Natural Resources Management.* London: Zed Books, 2001.

Benton, L. *A Search for Sovereignty: Law and Geography in European Empires, 1400–1900.* Cambridge: Cambridge University Press, 2009.

Bergamaschi, Isaline. "The Fall of a Donor Darling: The Role of Aid in Mali's Crisis." *Journal of Modern African Studies* 52, no. 3 (2014): 347–78.

Bergamaschi, Isaline. *Mali: Patterns and Limits of Donor-Driven Ownership.* Oxford: Oxford University Press, 2009.

Bilgin, Pinar. "Inquiring into Others' Conceptions of the International and Security." *PS: Political Science and Politics* 50, no. 3 (2017): 652–55.

Bilgin, Pinar. *The International in Security, Security in the International*. London: Routledge, 2016.

Bilgin, Pinar. "The 'Western-Centrism' of Security Studies: 'Blind Spot' or Constitutive Practice?" *Security Dialogue* 41, no. 6 (2010): 615–22.

Bilgin, Pinar, and Adam David Morton. "Historicising Representations of 'Failed States': Beyond the Cold-War Annexation of the Social Sciences?" *Third World Quarterly* 23, no. 1 (2002): 55–80.

Bleck, Jaimie. "Countries at the Crossroads 2011: Mali." *Freedom House* 11 (2011): 1–17.

Bøås, Morten. "Castles in the Sand: Informal Networks and Power Brokers in the Northern Mali Periphery." In *African Conflicts and Informal Power: Big Men and Networks*, edited by Mats Utas, 119–34. London: Zed Books, 2012.

Bøås, Morten. "Crime, Coping, and Resistance in the Mali-Sahel Periphery." *African Security* 8, no. 4 (2015): 299–319.

Bøås, Morten, Abdoul Wakhab Cissé, and Laouali Mahamane. "Explaining Violence in Tillabéri: Insurgent Appropriation of Local Grievances." *International Spectator* 55, no. 4 (2020): 118–32.

Bøås, Morten, and Francesco Strazzari. "Governance, Fragility and Insurgency in the Sahel: A Hybrid Political Order in the Making." *International Spectator* 55, no. 4 (2020): 1–17.

Bøås, Morten, and Liv Elin Torheim. "The Trouble in Mali: Corruption, Collusion, Resistance." *Third World Quarterly* 34, no. 7 (2013): 1279–92.

Bogosian, Catherine. "The 'Little Farming Soldiers': The Evolution of a Labor Army in Post-colonial Mali." *Mande Studies* 5, no. 1 (2003): 83–100.

Boilley, Pierre. "The Late Colonial State in the AOF and the Nomadic Societies." *Itinerario* 23 (1999): 98–109.

Boilley, Pierre. "Les Kel Adagh: Un siècle de dépendances, de la prise de Tombouctou (1893) au pacte national (1992); Étude des évolutions politiques, sociales et économiques d'une population Touarègue (Soudan Français, République du Mali)." PhD diss., Université Paris-Diderot, 1994.

Boilley, Pierre. "Nord-Mali: Les frontières coloniales de L'Azawad." *Canadian Journal of African Studies* 53, no. 3 (2019): 469–84.

Bourgeot, André. "Pasture in the Malian Gourma: Habitation by Humans and Animals." In *The Future of Pastoral Peoples: Proceedings of a Conference Held in Nairobi, Kenya, 4–8 August 1980*, edited by John G. Galaty, Dan Aronson, Philip Carl Salzman, and Amy Chouinard, 165–82. Ottawa: International Development Research Centre, 1981.

Bourgeot, André, and Henri Guillaume. "Identité touarègue: De l'aristocratie à la révolution." *Études rurales* 120, no. 1 (1990): 129–62.

Branch, Jordan. *The Cartographic State: Maps, Territory, and the Origins of Sovereignty*. Cambridge: Cambridge University Press, 2014.

Branch, Jordan. "'Colonial Reflection' and Territoriality: The Peripheral Origins of Sovereign Statehood." *European Journal of International Relations* 18, no. 2 (2010): 277–97.

Brantlinger, Patrick. "Victorians and Africans: The Genealogy of the Myth of the Dark Continent." *Critical Inquiry* 12, no. 1 (1985): 166–203.

Bratton, Michael, Massa Coulibaly, and Fabiana Machado. "Popular Perceptions of Good Governance in Mali." Afrobarometer Working Papers No. 9. Afrobarometer, Accra, Ghana, March 2000.

Brenner, Neil, and Stuart Elden. "Henri Lefebvre on State, Space, Territory." *International Political Sociology* 3, no. 4 (2009): 353–77.

Brink, Rogier van den, Daniel W. Bromley, and Jean-Paul Chives. "The Economics of Cain and Abel: Agro-pastoral Property Rights in the Sahel." *Journal of Development Studies* 31, no. 3 (1995): 373–99.

Brittany, Meché. "Bad Things Happen in the Desert: Mapping Security Regimes in the West African Sahel and the 'Problem' of Arid Spaces." In *A Research Agenda for Military Geographies*, edited by Rachel Woodward, 70–83. Cheltenham: Edward Elgar, 2019.

Brooks, George E. "A Provisional Historical Schema for Western Africa Based on Seven Climate Periods (ca. 9000 B.C. to the 19th Century)." *Cahiers d'études africaines* 26, nos. 1–2 (1986): 43–62.

Brown, William A. "The Caliphate of Hamdullahi." PhD diss., University of Wisconsin, 1969.

Bubandt, Nils. "Vernacular Security: The Politics of Feeling Safe in Global, National and Local Worlds." *Security Dialogue* 36, no. 3 (2005): 275–96.

Buell, Raymond Leslie. "'Backward' Peoples under the Mandate System." *Current History* 20, no. 3 (1924): 386–95.

Bunche, Ralph J. "Race and Imperialism." In *Black Scholars on the Line: Race, Social Science, and American Thought in the Twentieth Century*, edited by Jonathan Scott Holloway and Ben Keppel, 355–73. Notre Dame: University of Notre Dame Press, 2007.

Burgess, Stephen. "Military Intervention in Africa: French and US Approaches Compared." *Journal of European, Middle Eastern and African Affairs* 1, no. 1 (Spring 2019): 69–89.

Buzan, Barry, and George Lawson. "The Global Transformation: The Nineteenth Century and the Making of Modern International Relations." *International Studies Quarterly* 57, no. 3 (2013): 620–34.

Callahan, Michael Dennis. *Mandates and Empire: The League of Nations and Africa, 1914–1931*. Brighton: Sussex Academic Press, 2008.

Canut, Cécile. "Construction des discours identitaires au Mali: Ethnicisation et instrumentalisation des Senankuya." *Cahiers d'études africaines* 46, no. 184 (2006): 967–86.

Chafer, T. "France in Mali: Towards a New Africa Strategy?" *International Journal of Francophone Studies* 19, no. 2 (2016): 119–41.

Charbonneau, Bruno. "Counter-insurgency Governance in the Sahel." *International Affairs* 97, no. 6 (2021): 1805–23.

Chivvis, C. S. *The French War on Al Qa'ida in Africa*. Cambridge: Cambridge University Press, 2015.

Cohen, William B. "Imperial Mirage: The Western Sudan in French Thought and Action." *Journal of the Historical Society of Nigeria* 7, no. 3 (1974): 417–45.

Cold-Ravnkilde, Signe Marie, and Boubacar Ba. "Jihadist Ideological Conflict and Local Governance in Mali." *Studies in Conflict and Terrorism* 48, no. 3 (2025): 300–315.

Cold-Ravnkilde, Signe Marie, and Katja Lindskov Jacobsen. "Disentangling the Security Traffic Jam in the Sahel: Constitutive Effects of Contemporary Interventionism." *International Affairs* 96, no. 4 (2020): 855–74.

Cooper, Frederick. *Citizenship between Empire and Nation: Remaking France and French Africa, 1945–1960.* Princeton: Princeton University Press, 2014.

Cotula, Lorenzo, and Salmana Cissé. "Changes in 'Customary' Resource Tenure Systems in the Inner Niger Delta, Mali." *Journal of Legal Pluralism and Unofficial Law* 38, no. 52 (2006): 1–29.

Courtright, James. "Ethnic Killings by West African Armies Are Undermining Regional Security." *Foreign Policy*, March 7, 2023. https://foreignpolicy.com/2023/03/07/mali-burkina-faso-fulani-ethnic-killings-by-west-african-armies-are-undermining-regional-security/.

Crampton, Jeremy W. "The Cartographic Calculation of Space: Race Mapping and the Balkans at the Paris Peace Conference of 1919." *Social and Cultural Geography* 7, no. 5 (2006): 731–52.

Craven, Matthew. "Between Law and History: The Berlin Conference of 1884–1885 and the Logic of Free Trade." *London Review of International Law* 3, no. 1 (2015): 31–59.

Craven-Matthews, Catriona, and Pierre Englebert. "A Potemkin State in the Sahel? The Empirical and the Fictional in Malian State Reconstruction." *African Security* 11, no. 1 (2018): 1–31.

Crawford, Neta C. "Decolonization through Trusteeship: The Legacy of Ralph Bunche." In *Trustee for the Human Community: Ralph J. Bunche, the United Nations, and the Decolonization of Africa*, edited by Robert A. Hill and Edmond J. Keller, 93–115. Athens: Ohio University Press, 2010.

Crowe, S. E. *The Berlin West African Conference: 1884–1885.* London: Longmans, Green, 1942.

Crumley, Carole L. "Heterarchy and the Analysis of Complex Societies." *Archeological Papers of the American Anthropological Association* 6, no. 1 (1995): 1–5.

Danso, Kwaku, and Kwesi Aning. "African Experiences and Alternativity in International Relations Theorizing about Security." *International Affairs* 98, no. 1 (2022): 67–83.

Davis, Diana K. *The Arid Lands: History, Power, Knowledge.* Cambridge, MA: MIT Press, 2016.

Davis, Muriam Haleh. "The Sahara as the 'Cornerstone' of Eurafrica: European Integration and Technical Sovereignty Seen from the Desert." *Journal of European Integration History* 23, no. 1 (2017): 97–112.

Day, Adam. *States of Disorder, Ecosystems of Governance: Complexity Theory Applied to*

UN Statebuilding in the DRC and South Sudan. Oxford: Oxford University Press, 2022.

de Bruijn, Mirjam E., and Han J. W. M. van Dijk. *Arid Ways: Cultural Understandings of Insecurity in Fulbe Society, Central Mali*. Wageningen: Thela, 1995.

de Bruijn, Mirjam E., and Han J. W. M. van Dijk. "Changing Population Mobility in West Africa: Fulbe Pastoralists in Central and South Mali." *African Affairs* 102, no. 407 (2003): 285–307.

de Bruijn, Mirjam E., and Han J. W. M. van Dijk. "Ecology and Power in the Periphery of Maasina: The Case of the Hayre in the Nineteenth Century." *Journal of African History* 42, no. 2 (2001): 217–38.

de Bruijn, Mirjam E., and Han J. W. M. van Dijk. "Insecurity and Pastoral Development in the Sahel." *Development and Change* 30, no. 1 (1999): 115–39.

De Jorio, Rosa. "Narratives of the Nation and Democracy in Mali: A View from Modibo Keita's Memorial." *Cahiers d'études africaines* 43, no. 172 (2003): 827–55.

Dembele, Abdoulaye, Jaimie Bleck, and Sidiki Guindo. *Reconstructing the Malian State: Perspectives of Internally Displaced Persons; Results from a Survey Conducted June 2013*. Notre Dame, IN: Helen Kellogg Institute for International Studies, 2014.

Diagne, Souleymane Bachir. "Toward an Intellectual History of West Africa: The Meaning of Timbuktu." In *The Meanings of Timbuktu*, edited by Shamil Jeppie and Diagne, 19–27. Cape Town: HSRC Press, 2008.

Du Bois, W. E. B. "The African Roots of War." *The Atlantic*, May 1915.

Du Bois, W. E. B. "Of the Culture of White Folk." *Journal of Race Development* 7, no. 4 (1917): 434–47.

Du Bois, W. E. B. "Worlds of Color." *Foreign Affairs* 3, no. 3 (April 1925): 423–44.

Elden, Stuart. *Terror and Territory: The Spatial Extent of Sovereignty*. Minneapolis: University of Minnesota Press, 2009.

Ellis, Stephen. "Climate Variability and Complex Ecosystem Dynamics: Implications for Pastoral Development." In *Living with Uncertainty: New Directions in Pastoral Development in Africa*, edited by Ian Scoones, 37–46. London: Intermediate Technology Publications, 1995.

European Union External Action Service. *Strategy for Security and Development in the Sahel*. [Brussels]: EEAS, n.d. Accessed February 28, 2025. http://eeas.europa.eu/archives/docs/africa/docs/sahel_strategy_en.pdf.

Fabian, Johannes. *Time and the Other: How Anthropology Constructs Its Object*. New York: Columbia University Press, 1983.

Fanon, Frantz. *Wretched of the Earth*. New York: Grove Press, 1961.

Farrell, William B., and Carla M. Komich. *USAID/DCHA/CMM Assessment: Northern Mali*. Washington, DC: Management Systems International, 2004.

Ferguson, James, and Akhil Gupta. "Spatializing States: Toward an Ethnography of Neoliberal Governmentality." *American Ethnologist* 29, no. 4 (2002): 981–1002.

Fernandez-Gimenez, Maria E., and Sonya Le Febre. "Mobility in Pastoral Systems: Dynamic Flux or Downward Trend?" *International Journal of Sustainable Development and World Ecology* 13, no. 5 (2006): 341–62.

Filipovich, Jean. "Destined to Fail: Forced Settlement at the Office Du Niger, 1926–45." *Journal of African History* 42, no. 2 (2001): 239–60.

Fisch, J. "Africa as Terra Nullius: The Berlin Conference and International Law." In *Bismarck, Europe, and Africa: The Berlin Africa Conference 1884–1885 and the Onset of Partition*, edited by Stig Förster, Wolfgang J. Mommsen, and Ronald Robinson, 347–76. Oxford: Oxford University Press, 1988.

Fitzmaurice, Andrew. "The Genealogy of Terra Nullius." *Australian Historical Studies* 38, no. 129 (2007): 1–15.

Fitzmaurice, Andrew. "Liberalism and Empire in Nineteenth Century International Law." *American Historical Review* 117, no. 1 (2012): 122–40.

Fitzmaurice, Andrew. *Sovereignty, Property and Empire*. Cambridge: Cambridge University Press, 2014.

Fletcher, Robert S. G. "Decolonization and the Arid World." In *The Oxford Handbook of the Ends of Empire*, edited by Martin Thomas and Andrew S. Thompson, 373–90. Oxford: Oxford University Press, 2018.

Förster, Stig, Wolfgang J. Mommsen, and Ronald Robinson. *Bismarck, Europe, and Africa: The Berlin Africa Conference 1884–1885 and the Onset of Partition*. Oxford: Oxford University Press, 1988.

Frankema, Ewout, Jeffrey Williamson, and Pieter Woltjer. "An Economic Rationale for the West African Scramble? The Commercial Transition and the Commodity Price Boom of 1835–1885." *Journal of Economic History* 78, no. 1 (2018): 231–67.

Frowd, Philippe M., and Adam Sandor. "Militarism and Its Limits: Sociological Insights on Security Assemblages in the Sahel." *Security Dialogue* 49, nos. 1–2 (2018): 70–82.

Gagnol, Laurent, and Abdoulkader Afane. "When Injustice Is Spatial: Pastoral Nomadism and the Territorial Imperative in Niger's Sahara Region." *Spatial Justice* 2 (2010): 1–16.

Gallais, Jean. "Contribution à la connaissance de la perception spatialie chez les pasteurs du Sahel." *L'Espace géographique* 5, no. 1 (1976): 33–38.

Galli, Carlo. *Political Spaces and Global War*. Minneapolis: University of Minnesota Press, 2010.

Gallien, Max. "Informal Institutions and the Regulation of Smuggling in North Africa." *Perspectives on Politics* 18, no. 2 (2020): 492–508.

Gary-Tounkara, Daouda. "Quand les migrants demandent la route, Modibo Keita rétorque: 'Retournez à la terre!' Les 'baragnini' et la désertion du chantier national (1958–1968)." *Mande Studies* 5, no. 1 (2003): 49–64.

Gavin, R. J., and J. A. Betley, eds. *The Scramble for Africa: Documents on the Berlin West African Conference and Related Subjects, 1884/1885*. Ibadan: Ibadan University Press, 1973.

Gazit, Orit. "A Simmelian Approach to Space in World Politics." *International Theory* 10, no. 2 (2018): 219–52.

George, Alan. "'Making the Desert Bloom': A Myth Examined." *Journal of Palestine Studies* 8, no. 2 (1979): 88–100.

Getachew, Adom. *Worldmaking after Empire*. Princeton: Princeton University Press, 2019.

Glawion, Tim. *The Security Arena in Africa: Local Order-Making in the Central African Republic, Somaliland, and South Sudan*. Cambridge: Cambridge University Press, 2020.

Goettlich, Kerry. "The Colonial Origins of Modern Territoriality: Property Surveying in the Thirteen Colonies." *American Political Science Review* 116, no. 3 (2022): 911–26.

Goettlich, Kerry. "The Rise of Linear Borders in World Politics." *European Journal of International Relations* 25, no. 1 (2019): 203–28.

Gomez, Michael A. "Timbuktu under Imperial Songhay: A Reconsideration of Autonomy." *Journal of African History* 31, no. 1 (1990): 5–24.

Grégoire, Emmanuel. "Major Sahelian Trade Networks: Past and Present." In *Societies and Nature in the Sahel*, edited by Claude Raynaut, 90–108. London: Routledge, 1997.

Grémont, Charles. "Comment les Touaregs ont perdu le fleuve: Éclairage sur les pratiques et les représentations foncières dans le cercle de Gao (Mali), 19e–20e siècles." *Patrimonies naturels au Sud: Territoires, identités et stratégies locales*, edited by Marie-Christine Cormier-Salem, Dominique Juhé-Beaulaton, Jean Boutrais, and Bernard Roussel, 237–90. Montpellier: IRD éditions, 2005.

Grémont, Charles. *Les Touaregs Iwellemmedan, 1647–1896: Un ensemble politique de la boucle du Niger*. Paris: Karthala, 2010.

Grémont, Charles. "Mobility in Pastoral Societies of Northern Mali: Perspectives on Social and Political Rationales." *Canadian Journal of African Studies* 48, no. 1 (2014): 29–40.

Grémont, Charles. "Villages and Crossroads: Changing Territorialities among the Tuareg of Northern Mali." In *Saharan Frontiers: Space and Mobility in Northwest Africa*, edited by James McDougall and Judith Scheele, 131–45. Bloomington: Indiana University Press, 2012.

Grémont, Charles, Marty André, Mossa R. Ag, and Hamara Toure Younoussa. *Les liens sociaux au nord du Mali: Entre fleuves et dunes; Récits et témoignages*. Paris: Karthala, 2004.

Grovogui, Siba N. *Beyond Eurocentrism and Anarchy: Memories of International Order and Institutions*. New York: Palgrave Macmillan, 2006.

Grovogui, Siba N. "Come to Africa: A Hermeneutics of Race in International Theory." *Alternatives: Global, Local, Political* 26, no. 4 (2001): 425–48.

Grovogui, Siba N. "Dunes Shift, Humans Adapt: Political Transformations and Military Coups in the African Sahel." *CODESRIA Bulletin* 1 (2024): 23–26.

Grovogui, Siba N. "Regimes of Sovereignty: International Morality and the African Condition." *European Journal of International Relations* 8, no. 3 (2002): 315–38.

Grovogui, Siba N. *Sovereigns, Quasi Sovereigns, and Africans: Race and Self-Determination in International Law*. Minneapolis: University of Minnesota Press, 1996.

Grovogui, Siba N. "Your Blues Ain't My Blues: How 'International Security' Breeds

Conflicts in Africa." In *Reframing Contemporary Africa: Politics, Culture and Society in the Global Era*, edited by Peyi Soyinka-Airewele and Rita Kiki Edozie, 177–94. Washington, DC: CQ Press, 2010.

Guichaoua, Yvan, and Ferdaous Bouhlel. *Interactions between Civilians and Jihadists in Mali and Niger*. Canterbury: University of Kent, 2023.

Gutelius, David. "Islam in Northern Mali and the War on Terror." *Journal of Contemporary African Studies* 25, no. 1 (2007): 59–76.

Hall, Bruce S. "Arguing Sovereignty in Songhay." *Afriques: Débats, methods et terraines d'histoire* 4 (2013): 2–17. https://doi.org/10.4000/afriques.1121.

Hall, Bruce S. "Bellah Histories of Decolonization, Iklan Paths to Freedom: The Meanings of Race and Slavery in the Late-Colonial Niger Bend (Mali), 1944–1960." *International Journal of African Historical Studies* 44, no. 1 (2011): 61–87.

Hall, Bruce S. *A History of Race in Muslim West Africa, 1600–1960*. Cambridge: Cambridge University Press, 2011.

Hall, Stuart. "Who Needs 'Identity'?" In *Questions of Cultural Identity*, edited by Hall and Paul Du Gay, 1–17. London: Sage, 1996.

Hansen, Eva. "Farmer-Herder Relations, Land Governance and the National Conflict in Mali." *Journal of Peasant Studies* 51, no. 4 (2024): 1046–71.

Hansen, Peo, and Stefan Jonsson. *Eurafrica: The Untold History of European Integration and Colonialism*. London: Bloomsbury, 2014.

Hansrod, Zeenat. "New Sahel Confederation Challenges Regional Order as ECOWAS Seeks Dialogue." *RFI*, July 7, 2024.

Hart, Gillian. "Denaturalizing Dispossession: Critical Ethnography in the Age of Resurgent Imperialism." *Antipode* 38, no. 5 (2006): 977–1004.

Herbst, Jeffrey. *States and Power in Africa: Comparative Lessons in Authority and Control*. Princeton: Princeton University Press, 2014.

Herz, John H. "Rise and Demise of the Territorial State." *World Politics* 9, no. 4 (1957): 473–93.

Hill, Jonathon. "Beyond the Other? A Postcolonial Critique of the Failed State Thesis." *African Identities* (2005): 139–54.

Hobson, John Atkinson. *Imperialism: A Study*. New York: James Pott, 1902.

Hobson, John Atkinson. *Towards International Government*. London: Macmillan, 1915.

Hochschild, Adam. *King Leopold's Ghost: A Story of Greed, Terror, and Heroism in Colonial Africa*. New York: Harper Collins, 1999.

Human Rights Watch. "Burkina Faso: Army Massacres 223 Villagers." April 25, 2024. https://www.hrw.org/news/2024/04/25/burkina-faso-army-massacres-223-villagers.

Human Rights Watch. "Mali: Islamist Armed Groups, Ethnic Militias Commit Atrocities." May 8, 2024. https://www.hrw.org/news/2024/05/08/mali-islamist--armed-groups-ethnic-militias-commit-atrocities.

Hunwick, John O. "Ahmad Baba and the Moroccan Invasion of the Sudan (1591)." *Journal of the Historical Society of Nigeria* 2, no. 3 (1962): 311–28.

Hunwick, John O. *Timbuktu and the Songhay Empire: Al-Sa'di's Ta'rīkh Al-Sūdān down to 1613, and Other Contemporary Documents.* Leiden: Brill, 1999.

Hüsken, Thomas, and Georg Klute. "Political Orders in the Making: Emerging Forms of Political Organization from Libya to Northern Mali." *African Security* 8, no. 4 (2015): 320–37.

Huysmans, Jef. "Motioning the Politics of Security: The Primacy of Movement and the Subject of Security." *Security Dialogue* 53, no. 3 (2021): 238–55.

Idelman, Eric. *Decentralisation and Boundary Setting in Mali: The Case of Kita District.* London: International Institute for Environment and Development, 2009. https://www.iied.org/12558iied.

Idrissa, Rahmane. "Yesterday Meets Tomorrow in Sahelian Intellectual Currents." In *The Oxford Handbook of the African Sahel*, edited by Leonardo A. Villalón, 492–510. Oxford: Oxford University Press, 2021.

Idrissa, Rahmane. "The Sahel: A Cognitive Mapping." *New Left Review*, no. 132 (2021): 5–39.

Inayatullah, Naeem, and David L. Blaney. *International Relations and the Problem of Difference.* New York: Routledge, 2004.

International Crisis Group. *Mali: Avoiding Escalation.* Africa Report No. 189. Brussels: ICG, July 18, 2012.

Ireland, Alleyne. "On the Need for a Scientific Study of Colonial Administration." *Proceedings of the American Political Science Association* 3, no. 3 (1906): 210–21.

Jackson, Robert H. *Quasi-States: Sovereignty, International Relations, and the Third World.* Cambridge: Cambridge University Press, 1990.

Jahn, Beate. "Barbarian Thoughts: Imperialism in the Philosophy of John Stuart Mill." *Review of International Studies* 31, no. 3 (2005): 599–618.

Jahn, Beate. "IR and the State of Nature: The Cultural Origins of a Ruling Ideology." *Review of International Studies* 25, no. 3 (1999): 411–34.

Jarvis, Lee. "Toward a Vernacular Security Studies: Origins, Interlocutors, Contributions, and Challenges." *International Studies Review* 21, no. 1 (2019): 107–26.

Johnson, Charles M., Jr., Godwin Agbara, Aniruddha Dasgupta, Kendal Robinson, Ashley Alley, Martin de Alteriis, Karen Deans, and Etana Finkler. *Combating Terrorism: US Efforts in Northwest Africa Would Be Strengthened by Enhanced Program Management.* Washington, DC: Government Accountability Office, 2014. https://www.gao.gov/products/gao-14-518.

Johnson, Marion. "The Economic Foundations of an Islamic Theocracy—the Case of Masina." *Journal of African History* 17, no. 4 (1976): 481–95.

Jones, Branwen Gruffydd. "Africa and the Poverty of International Relations." *Third World Quarterly* 26, no. 6 (2005): 987–1003.

Jones, Branwen Gruffydd. "The Global Political Economy of Social Crisis: Towards a Critique of the 'Failed State' Ideology." *Review of International Political Economy* 15, no. 2 (2008): 180–205.

Jones, Branwen Gruffydd. " 'Good Governance' and 'State Failure': The Pseudoscience of Statesmen in Our Times." In *Race and Racism in International Relations: Confronting the Global Colour Line*, edited by Alexander Anievas, Nivi Manchanda, and Robbie Shilliam, 62–80. London: Routledge, 2014.

Jones, Brynmor. "Desiccation and the West African Colonies." *Geographical Journal* 91, no. 5 (1938): 401–23.

Kane, Ousmane. *Beyond Timbuktu: An Intellectual History of Muslim West Africa*. Cambridge, MA: Harvard University Press, 2016.

Kanya-Forstner, A. S. *The Conquest of Western Sudan: A Study in French Military Imperialism*. Cambridge: Cambridge University Press, 1969.

Keenan, Jeremy. *The Dark Sahara: America's War on Terror in the Sahara*. New York: Pluto, 2009.

Keenan, Jeremy. "Uranium Goes Critical in Niger: Tuareg Rebellions Threaten Sahelian Conflagration." *Review of African Political Economy* 35, no. 117 (2008): 449–66.

Keita, Modibo. "The Foreign Policy of Mali." *International Affairs* 37, no. 4 (1961): 432–39.

Keïta, Naffet. *Agreement for Peace and Reconciliation in Mali Resulting from the Algiers Process: Between Euphoria and Skepticism; Traces of Peace*. FES Peace and Security Series No. 32. Bonn: Friedrich-Ebert-Stiftung, 2018. https://library.fes.de/pdf--files/bueros/fes-pscc/14425.pdf.

Keïta, Naffet. "De l'identitaire au problème de la territorialité: L'OCRS et les sociétés Kel Tamacheq du Mali." In *Hommes et sociétés*, edited by GEMDEV and the University of Mali, 91–121. [Paris]: Karthala, 2005.

Keïta, Naffet. "La gouvernance de la sécurité au Mali: entre liberalisation et/ou privatisation des offres de sécurité et quête de sécurité humain en question." *Afrique et développement* 42, no. 3 (2017): 249–68.

Kennedy, Dane. *Mungo Park's Ghost: The Haunted Hubris of British Explorers in Nineteenth-Century Africa*. Cambridge: Cambridge University Press, 2024.

Khatchadourian, Raf. "Pursuing Terrorists in the Great Desert." *Village Voice*, August 30, 2006.

Klein, Martin A. "The Impact of the Atlantic Slave Trade on the Societies of the Western Sudan." *Social Science History* 14, no. 2 (1990): 231–53.

Klute, Georg. "De la chefferie administrative à la parasouveraineté régionale." In *Horizons nomades en Afrique sahélienne*, edited by André Bourgeot, 167–81. Paris: Karthala, 1999.

Klute, Georg. "Hostilités et alliances. Archéologie de la dissidence des Touaregs Au Mali." *Cahiers d'études africaines* 35, no. 137 (1995): 55–71.

Klute, Georg, and Baz Lecocq. "Tuareg Separatism in Mali." *International Journal* 68, no. 3 (September 2013): 424–32.

Klute, Georg, and Trutz von Trotha. "Roads to Peace: From Small War to Parasovereign Peace in the North of Mali." In *Healing the Wounds: Essays on the Reconstruction of Societies after War*, edited by Marie-Claire Foblets and von Trotha, 109–43. Portland: Hart, 2004.

Koopman, Sara. "Alter-Geopolitics: Other Securities Are Happening." *Geoforum* 42, no. 3 (2011): 274–84.

Koskenniemi, Martti, Walter Rech, and Manuel Jiménez Fonseca, eds. *International Law and Empire: Historical Explorations*. Oxford: Oxford University Press, 2017.

Kramer, Reed. "National Security Review 30: American Policy toward Africa in the 1990s—Key Findings." *Africa News Service*, March 28, 1993.

Lacher, Wolfram. "Actually Existing Security: The Political Economy of the Saharan Threat." *Security Dialogue* 39, no. 4 (2008): 383–405.

Lacher, Wolfram. *Organized Crime and Conflict in the Sahel-Sahara Region*. The Carnegie Papers Middle East. Washington, DC: Carnegie Endowment for International Peace, 2012.

Lamb, Robert. *Ungoverned Areas and Threats from Safe Havens*. Washington, DC: Office of the Under Secretary of Defense for Policy, 2008.

Lambach, Daniel. "Space, Scale, and Global Politics: Towards a Critical Approach to Space in International Relations." *Review of International Studies* 48, no. 2 (2022): 282–300.

Lecocq, Baz. *Disputed Desert: Decolonisation, Competing Nationalisms and Tuareg Rebellions in Northern Mali*. Leiden: Brill, 2010.

Lecocq, Baz. "From Colonialism to Keita: Comparing Pre- and Post-independence Regimes (1946–1968)." *Mande Studies* 5, no. 1 (2003): 29–47.

Lecocq, Baz. "This Country Is Your Country: Territory, Borders, and Decentralisation in Tuareg Politics." *Itinerario* 27, no. 1 (2003): 59–78.

Lecocq, Baz. "Unemployed Intellectuals in the Sahara: The Teshumara Nationalist Movement and the Revolutions in Tuareg Society." *International Review of Social History* 49, no. 12 (2004): 87–109.

Lecocq, Baz, Gregory Mann, Bruce Whitehouse, Dida Badi, Lott Pelckmans, Nadia Belalimat, Bruce Hall, and Wolfram Lacher. "One Hippopotamus and Eight Blind Analysts: A Multivocal Analysis of the 2012 Political Crisis in the Divided Republic of Mali." *Review of African Political Economy* 40, no. 137 (2013): 343–57.

Lefebvre, Henri. *State, Space, World: Selected Essays*. Edited by Neil Brenner and Stuart Elden, translated by Gerald Moore, Brenner, and Elden. Minneapolis: University of Minnesota Press, 2009.

Legrosse, Pascal. "Les règles d'accès des troupeaux Peuls aux paturages du delta: Central du Niger (Mali)." In *Managing Mobility in African Rangelands: The Legitimization of Transhumance*, edited by Maryam Niamir-Fuller, 76–96. London: Intermediate Technology Publications, 1999.

Lindley, Mark Frank. *The Acquisition and Government of Backward Territory in International Law: Being a Treatise on the Law and Practice Relating to Colonial Expansion*. New York: Longmans, Green, 1926.

Lippmann, Walter. *The Stakes of Diplomacy*. New York: Henry Holt, 1915.

Lode, Kare. *Civil Society Takes Responsibility: Popular Involvement in the Peace Process in Mali*. Oslo: Norwegian Church Aid and PRIO, 1997. https://www.prio.org/publications/7216.

Long, David, and Brian C. Schmidt. *Imperialism and Internationalism in the Discipline of International Relations*. New York: State University of New York Press, 2005.

Louis, William Roger. "African Origins of the Mandates Idea." *International Organization* 19, no. 1 (1965): 20–36.

Louis, William Roger. "The Berlin Congo Conference." In *France and Britain in Africa: Imperial Rivalry and Colonial Rule*, edited by Prosser Gifford and Louis, 167–220. New Haven: Yale University Press, 1971.

Louis, William Roger. "The Imperialism of Decolonization." *Journal of Imperial and Commonwealth History* 22, no. 3 (1994): 462–511.

Lovejoy, Paul E. "Commercial Sectors in the Economy of the Nineteenth-Century Central Sudan: The Trans-Saharan Trade and the Desert-Side Salt Trade." *African Economic History*, no. 13 (1984): 85–116.

Lovejoy, Paul E. "Islam, Slavery, and Political Transformation in West Africa: Constraints on the Trans-Atlantic Slave Trade." *Outre-mers* 89, no. 336 (2002): 247–82.

Lovejoy, Paul E. *Jihād in West Africa during the Age of Revolutions*. Athens: Ohio University Press, 2016.

Lovejoy, Paul E. "The Role of the Wangara in the Economic Transformation of the Central Sudan in the Fifteenth and Sixteenth Centuries." *Journal of African History* 19, no. 2 (1978): 173–93.

Lovejoy, Paul E. *Transformations in Slavery: A History of Slavery in Africa*. New York: Cambridge University Press, 2011.

Lovejoy, Paul E., and Stephen Baier. "The Desert-Side Economy of the Central Sudan." *International Journal of African Historical Studies* 8, no. 4 (1975): 551–81.

Lydon, Ghislaine. *On Trans-Saharan Trails*. Cambridge: Cambridge University Press, 2009.

Magassa, Hamidou, and Stefan Meyer. "The Impact of Aid Policies on Domestic Democratisation Processes: The Case of Mali." FRIDE Working Paper 50, Fundacion para las Relaciones Internacionales y el Diálogo Exterior, 2008.

Mamdani, Mahmood. *Neither Settler nor Native*. Cambridge, MA: Belknap Press of Harvard University Press, 2020.

Mann, Gregory. *From Empires to NGOs in the West African Sahel*. Cambridge: Cambridge University Press, 2014.

Mazower, Mark. *Governing the World: The History of an Idea*. New York: Penguin Books, 2013.

Mazower, Mark. *No Enchanted Palace: The End of Empire and the Ideological Origins of the United Nations*. Princeton: Princeton University Press, 2009.

Mbembé, J.-A., and Steven Rendall. "At the Edge of the World: Boundaries, Territoriality, and Sovereignty in Africa." *Public Culture* 12, no. 1 (2000): 259–84.

McDougall, E. Ann. "Class and Credit in a Regional Salt Economy: 'The Story of My Father'; Tishit and the Desert Salt Trade, Mauritania-Mali." *African Economic History* 49, no. 1 (2021): 192–221.

McDougall, E. Ann. "The Sahara Reconsidered: Pastoralism, Politics and Salt from the Ninth through the Twelfth Centuries." In "Business Empires in Equatorial Africa," edited by W. G. Clarence-Smith. Special issue, *African Economic History*, no. 12 (1983): 263–86.

McDougall, E. Ann. "Salt, Saharans, and the Trans-Saharan Slave Trade: Nineteenth Century Developments." *Slavery and Abolition* 13, no. 1 (1992): 61–88.

McDougall, E. Ann. "Salts of the Western Sahara: Myths, Mysteries, and Historical Significance." *International Journal of African Historical Studies* 23, no. 2 (1990): 231–57.

McDougall, E. Ann. "The View from Awdaghust: War, Trade and Social Change in the Southwestern Sahara, from the Eighth to the Fifteenth Century." *Journal of African History* 26, no. 1 (1985): 1–31.

McDougall, James, and Judith Scheele. *Saharan Frontiers: Space and Mobility in Northwest Africa*. Bloomington: Indiana University Press, 2012.

McGovern, Mike. *Islamist Terror in the Sahel: Fact or Fiction?* Africa Report No. 92. Brussels: International Crisis Group, March 31, 2005.

McIntosh, Roderick James. *The Peoples of the Middle Niger: The Island of Gold*. Malden, MA: Blackwell, 1998.

McNeill, Casey. "'Ça devient le Texas la-bas': Territoriality and the Diagnosis of Crisis in the Sahel." In *Identités sahéliennes en temps de crise*, edited by Baz Lecocq and Amy Niang, 227–55. Berlin: Lit Verlag, 2019.

McNeill, Casey. "Deterritorialized Threats and the 'Territorial Trap': The Geographical Imaginaries of Piracy in the Gulf of Aden." *Alternatives: Global, Local, Political* 48, no. 2 (2023): 170–88.

McNeill, Casey. "'Playing the Away Game': AFRICOM in the Sahara-Sahel." *Political Geography* 58 (May 2017): 46–55.

Mitchell, Audra. "Only Human? A Worldly Approach to Security." *Security Dialogue* 45, no. 1 (2014): 5–21.

Moorehead, Richard. "Mali." In *Custodians of the Commons: Pastoral Land Tenure in Africa*, edited by Lane Charles, 46–70. London: Taylor and Francis, 2014.

Moorehead, Richard. "Structural Chaos: Community and State Management of Common Property in Mali." PhD diss., University of Sussex, 1997.

Morel, Edmund Dene. *Africa and the Peace of Europe*. London: National Labour Press, 1917.

Morel, Edmund Dene. *Red Rubber: The Story of the Rubber Slave Trade Which Flourished on the Congo for Twenty Years, 1890–1910*. Manchester: National Labour Press, 1919.

Mundy, Jacob. "Introduction: Securitizing the Sahara." *Concerned Africa Scholars Bulletin*, no. 85 (Spring 2010): 1–11.

Mutua, Makau wa. "Why Redraw the Map of Africa: A Moral and Legal Inquiry." *Michigan Journal of International Law* 16, no. 4 (1995): 1113–76.

National Security Council. *Defense Planning Guidance, FY 1994–1999*. [Washington, DC]: NSC, April 16, 1992. National Archives. www.archives.gov/files/declassification/iscap/pdf/2008-003-docs1-12.pdf.

Newbury, C. W. "The Development of French Policy on the Lower and Upper Niger, 1880–98." *Journal of Modern History* 31, no. 1 (1959): 16–26.

Niamir-Fuller, Maryam. "Managing Mobility in African Rangelands." In *Property Rights, Risk and Livestock Development in Africa*, edited by Nancy McCarthy, Brent Swallow, Michael Kirk, and Peter Hazell, 102–31. Washington, DC: International Food Policy Research Institute, 1999.

Niamir-Fuller, Maryam, and Matthew Turner. "A Review of Recent Literature on Pastoralism and Transhumance in Africa." In *Managing Mobility in African Rangelands: The Legitimization of Transhumance*, edited by Niamir-Fuller, 18–46. London: Intermediate Technology Publications, 1999.

Niamir-Fuller, Maryam. "The Resilience of Pastoral Herding in Sahelian Africa." In *Linking Social and Ecological Systems: Management Practices and Social Mechanisms for Building Resilience*, edited by Fikret Berkes and Carl Folke, 250–84. Cambridge: Cambridge University Press, 1998.

Niang, Amy. "The Imperative of African Perspectives on International Relations." *Politics* 36, no. 4 (2016): 453–66.

Niang, Amy. "Le 'boom' des saisons dans l'espace sahélo-saharien." *Afrique Contemporaine* 245, no. 1 (2013): 53–69.

Niang, Amy. "The Political Economy of Ransoming in the Sahel: The History, the Ethics and the Practice." *African Economic History* 42 (2014): 157–83.

Niang, Amy. *The Postcolonial African State in Transition: Stateness and Modes of Sovereignty.* Lanham: Rowman and Littlefield, 2018.

Niang, Amy. "Ransoming, Compensatory Violence, and Humanitarianism in the Sahel." *Alternatives: Global, Local, Political* 39, no. 4 (2014): 231–51.

Niang, Amy. "Rehistoricizing the Sovereignty Principle: Stature, Decline, and Anxieties about a Foundational Norm." In *Recentering Africa in International Relations*, edited by Marta Iniguez de Heredia and Zubairu Wai, 121–44. New York: Palgrave MacMillan, 2019.

Niang, Amy. "Space and the Geopolitical." *Millennium: Journal of International Studies* 51, no. 1 (2023): 284–304.

Niang, Amy. "Stateness and Borderness in Mediation: Productions and Contestations of Space in the Sahel." Working Papers Series No. 26, Adaptation and Creativity in Africa: Technologies and Significations in the Making of Order and Disorder, German Research Foundation, Berlin, 2018.

Nicholson, Sharon. "Climatic Variations in the Sahel and Other African Regions during the Past Five Centuries." *Journal of Arid Environments* 1, no. 1 (1978): 3–24.

Nijenhuis, Karin. "Does Decentralisation Serve Everyone? The Struggle for Power in a Malian Village." *European Journal of Development Research* 15, no. 2 (2003): 67–92.

Nisancioglu, Karem. "Racial Sovereignty." *European Journal of International Relations* 26, no. 1 (2020): 39–63.

Nobili, Mauro. *Sultan, Caliph and the Renewer of the Faith: Ahmad Lobbo, the Tarikh al-Fattish and the Making of an Islamic State in West Africa.* Cambridge: Cambridge University Press, 2020.

Nuzzo, Luigi. "Territory, Sovereignty, and the Construction of the Colonial Space." In *International Law and Empire: Historical Explorations*, edited by Martti Koskenniemi, Walter Rech, and Manuel Jiménez Fonseca, 263–92. Oxford: Oxford University Press, 2017.

Nwaubani, Ebere. *The United States and Decolonization in West Africa, 1950–1960.* Cambridge, MA: Harvard University Press, 2001.

Nyman, Jonna. "The Everyday Life of Security: Capturing Space, Practice, and Affect." *International Political Sociology* 15, no. 3 (2021): 313–37.

Obichere, Boniface I. *West African States and European Expansion: The Dahomey-Niger Hinterland, 1885–1898.* New Haven: Yale University Press, 1971.

Office of the Secretary of Defense. *Quadrennial Defense Review Report.* Washington, DC: Department of Defense, 1997.

Oloruntimehin, B. O. "Resistance Movements in the Tukulor Empire." *Cahiers d'études africaines* 8, no. 29 (1968): 123–43.

Oloruntimehin, B. O. *The Segu Tukulor Empire.* London: Longman, 1972.

Opondo, Sam Okoth. "Decolonizing Diplomacy: Reflections on African Estrangement and Exclusion." In *Sustainable Diplomacies*, edited by Costas Constantinou and James Der Derien, 109–27. Basingstoke: Palgrave MacMillan, 2010.

Orford, Anne. "Regional Orders, Geopolitics, and the Future of International Law." *Current Legal Problems* 74, no. 1 (2021): 149–94.

Pasha, Mustapha Kamal. "Security as Hegemony." *Alternatives: Global, Local, Political* 21, no. 3 (1996): 283–302.

Pedersen, Susan. *The Guardians.* Oxford: Oxford University Press, 2015.

Perrier, Greg. "New Directions in Range Management Planning in Africa." In *Living with Uncertainty: New Directions in Pastoral Development in Africa*, edited by Ian Scoones, 47–57. London: Intermediate Technology Publications, 1995.

Persaud, Randolph B. "Killing the Third World: Civilisational Security as US Grand Strategy." *Third World Quarterly* 40, no. 2 (2019): 266–83, 428.

Persaud, Randolph B., and Rob B. J. Walker. "Apertura: Race in International Relations." *Alternatives* 26, no. 4 (2001): 373–76.

Pitts, Jennifer. "Political Theory of Empire and Imperialism." *Annual Review of Political Science* 13, no. 1 (2010): 211–35.

Poulton, Robin-Edward, and Ibrahim ag Youssouf. *A Peace of Timbuktu: Democratic Governance, Development and African Peacemaking.* Geneva: United Nations Institute for Disarmament Research, 1998.

Powell, Stewart. "Swamp of Terror in the Sahara." *Air Force Magazine*, November 2004.

Présidence de la République du Mali (website). "Premier sommet des chefs d'état de l'alliance des états du sahel Niamey, le 06 juillet 2024, communiqué final." 2024. https://koulouba.ml/premier-sommet-des-chefs-detat-de-lalliance-des-etats-du -sahel-niamey-le-06-juillet-2024-communique-final/.

Quijano, Anibal, and Michael Ennis. "Coloniality of Power, Eurocentrism, and Latin America." *Nepantla: Views from the South* 1, no. 3 (2000): 533–80.

Rabasa, Angel, Steven Boraz, Peter Chalk, Kim Cragin, Theodore W. Karasik, Jennifer D. P. Moroney, Kevin A. O'Brien, and John E. Peters. *Ungoverned Territories: Understanding and Reducing Terrorism Risks.* Washington, DC: RAND, 2007.

Raineri, Luca. "Gold Mining in the Sahara-Sahel: The Political Geography of State-Making and Unmaking." *International Spectator* 55, no. 4 (2020): 100–117.

Raineri, Luca, and Edoardo Baldaro. "The Place of Africa in International Relations: The Centrality of the Margins in Global IR." *Italian Political Science Review* 52, no. 2 (2022): 236–51.

Raineri, Luca, and Francesco Strazzari. "(B)ordering Hybrid Security? EU Stabilisation Practices in the Sahara-Sahel Region." *Ethnopolitics* 18, no. 5 (2019): 544–59.

Raineri, Luca, and Francesco Strazzari. "State, Secession, and Jihad: The Micropolitical Economy of Conflict in Northern Mali." *African Security* 8, no. 4 (2015): 249–71.

Raynaut, Claude, Emmanuel Grégoire, Pierre Janin, Jean Koechlin, and P. Lavigne Delville. *Societies and Nature in the Sahel.* London: Routledge, 1997.

Reinsch, Paul Samuel. *Colonial Administration.* New York: Macmillan, 1905.

Retaillé, Denis. "Afrique: Le besoin de parler autrement qu'en surface." *Espaces Temps* 51, no. 1 (1993): 52–62.

Retaillé, Denis, and Olivier Walther. "Spaces of Uncertainty: A Model of Mobile Space in the Sahel." *Singapore Journal of Tropical Geography* 32, no. 1 (2011): 85–101.

Rid, Thomas. "Razzia: A Turning Point in Modern Strategy." *Terrorism and Political Violence* 21, no. 4 (2009): 617–35.

Roberts, Richard L. "Production and Reproduction of Warrior States: Segu Bambara and Segu Tokolor, C. 1712–1890." *International Journal of African Historical Studies* 13, no. 3 (1980): 389–419.

Roberts, Richard L. *Warriors, Merchants, and Slaves: The State and the Economy in the Middle Niger Valley, 1700–1914.* Stanford: Stanford University Press, 1987.

Robinson, Cedric J. *The Terms of Order: Political Science and the Myth of Leadership.* Chapel Hill: University of North Carolina Press, 2016.

Robinson, David. *The Holy War of Umar Tal: The Western Sudan in the Mid-Nineteenth Century.* Oxford: Oxford University Press, 1985.

Rossi, Benedetta. "Kinetocracy: The Government of Mobility at the Desert's Edge." In *Mobility Makes States: Migration and Power in Africa,* edited by Darshan Vigneswaran and Joel Quirk, 147–68. Philadelphia: University of Pennsylvania Press, 2015.

Ruggie, John Gerard. "Territoriality and Beyond: Problematizing Modernity in International Relations." *International Organization* 47, no. 1 (1993): 139–74.

Saad, Elias N. *Social History of Timbuktu: The Role of Muslim Scholars and Notables, 1400–1900.* Cambridge: Cambridge University Press, 1983.

Salomon, Stefan. "The Construction of Territory in Nineteenth and Early Twentieth Century International Legal Doctrine." *Zeitschrift für öffentliches Recht* 77, no. 1 (2022): 59–91.

Sampson, Aaron Beers. "Tropical Anarchy: Waltz, Wendt, and the Way We Imagine International Politics." *Alternatives: Global, Local, Political* 27, no. 4 (2002): 429–57.

Sandor, Adam. "The Power of Rumour(s) in International Interventions: MINUS-MA's Management of Mali's Rumour Mill." *International Affairs* 96, no. 4 (2020): 913–34.

Sanneh, L. O. *Beyond Jihad: The Pacifist Tradition in West African Islam.* Oxford: Oxford University Press, 2016.

Scheele, Judith. "Circulations marchandes au Sahara: Entre licite et illicite." *Hérodote* 142, no. 3 (2011): 143–62.

Scheele, Judith. "Garage or Caravanserail: Saharan Connectivity in al-Khalil, Northern Mali." In *Saharan Frontiers: Space and Mobility in Northwest Africa*, edited by James McDougall and Scheele, 222–37. Bloomington: Indiana University Press, 2012.

Scheele, Judith. "Northwest African Perspectives on the Concept of the State." *HAU: Journal of Ethnographic Theory* 12, no. 3 (2022): 732–46.

Scheele, Judith. *Smugglers and Saints of the Sahara: Regional Connectivity in the Twentieth Century.* Cambridge: Cambridge University Press, 2012.

Scheele, Judith. "State-Like and State Dislike in the Anthropological Margins." *Journal of the Royal Anthropological Institute* 27, no. 4 (2021): 909–27.

Scheele, Judith. "Trade, Mobility and Migration." In *Landscapes and Landforms of the Central Sahara*, edited by Jasper Knight, Stefania Merlo, and Andrea Zerboni, 193–98. Cham: Springer, 2023.

Scheele, Judith. "Traders, Saints, and Irrigation: Reflections on Saharan Connectivity." *Journal of African History* 51, no. 3 (2010): 281–300.

Schmidle, Nicholas. "The Saharan Conundrum." *New York Times Magazine*, February 13, 2009. https://www.nytimes.com/2009/02/15/magazine/15Africa-t.html.

Schmidt, Brian. *The Political Discourse of Anarchy: A Disciplinary History of International Relations.* Albany: State University of New York Press, 1998.

Schmitt, Carl. *The Nomos of the Earth in the International Law of the* Jus Publicum Europaeum. New York: Telos Press, 2006.

Schmitz, Jean. "L'État géomètre: Les leydi des Peul du Fuuta Tooro (Sénégal) et du Maasina (Mali)." *Cahiers d'études africaines* 26, no. 103 (1986): 349–94.

Scoones, Ian. "New Directions in Pastoral Development in Africa." In *Living with Uncertainty: New Directions in Pastoral Development in Africa*, edited by Scoones, 1–36. London: Intermediate Technology Publications, 1995.

Scott, James C. *Against the Grain: A Deep History of the Earliest States.* New Haven: Yale University Press, 2017.

Scott, James C. *The Art of Not Being Governed: An Anarchist History of Upland Southeast Asia.* New Haven: Yale University Press, 2009.

Sèbe, Berny. "In the Shadow of the Algerian War: The United States and the Common Organisation of Saharan Regions (Ocrs), 1957–62." *Journal of Imperial and Commonwealth History* 38, no. 2 (2010): 303–22.

Seely, Jennifer C. "A Political Analysis of Decentralisation: Coopting the Tuareg Threat in Mali." *Journal of Modern African Studies* 39, no. 3 (2001): 499–524.

Shah, Nisha. *"Terra Infirma." Political Geography* 29, no. 6 (2010): 352–55.

Shah, Nisha. "The Territorial Trap of the Territorial Trap: Global Transformation and the Problem of the State's Two Territories." *International Political Sociology* 6, no. 1 (2012): 57–76.

Smith, Leonard V. "Sovereignty under the League of Nations Mandates: The Jurists' Debates." *Journal of the History of International Law* 21, no. 4 (2019): 563–87.

Smith, Neil. *American Empire: Roosevelt's Geographer and the Prelude to Globalization.* Berkeley: University of California Press, 2003.

Snyder, Francis G. "The Political Thought of Modibo Keita." *Journal of Modern African Studies* 5, no. 1 (1967): 79–106.

Stewart, C. C. "Frontier Disputes and Problems of Legitimation: Sokoto-Masina Relations 1817–1837." *Journal of African History* 17, no. 4 (1976): 497–514.

Strazzari, Francesco. *Azawad and the Rights of Passage: The Role of Illicit Trade in the Logic of Armed Group Formation in Northern Mali.* Oslo: Norwegian Peacebuilding Resource Center, 2015.

Strazzari, Francesco, and G. Zanoletti. "North Africa: Organized Crime, the Sahel-Sahara Region and State (Un)making." In *Handbook of Organized Crime and Politics*, edited by Felia Allum and Stan Gilmour, 287–308. Northampton, MA: Edward Elgar, 2019.

Suleiman, Muhammad Dan. "Eurocentrism, Africanity and 'the Jihad': Towards an Africa Worldview on Jihadism." *Méthod(e)s: African Review of Social Sciences Methodology* 2, nos. 1–2 (2017): 41–61.

Sweet, Louise E. "Camel Raiding of North Arabian Bedouin: A Mechanism of Ecological Adaptation." *American Anthropologist* 67, no. 5 (1965): 1132–50.

Syed, Amir. "Al-Hajj Umar Tal and the Realm of the Written: Mastery, Mobility and Islamic Authority in 19th Century West Africa." PhD diss., University of Michigan, 2017.

Syed, Amir. "Political Theology in Nineteenth-Century West Africa: Al-Ḥājj ʿUmar, the Bayān Mā Waqaʿa, and the Conquest of the Caliphate of Ḥamdallāhi." *Journal of African History* 62, no. 3 (2021): 358–76.

Tankel, Stephen. "US Counterterrorism in the Sahel: From Indirect to Direct Intervention." *International Affairs* 96, no. 4 (2020): 875–93.

Tapscott, Rebecca. "Vigilantes and the State: Understanding Violence through a Security Assemblages Approach." *Perspectives on Politics* 21, no. 1 (2023): 209–24.

Thakur, Vineet, and Peter C. J. Vale. *South Africa, Race and the Making of International Relations.* London: Rowman and Littlefield, 2020.

Thioub, Ibrahima. "Stigmas and Memory of Slavery in West Africa: Skin Color and Blood as Social Fracture Lines." *New Global Studies* 6, no. 3 (2012): 2–18.

Thurston, Alexander. "Illiberalism and Post-conflict Settlements with Jihadists: A Malian Case Study." *Third World Quarterly* 43, no. 10 (2022): 2396–412.

Timpong-Jones, Eric Cofie, Igshaan Samuels, Felix Owusu Sarkwa, Kwame Oppong-Anane, and Ayodele Oluwakemi Majekodumni. "Transhumance Pastoralism in West Africa—Its Importance, Policies and Challenges." *African Journal of Range and Forage Science* 40, no. 1 (2023): 114–28.

Tinti, Peter. *Illicit Trafficking and Instability in Mali: Past, Present, Future*. Geneva: Global Initiative against Transnational Organized Crime, 2014.

Turner, Matthew D. "Conflict, Environmental Change, and Social Institutions in Dryland Africa: Limitations of the Community Resource Management Approach." *Society and Natural Resources* 12, no. 7 (1999): 643–57.

Turner, Matthew D. "The Micropolitics of Common Property Management on the Maasina Floodplains of Central Mali." *Canadian Journal of African Studies* 40, no. 1 (2006): 41–75.

Turner, Matthew D. "Political Ecology and the Moral Dimensions of 'Resource Conflicts': The Case of Farmer-Herder Conflicts in the Sahel." *Political Geography* 23, no. 7 (2004): 863–89.

Turner, Matthew D. "The Role of Social Networks, Indefinite Boundaries and Political Bargaining in Maintaining the Ecological and Economic Resilience of the Transhumance Systems of Sudano-Sahelian West Africa." In *Managing Mobility in African Rangelands: The Legitimization of Transhumance*, edited by Maryam Niamir-Fuller, 97–123. London: Intermediate Technology Publications, 1999.

Turner, Matthew D., and Eva Schlecht. "Livestock Mobility in Sub-Saharan Africa: A Critical Review." *Pastoralism* 9, no. 13 (2019): 1–15.

Twiss, Travers. *An International Protectorate of the Congo River*. London: Pewtress, 1883.

Unangst, Matthew. "Hinterland: The Political History of a Geographic Category from the Scramble for Africa to Afro-Asian Solidarity." *Journal of Global History* 17, no. 3 (2022): 496–514.

United Nations. "Mali." Geospatial Network, February 1, 2020. https://www.un.org/geospatial/content/mali.

US Embassy Bamako. "The Deputy Secretary in Mali: Meetings with President Toure and Foreign Minister." Cable 07BAMAKO1361, November 28, 2007. WikiLeaks. https://wikileaks.org/plusd/cables/07BAMAKO1361_a.html.

US Embassy Bamako. "Of Tuaregs and Terrorists: A Rebel's View of Unrest in the North and AQIM." Cable 08BAMAKO0462, May 21, 2008. WikiLeaks. https://search.wikileaks.org/plusd/cables/08BAMAKO462_a.html.

US Embassy Bamako. "Working with the Malians on Sahel Security." Cable 08BAMAKO485, May 30, 2008. WikiLeaks. https://search.wikileaks.org/plusd/cables/08BAMAKO485_a.html.

Uzoigwe, G. N. "Spheres of Influence and the Doctrine of the Hinterland in the Partition of Africa." *Journal of African Studies* 3, no. 2 (1976): 183–203.

van Beusekom, Monica M. "*Colonisation Indigène*: French Rural Development Ideology at the Office Du Niger, 1920–1940." *International Journal of African Historical Studies* 30, no. 2 (1997): 299–323.

van Beusekom, Monica M. "From Underpopulation to Overpopulation: French Perceptions of Population, Environment, and Agricultural Development in French Soudan (Mali), 1900–1960." *Environmental History* 4, no. 2 (1999): 198–219.

van Beusekom, Monica M. "Individualism, Community, and Cooperatives in the Development Thinking of the Union Soudanaise–RDA, 1946–1960." *African Studies Review* 51, no. 2 (2008): 1–25.

van der Made, Jan. "Russian Wagner Group Reports Massive Losses in Mali." *RFI*, July 31, 2024.

Vandersmissen, Jan. "The King's Most Eloquent Campaigner: Emile De Laveleye, Leopold II and the Creation of the Congo Free State." *Revue belge d'histoire contemporaine* 41, no. 1 (2011): 7–57.

Van de Walle, Nicolas. "Foreign Aid in Dangerous Places: The Donors and Mali's Democracy." WIDER Working Paper 2012/61, United Nations University World Institute for Development Economics Research, 2012.

Vedeld, Trond. "History, Continuity and Change in Fulani Resource Regimes." In *Politics, Property and Production in the West African Sahel: Understanding Natural Resources Management*, edited by Tor A. Benjaminsen and Christian Lund, 117–43. London: Zed Books, 2001.

Venturi, Bernardo, and Nana Toure. "The Great Illusion: Security Sector Reform in the Sahel." *International Spectator* 55, no. 4 (2020): 54–68.

Véron, Jean-Bernard. "Les dynamiques du pastoralisme au sahel." *Afrique contemporaine* 1, no. 249 (2014): 11–19.

Villalón, Leonardo A., and Abdourahmane Idrissa. "The Tribulations of a Successful Transition: Institutional Dynamics and Elite Rivalry in Mali." In *The Fate of Africa's Democratic Experiments: Elites and Institutions*, edited by Villalón and Peter Von Doepp, 49–74. Bloomington: Indiana University Press, 2005.

Vitalis, Robert. "The Noble American Science of Imperial Relations and Its Laws of Race Development." *Comparative Studies in Society and History* 52, no. 4 (2010): 909–38.

Vitalis, Robert. *White World Order, Black Power Politics: The Birth of American International Relations*. Ithaca: Cornell University Press, 2015.

Vora, Neha, and Natalie Koch. "The Political Lives of Deserts." *Annals of the American Association of Geographers* 111, no. 1 (2021): 87–104.

Wai, Zubairu. "Africa in/and International Relations: An Introduction." In *Recentering Africa in International Relations: Beyond Lack, Peripherality, and Failure*, edited by Marta Iñiguez de Heredia and Wai, 1–29. New York: Palgrave MacMillan, 2019.

Walker, R. B. J. *After the Globe, before the World*. London: Routledge, 2010.

Walker, R. B. J. *Inside/Outside: International Relations and Political Theory*. Cambridge: Cambridge University Press, 1993.

Walther, Olivier J., Allen M. Howard, and Denis Retaillé. "West African Spatial Patterns of Economic Activities: Combining the 'Spatial Factor' and 'Mobile Space' Approaches." *African Studies* 74, no. 3 (2015): 346–65.

Walther, Olivier J., and Denis Retaillé. "Mapping the Sahelian Space." In *The Oxford Handbook of the African Sahel*, edited by Leonardo A. Villalón, 15–34. Oxford: Oxford University Press, 2021.

Ward, Stuart. "The European Provenance of Decolonization." *Past and Present* 230, no. 1 (2016): 227–60.

Ware, Rudolph T. *The Walking Qur'an: Islamic Education, Embodied Knowledge, and History in West Africa*. Chapel Hill: University of North Carolina Press, 2014.

Warscheid, Ismail. "The West African Jihād Movements and the Islamic Legal Literature of the Southwestern Sahara (1650–1850)." *Journal of West African History* 6, no. 2 (2020): 33–60.

Webb, James L. A. *Desert Frontier: Ecological and Economic Change along the Western Sahel, 1600–1850*. Madison: University of Wisconsin Press, 1995.

Wempe, Sean Andrew. "A League to Preserve Empires: Understanding the Mandates System and Avenues for Further Scholarly Inquiry." *American Historical Review* 124, no. 5 (December 2019): 1723–31.

Whitehouse, Bruce, and Francesco Strazzari. "Introduction: Rethinking Challenges to State Sovereignty in Mali and Northwest Africa." *African Security* 8, no. 4 (2015): 213–26.

Wilson-Fall, Wendy. "Pastoralist Societies in the Sahel." In *The Oxford Handbook of the African Sahel*, edited by Leonardo A. Villalón, 667–82. Oxford: Oxford University Press, 2021.

Wing, Susanna D. *Constructing Democracy in Transitioning Societies of Africa: Constitutionalism and Deliberation in Mali*. New York: Palgrave Macmillan, 2008.

Wing, Susanna D. "French Intervention in Mali: Strategic Alliances, Long-Term Regional Presence?" *Small Wars and Insurgencies* 27, no. 1 (2016): 59–80.

Wing, Susanna D. *Governance and Intervention in Mali: Elusive Security*. New York: Routledge, 2024.

Wing, Susanna D. "Mali: Politics of a Crisis." *African Affairs* 112, no. 448 (2013): 476–85.

Withers, Charles W. J. *Majestic River: Mungo Park and the Exploration of the Niger*. Havertown: Birlinn, 2022.

Woolf, Leonard. *Empire and Commerce in Africa: A Study in Economic Imperialism*. Westminster: George Allen and Unwin, 1920.

Wright, Quincy. *Mandates under the League of Nations*. 1930; repr., New York: Greenwood Press, 1968.

Yao, Joanne. "'Conquest from Barbarism': The Danube Commission, International Order and the Control of Nature as a Standard of Civilization." *European Journal of International Relations* 25, no. 2 (2018): 335–59.

Yao, Joanne. *The Ideal River: How Control of Nature Shaped the International Order*. Manchester: Manchester University Press, 2022.

Yao, Joanne. "The Power of Geographical Imaginaries in the European International Order: Colonialism, the 1884–85 Berlin Conference, and Model International Organizations." *International Organization* 76, no. 4 (2022): 901–28.

Zoubir, Yahia H. "The United States and Algeria: A New Strategic Partnership." *Journal of Middle Eastern and Islamic Studies* 5, no. 4 (2011): 1–27.

Zoubir, Yahia H. "The United States and Maghreb-Sahel Security." *International Affairs* 85, no. 5 (2009): 977–95.

Index

Page numbers in *italics* refer to illustrations.